THE TESTING CHARADE

THE TESTING CHARADE

Pretending to Make Schools Better

DANIEL KORETZ

The University of Chicago Press
Chicago and London

The University of Chicago Press, Chicago 60637
The University of Chicago Press, Ltd., London

For more information, contact the University of Chicago Press, 1427 E. 60th St., Chicago, IL 60637.

Published 2017
Printed in the United States of America

26 25 24 23 22 21 20 19 18 17   1 2 3 4 5

ISBN-13: 978-0-226-40871-2 (cloth)
ISBN-13: 978-0-226-40885-9 (e-book)
DOI: 10.7208/chicago/9780226408859.001.0001

Library of Congress Cataloging-in-Publication Data

Names: Koretz, Daniel M., author.
Title: The testing charade : pretending to make schools better / Daniel Koretz.
Description: Chicago ; London : The University of Chicago Press, 2017. | Includes bibliographical references and index.
Identifiers: LCCN 2017012607 | ISBN 9780226408712 (cloth : alk. paper) | ISBN 9780226408859 (e-book)
Subjects: LCSH: Educational tests and measurements—United States. | Educational accountability—United States.
Classification: LCC LB3051 .K668 2017 | DDC 371.260973—dc23
LC record available at https://lccn.loc.gov/2017012607

♾ This paper meets the requirements of ANSI/NISO Z39.48-1992 (Permanence of Paper).

CONTENTS

ACKNOWLEDGMENTS

I am grateful to my editor, Elizabeth Branch Dyson, for much more than the months of helpful guidance she provided while I was writing this book. I doubt I would have written it at all were it not for her. Some years ago Elizabeth, whom I had never met, contacted me out of the blue to ask to meet with me during an upcoming trip to Cambridge. She told me that she thought I had been "pulling my punches" in writing about the failures of test-based accountability in the past and that she wanted to sign me for a book in which I didn't. She was right. I had written about the problems of high-stakes testing for twenty-five years, but I had tried to keep my writing carefully measured, as is the norm in academia. The prospect of finally using honest adjectives to describe the harm high-stakes testing has done to students and teachers was alluring, but nonetheless I wavered for a few years. Elizabeth didn't give up: she spent many hours over several years talking with me about the idea. So thank you, Elizabeth.

I want to thank Aliya Pilchen, Christina Simpson, Luke Dorfman, and Tasmin Dhaliwal, who investigated cheating, stress on students, the corruption of the notion of good teaching, and test preparation strategies as participants in a seminar I led at the Harvard Graduate School of Education. All four made contributions to this book, and Aliya's was so substantial that she is the coauthor of the chapter on cheating.

This is a decidedly nonacademic book, and it calls into question a substantial amount of the current large-scale testing in the United States. For both reasons, I expected many of my professional colleagues to look down their noses at the effort. None did. On the contrary, without exception they urged me to write it. I'm grateful for their support.

Finally, I want to thank my wife, Doreen Koretz. Having been through it before, she knew all too well what would be in store, but she urged me to go ahead regardless and supported me throughout with her characteristic patience.

1

BEYOND ALL REASON

Pressure to raise scores on achievement tests dominates American education today. It shapes what is taught and how it is taught. It influences the problems students are given in math class (often questions from earlier tests), the materials they are given to read, the essays and other work they are required to produce, and often the manner in which teachers grade this work. It determines which educators are rewarded, punished, and even fired. In many cases it determines which students are promoted or graduate. This is the result of decades of "education reforms" that progressively expanded the amount of externally imposed testing and ratcheted up the pressure to raise scores. Although some people mistakenly identify these test-based reforms with the federal No Child Left Behind Act (NCLB) enacted in 2001, they began years earlier, and they will continue under the somewhat less draconian Every Student Succeeds Act (ESSA) that replaced NCLB in 2015.

A few examples will illustrate how extreme—often simply absurd—this focus on testing has become.

In 2012 two high schools in the Anaheim School District issued ID cards and day planners to students that were color-coded based on the students' performance on the previous year's standardized tests: platinum for those who scored at the "advanced" level, gold for those who scored "proficient," and white for everyone else. Students with premium cards were allowed to use a shorter lunch line and received discounts on entry to football games and other school activities.[1]

Newspapers are replete with reports of students who are so stressed by testing that they become ill during testing or refuse to come to school. In 2013, for example, eight New York school principals jointly sent a letter to parents that included this: "We know that many children cried during or after testing, and others vomited or lost control of their bowels or bladders. Others simply gave up. One teacher reported that a student kept banging his head on the desk, and wrote, 'This is too hard,' and 'I can't do this,' throughout his test booklet."[2]

In many schools it is not just testing itself that stresses students; they are also stressed by the unrelenting focus on scores and on their degree of preparation for the end-of-year accountability tests. For example, some schools post "data walls" that show each student's performance on practice tests used to prepare kids for the main event at the end of the year. This is intended to be motivating, but it shames some students. One third-grade teacher who caved in to pressure to post a data wall wrote this:

> [One student,] I'll call her Janie, immediately noticed the two poster-size charts I'd hung low on the wall. Still wearing her jacket, she let her backpack drop to the floor and raised one finger to touch her name on the math achievement chart. Slowly, she traced the row of dots representing her scores for each state standard on the latest practice test. Red, red, yellow, red, green, red, red. Janie is a child capable of much drama, but that morning she just lowered her gaze to the floor and shuffled to her chair....
>
> Even an adult faced with a row of red dots after her name for all her peers to see would have to dig deep into her hard-won sense of self to put into context what those red dots meant in her life and what she would do about them. An 8-year-old just feels shame.[3]

The press to test students has sometimes been taken to lengths that are both absurd and cruel. Valerie Strauss of the *Washington Post* wrote a number of reports about students with severe cognitive disabilities—one born with only a brain stem—who were forced to take high-stakes tests. When one of them lay dying in a morphine coma, the school district refused to accept his mother's explanation that he was in hospice care and demanded written confirmation from the hospice agency that the student was indeed dying.[4]

Shauna Paedae is a National Board Certified mathematics teacher with a bachelor's degree in mathematics, a master's degree in statistics, and three decades of experience as a teacher. During the 2011–12 school year she taught advanced mathematics in a high school in Pensacola, Florida: International Baccalaureate Mathematical Studies, Calculus, and Algebra 2. All but two of her students were in the eleventh and twelfth grades. That year 50 percent of her performance evaluation was based on a "value added measure" (VAM), a measure intended to show how much her teaching had contributed to students' performance gains on the Florida Comprehensive Assessment Test (FCAT). However, there were no FCAT mathematics tests administered above grade 8. Instead her district based her VAM on the school-wide performance of students taking the tenth-grade FCAT *reading* test—a test in a different subject administered, with only two exceptions, to different students in an earlier grade.

Kim Cook is a first-grade teacher in Alachua County, Florida, who was selected as her school's Teacher of the Year in 2012–13. In 2011–12 she had the same problem as Shauna: there are no FCAT tests in first grade. They are first administered in the third grade, and because Kim's school enrolls only students in preschool through second grade, no students in her school took the FCATs. Her school board resolved this problem by basing 40 percent of her evaluation on the test scores of fourth- and fifth-grade students *in another school.*

Paedae and Cook were among a group of plaintiffs who sued the Florida commissioner of education, members of the state board of education, and their local school boards in 2013 in an attempt to put an end to the absurd practice of evaluating teachers based on the performance of students they don't even teach, often in subjects they don't teach, and sometimes in different schools.[5]

They lost.

In August 2014 Rebecca Holcombe, the Vermont secretary of education, reported seemingly dire information about the performance of the state's schools. Like all states, Vermont accepts certain federal funds that require the state to follow the test-based accountability requirements of federal law—NLCB at that time, and now ESSA. Holcombe reported that under the terms of NCLB, *every school in the state* that had administered the state tests was classified as a low-performing school in need of improvement by the US Department of Education and was therefore subject to a series of escalating sanctions.

This bleak news, however, followed by less than a year another report from the US Department of Education indicating that in eighth-grade mathematics Vermont is very high performing, not only in comparison to other states but by international standards as well. For half a century the department has sponsored the National Assessment of Educational Progress (NAEP), a set of tests administered to representative samples of students across the country. The NAEP is widely considered the best test for monitoring overall trends in the performance of American students. The department linked the NAEP to the Trends in International Mathematics and Science Study (TIMSS) assessment, one of the two leading international comparative tests, "to provide each state with a way to examine how their students compare academically with their peers around the world in mathematics and science."[6] The study included all fifty states as well as forty-seven countries. In eighth-grade mathematics Vermont ranked seventh; its average score was exceeded only by of Massachusetts and five East Asian countries that always score near the top in international comparisons of mathematics achievement: Japan, Hong Kong, Taipei, Singapore, and Korea. Vermont outscored Finland, often held up as a high-achieving country the United States should emulate, by a large margin.

Thus Holcombe had to report to parents and the public that in terms of the accountability policies that were mandated by law, every school in one of the highest-performing jurisdictions in the world—even the schools that were at the very top of Vermont's very high distribution of scores—were performing so badly that they deserved sanctions. To her credit, Holcombe (a former student of mine) resolved this absurd contradiction in a reasonable if understated way. She wrote, "The Vermont Agency of Education does not agree with this federal policy, nor do we agree that all of our schools are low performing." Her sensible response, however, was very much an exception.

These examples, while extreme, are not anomalous. For example, Tennessee, like Florida, evaluates some teachers based on the scores obtained by students they don't teach, and in Tennessee as well, a lawsuit challenging this policy failed.[7] New York State required that all teachers be evaluated with scores and gave districts the choice between finding tests for teachers for whom they had none—art teachers, for example—and evaluating those teachers with the scores of other teachers' students. New York City opted to follow the Florida model, with the exception that scores had to be from the same school. Vermont wasn't alone in having high-performing schools classified as failures under the provisions of NCLB; Washington, also a high-performing state, had nearly 90 percent of its schools classified as in need of improvement. There are abundant newspaper reports of teachers who are falsely classified as failing despite ample evidence that they are actually highly effective. Reports of students having somatic symptoms because of anxiety about high-stakes tests, or being forced to take them despite being ill, have appeared often in the media. And for every example that is so extreme as to be newsworthy, there are countless other unreported instances of misused test scores or undesirable responses to testing occurring in schools across the nation every day.

Test-based accountability has become an end in itself in American education, unmoored from clear thinking about what should be measured, how it should be measured, or how testing can fit into a rational plan for evaluating and improving our schools. It is hard to overstate how much this matters—for children, for educators, and for the American public.

The rationale for these policies is deceptively simple. American schools are not performing as well as we would like. They do not fare well in international comparisons, and there are appalling inequities across schools and districts in both opportunities for students and student performance. These problems have been amply documented. The prescription that has been imposed on educators and children in response is seductively simple: measure student performance using standardized tests and use those measurements to create incentives for higher performance. If we reward people for producing what we want, the logic goes, they will produce more of it. Schools will get better, and students will learn more.

However, this reasoning isn't just simple, it's simplistic—and the evidence is overwhelming that this approach has failed. That is not to say it hasn't produced any improvements. It has. But these improvements are few and small. Hard evidence is limited, a consequence of our failure as a nation to evaluate these programs appropriately before imposing them on all children. The best estimate is that test-based accountability may have produced modest gains in elementary-school mathematics but no appreciable gains in either reading or high-school mathematics—even though reading and mathematics have been its primary focus. These meager positive effects must be balanced against the many widespread and serious negative effects. Test-based accountability has led teachers to waste time on all manner of undesirable test preparation—for example, teaching children tricks to answer multiple-choice questions or ways to game the rules used to score the tests. Testing and test preparation have displaced a sizable share of actual instruction, in a school year that is already short by international standards. Test-based accountability has led to a corruption of the ideals of teaching. In an apparently increasing number of cases, it has led to manipulation of the tested population (for example, finding ways to keep low achievers from being tested) and outright cheating, some instances of which have led to criminal charges and even imprisonment. And it has created gratuitous and often enormous stress for educators, parents, and, most important, students.

Ironically, our heavy-handed use of tests for accountability has also undermined precisely the function that testing is best designed to serve: providing trustworthy information about student achievement. It has led to "score inflation": increases in scores much higher than the actual improvements in achievement that they are supposedly measuring. This problem was predicted by measurement experts nearly seventy years ago, and we have more than twenty years of research showing that false gains are common and often very large. It's not uncommon for gains on high-stakes tests to be several times as large as they should be. The result is illusions of progress: student performance appears to be improving far more than it really is. This cheats parents, students, and the public at large, who are being given a steady stream of seriously misleading good news.

Perhaps even worse, these bogus score gains are more severe in some schools than in others. The purpose of test-based accountability system is to reward effective practice and encourage improvements. However, because score inflation varies from school to school and system to system, the wrong schools and programs are sometimes rewarded or punished, and the wrong practices may be touted as successful and emulated. And an increasing amount of evidence suggests that on average, schools that serve disadvantaged students engage in more test preparation and therefore inflate scores more, creating an illusion that the gap in achievement between disadvantaged and advantaged children is shrinking more than it is. This is another irony, as one of the primary justifications for the current test-based accountability programs has been to improve equity.

The evidence of these failures has been accumulating for more than a quarter century. Yet it is routinely ignored—in the design of educational programs, in public reporting of educational "progress," and in decisions about the fates of schools, students, and educators.

Don't make the mistake of thinking that these problems will disappear now that NCLB has finally been replaced. Test-based accountability was well established in this country before NCLB, and it will continue now that ESSA has replaced it. It's true that NCLB was a very poorly crafted set of policies—a train wreck waiting to happen, some of us said when it was enacted—and it did substantial harm. ESSA does remove some of the more draconian elements of NCLB, and that may help lessen some of the problems I describe here. Nevertheless, ESSA continues the basic model of test-based accountability, while returning to states just a fraction of the discretion they had in implementing this model before NCLB was enacted. Individual states started this ball rolling decades ago, so there isn't much reason to expect that they would turn in a fundamentally different direction now, even if ESSA permitted them to. And in any case, it doesn't let them change course anywhere nearly as much as I argue they should.

This book documents the failures of test-based accountability. I will describe some of the most egregious misuses and outright abuses of testing, and I will document some of the most serious negative effects. I'll explain why these effects have occurred. To put these harms into perspective, I will also describe the modest positive effects the testing policies have had.

Supporters of our current system will no doubt want to dismiss this book as yet another anti-testing or anti-accountability screed. It's neither. Standardized tests, *if properly used*, are a valuable and in some instances irreplaceable tool. They provide us with important information that is not available from other sources. For example, we all know that there is a troubling, large, and persistent gap in performance between white students and some minority students. How do we know that? Standardized tests. We've known for decades that American students don't perform as well in mathematics as students in many other countries. How do we know? Again, standardized tests. And the information in this book, as damning as it is regarding our current accountability system, is not an argument against accountability. My experience as a public school teacher, my years as the parent of children in public schools, and my decades of work as a researcher in education have made clear to me the need for more rigorous and effective accountability in public education.

Moreover, I am not questioning the motives of the many people who pushed for imposing test-based accountability on schools. Many, I know for a fact, had the best of intentions: they wanted to improve the quality of schools, to help all students learn more, and to narrow the gaps between advantaged and disadvantaged students.

However, neither good intentions nor the value of well-used tests justifies continuing to ignore the absurdities and failures of the current system and the real harms it is causing. Imagine that you go to see your doctor because of a chronic problem, and from a wide variety of available treatments she selects a medication that in your case turns out not to provide much benefit and has many serious, even debilitating side effects. Would you tell the doctor to stick with this medication because some treatment is needed, or would you ask her to try something else? It's time for us to switch prescriptions, to put in place accountability systems that encourage teachers to act in ways that we *do* want and that produce students who are more capable—not just higher-scoring on a few tests but more knowledgeable, more able to learn on their own, more able to think critically, and therefore more successful, not only in their later work but also as citizens. To do this, we have to start by confronting honestly the failures that stare us in the face.

The next few chapters provide a little background that you need to understand the arguments that follow. They are followed by a number of chapters laying out some of the most serious failures of test-based accountability. In a final section, I offer some suggestions about more rational ways to go about improving our schools.

⊏2⊐

WHAT *IS* A TEST?

What *is* a test?

This may seem like a foolish question. Anyone who has spent time in American schools recently has been inundated with information about tests. Many readers have taken far more tests than they can recall. And readers who follow education can rattle off the names of many: SAT, ACT, NAEP, TIMSS, their own state's tests, the AP tests, and on and on. Of course everyone knows what tests are.

Or maybe not.

Everyone knows a test when they see it. However, understanding tests is very different from recognizing them, and unfortunately, many of the people with their hands on the levers in education don't understand what tests are and what they can and can't do. Many think that testing is simpler and more straightforward than it is. A good example was a claim by George W. Bush when NCLB was being debated. "A reading comprehension test is a reading comprehension test. And a math test in the fourth grade—there's not many ways you can foul up a test. It's pretty easy to 'norm'" scores.[1] Not one of these three assertions is remotely correct.

Why does this lack of understanding matter? Because it underlies a great deal of what has gone wrong in US education reform. It has led to inappropriate uses of testing, distortions of educational practice, and bogus data supposedly showing large gains in student learning and a narrowing of the gap between disadvantaged kids and others. It also goes a long way to explaining why the positive effects of reform have been so meager. Simply put, the pervasive misunderstanding of testing is a key to the failure of education reform.

If the people pulling the strings had understood testing, *and if they had made decisions consistent with what tests really are*, we would not be confronting the decades of failure that we now see.

So what really is an achievement test?

Let's start with an analogy that is helpful if not entirely apt: political polls. Every election year, people want to know who is winning, starting long before the election is actually held. Newspapers report polls much like major league baseball standings, often devoting far more space to who is supposedly ahead or behind than they do to what candidates actually promise to do.

This desire creates a big market for information, and pollsters make a living telling us how candidates are faring. Lately, these predictions have become increasingly risky. To give just one reason, pollsters often try to reach a representative group of people by landline phone, but fewer people each year have landline phones, and those who don't have them differ from those who do. For example, they tend to be younger. Every year, when I discuss these issues in class, I ask for a show of hands: who has a landline phone? Virtually none of the students—graduate students with an average age of twenty-nine or so—raise a hand. So, for this reason and others, polling often fails, giving us badly misleading predictions. Of course we saw the failure of polling in the 2016 US presidential election, which almost all pollsters called incorrectly, and there have been other cases as well, for example, the 2015 election in Israel, the Brexit referendum in Britain, and the 2016 referendum in Colombia about the first peace agreement between the government and the FARC guerrillas. These problems notwithstanding, polling is a good starting point for understanding standardized tests.

Pollsters confront an obvious problem that makes it impossible to know with certainty what the vote will be. There are far too many people to poll—roughly 125,000,000 in a US presidential election, and smaller but still unmanageable numbers in most elections. The solution is to contact a small number of the potential voters. A *very* small number. In the next election cycle, when you are bombarded with poll results, check the numbers. Most of the good polls will be based on samples of only 800 to 1,200 people. This is the essence of polling: use the responses of a small sample of people to predict what the entire population will do. The results of the poll are valuable *only* to the extent that they give us a good prediction of the unmeasured behavior of the vast majority of voters, whom the pollsters don't contact.

Achievement tests are in many ways like polls, and this analogy is a helpful starting point for understanding them. Large-scale tests are typically used to estimate mastery of some large area of study, called a "domain" in the testing world. These may reflect a full year of work (algebra) or more (skills in reading and language arts developed over a period of years). There is no way to test the entire domain. There just isn't time, even with the excessive amount of time many American schools now devote to testing. So we test a small part of the domain and use the tested part to estimate how well students would have done if we had tested the whole thing. Rather than sampling a small number of people to represent a population as pollsters do, the authors of tests sample a small amount of content to represent the larger domain. Most of the domain remains untested, just as most voters are not reached by pollsters.

And just as the people polled matter only because they allow us to predict how everyone will vote, the items on a test matter *only to the extent that they allow us to predict mastery of the larger subject area from which they are sampled.* Performance on the specific tasks included in a given test isn't what matters. The tested tasks are just like your 800 polled voters. In themselves these 800 don't much matter, but the huge number of voters they represent certainly do. If all goes well—and, you'll see later on, all has most definitely not been going well—performance on the tasks on a test is likewise an indication of something that *does* matter.

The content sampled by the test can take many different forms—complex multistep problems, essays, simple multiple-choice tasks, and much more. These are typically called *items* or *tasks* in the testing business, for the simple reason that they often don't take the form of questions. I'll use the two terms interchangeably. The principle is the same regardless of the form this sampled content takes: the items that appear on the test are intended to represent the whole domain, including—and primarily—what isn't included.

Before turning to why this matters so much for test-based accountability—and it matters hugely—I have to explain one way in which this analogy to polling breaks down. If all goes well, the sample in a poll is reasonably representative of the population from which it is drawn. In contrast, the sampling of content used to create most tests is not fully representative of what we want students to accomplish or schools to produce. Of course (I say "of course" because this is obvious, not because reformers have paid much attention to it), education has many other goals beyond achievement in a few tested subjects. But even if one looks only at achievement in those subjects, tests are not fully representative of the domains they are intended to represent. There are a few reasons for this.

First, standardized testing has inherent limitations. Some things (for example, factual knowledge) are very easy to test. Other things (complex analytical thinking and problem solving) are much more difficult to test, and some aren't practical to test in this way at all. They can be assessed, but standardized tests aren't the right tool for doing that.

Second, in constructing a test the authors must make a very large number of decisions about the content that is included, the ways that content is represented, the responses required of students, and how students' responses will be scored. Some of these decisions are entirely intentional; just as a pollster aims for a particular mix of older and younger voters, the test's authors may have been given instructions about, for example, what fraction of an eighth-grade math test should comprise items about elementary algebra. However, there are many more minor decisions, some frankly incidental, that further narrow what is tested. For example, years ago a Boston math teacher said to one of my students, "Why would I teach irregular polygons?" She wasn't suggesting that they are unimportant. Her point was that she had noticed that the item-writers for the state test always happened to use regular polygons. These decisions may seem like arcane details, but they aren't: in a high-stakes environment, they matter a great deal, and they are the root of some of the major failures of test-based accountability.

What I have just explained—the sampling of content needed to create a test—is the single most important thing to understand about standardized testing, and it is the root of many of the problems that I describe in the following chapters. Test-based accountability didn't fail because testing is something evil or pernicious, as some critics would have it. Used sensibly, tests can be tremendously informative, and they can be powerful tools for improving education. The reforms have failed because tests are so much less than those pushing for test-based accountability want them to be. Testing simply can't carry the freight that has been piled onto it. The failure to understand this, or a willful decision to ignore it, can explain much of what has gone wrong.

Three of the consequences of sampling are particularly important for the arguments in this book.

The first consequence is simply imprecision, or "error." In lay speech, "error" means that something is wrong. "That's my error" is synonymous with "I made a mistake." When statisticians speak of error, however, they mean imprecision, not a systematic bias. When a pollster reports a "margin of error," she is not conceding that she screwed up. She is simply saying that the poll is necessarily imprecise, and if you did it over and over again with different samples of people, the results would vary. How much? That's the "margin of error."

Likewise, test scores have a margin of error. When a student scores 600 on the SAT, we don't know that this is her "true" score, and almost invariably, if she takes the test again, she will get a different score. Testing experts have spent generations figuring out how to quantify this error, and we are pretty good at it, so we know that in some cases it is severe.

Unfortunately for those running schools or education systems, it is not just the scores of individual kids that include error. Everything based on those scores does too. Some of the measures we now use to control schools have more error than others. One of the worst in this respect is the "value-added" estimates used to evaluate teachers in many states. These are highly imprecise, and ratings of many teachers fluctuate dramatically, sometimes wildly, from year to year. A measure that wobbles wildly from year to year isn't a solid basis for deciding how competent a teacher is.

There are a number of sensible ways to deal with this error, but ignoring it—which has all too often been the path chosen—is not one of them.

The second consequence arises because the tested samples of content and skills are not fully representative, either of the goals of schooling broadly or of student achievement more narrowly. This may sound obvious, but it isn't always clear to people just how far short standardized tests fall. For a reminder, it's worth turning to a remarkable chapter about testing published well over half a century ago by E. F. Lindquist, a member of the faculty at the University of Iowa. Lindquist is not a household name, but he was one of the most important figures in the history of standardized achievement testing. It may not be an exaggeration to say that Lindquist did more than any other single person to foster the use of standardized tests in the United States. He was, among other things, the creator of the Iowa Tests of Basic Skills—the standardized test I took in elementary school, and still one of the most widely used tests in grades 3 through 8—as well as the ACT college-admissions test and the original GED (General Educational Development test), the widely used high-school equivalency test. I'll cite Lindquist not only because he thought deeply about both the usefulness and the limits of standardized testing, but also because his views obviously can't be dismissed as those of someone who is anti-testing. That will become even more important in later chapters, when I show that Lindquist warned about one of the key failures of recent education reforms at least as early as 1951.

Lindquist started by asking: if we wanted to measure "educational development," what would we ideally measure? He pointed out that "intellectual development" is only one goal of schooling and that we hold many other goals, including, for example, managerial or executive abilities and artistic abilities. Even in the area of intellectual development, what we really care about most is what he called "criterion behaviors": the knowledge and skills that students are able to apply once they leave school. We can't wait until students enter college or the workplace to do that—and wouldn't be able to do it well even if we did wait—so instead we measure mastery of the school curriculum while kids are still in school. Moreover, even within that far narrower range, there is a great deal of student learning that we simply can't measure well with standardized instruments. People have been struggling to push the envelope for many years, and at this point we can measure more than Lindquist could more than half a century ago, but it remains true—and it will for the foreseeable future—that there is a great deal that is important but that we can't measure with standardized tests.[2]

What does this imply about the appropriate use of standardized tests? Clearly Lindquist, who worked with remarkable success throughout his entire career to spread the use of standardized tests and who made a good bit of money selling them, wasn't arguing that these limitations are reasons not to use tests. Neither am I. Rather, he argued that these limitations mean that *test scores should always be used as incomplete measures of student achievement.* His successors in the Iowa Testing Program have continued to make the same argument ever since. For example, more than forty years after Lindquist published his discussion of these issues, the manual for a then-current version of the ITBS warned school administrators that "though standardized achievement scores *cannot and should not replace teacher observations and classroom assessment information*, they provide unique supplementary information" (emphasis added).[3] This remains axiomatic in the profession of testing, although many in the profession no longer remind education policy makers of it.

The bottom line: the information yielded by tests, while very useful, is *never* by itself adequate for evaluating programs, schools, or educators. Self-evident as this should be, it has been widely ignored in recent years. Indeed, ignoring this obvious warning has been the bedrock of test-based education reform. Yes, some systems have added other measures of school performance even during the NCLB era. Its successor, ESSA, explicitly permits states to include one measure not based on test scores in its accountability system, but it largely leaves it to states to decide what that might be, and it requires that test-based indicators—and, in the case of high schools, graduation rates—together be given "much greater weight" than any additional indicator a state may choose.[4] Despite these wrinkles, the core logic of reform has been to treat a small number of test scores, either alone or with minor additions, as an adequate measure of school quality. Low scores alone have been enough to cost educators their jobs and to close schools.

Think about it: some of the people who were most influential in the development of standardized testing, and whose professional reputations and incomes depended on the tests they sold, warned that we should *never* use test scores precisely the way they are now used. That this warning is ignored doesn't stem from improvements in testing. It just shows a lamentable willingness to ignore the unavoidable limitations of standardized tests.

The most worrisome of the three consequences is the perverse incentives that test-based accountability has created for educators. These incentives are responsible for the fraudulent performance gains that have helped to maintain test-based accountability in the face of its many failures. The problem is simple: *high-stakes testing creates strong incentives to focus on the tested sample rather than the domain it is intended to represent.* If you teach a domain better—say, geometry—scores on a good test of that area will go up. However, if you directly teach the small sample measured by a particular test—for example, memorization of the fact that vertical angles are equal—scores will increase, often dramatically, but mastery of geometry as a whole will not improve much, if at all.

It is much as though a campaign tried to win an election by convincing the eight hundred polled people—and *only* those eight hundred people—to vote for their candidate.

This is the core of inappropriate test preparation, which is epidemic in American schools today. People in the testing field have warned about this problem well over half a century.

Supporters of reform often argue that teaching to the test is fine as long as the test includes important knowledge and skills. And they will also maintain that teachers who teach the tested content well also teach untested material well. Both of these defenses are nonsense. Bad test prep and the score inflation it often produces do not require "bad" tests, although bad tests can certainly make these problems worse. And while many teachers who teach tested content well *can* also teach untested material well, they often don't, because the system has given them strong incentives not to. Indeed, the system has given them incentives to teach the tested material poorly, in ways that I will describe a bit later. As long as the details of sampling are predictable—and test prep companies are very good at finding predictable patterns in tests—teaching to the specifics of the test will inflate scores. In many cases, all you need to do to make the resulting bogus gains vanish is substitute another test from a different developer.

And we shouldn't let fake score gains, as important as they are, blind us to the other, perhaps even more important, reason to worry about these perverse incentives. Bad test prep, even when it fails to inflate scores, robs students of the useful instruction they need and deserve.

⊏ 3 ⊐

THE EVOLUTION OF TEST-BASED "REFORM"

How can we discuss the failure of "education reform" as one thing when there have been so many different reforms in recent years? We've seen "minimum-competency" high-school exit exams, the performance-assessment movement, standards-based reform, teacher evaluations based on "value-added" estimates of their kids' gains in test scores, charter schools, public-school voucher programs, the small-schools movement, the Common Core standards, and the current focus on "college and career readiness," to name just some.

This variety, however, obscures the main story.

If you ask, "What dominates everyday life in schools?," the answer is much simpler: tests. Walk into almost any school, and you will enter a world that revolves around testing and test scores, day after day and month after month. The state-mandated accountability tests administered every spring are the ultimate cause of all of this, but many districts add their own "benchmark" or "interim" assessments during the year to gauge how well students are progressing toward the main event. Kids spend a lot of time taking these tests. And in many schools they spend vastly more time yet—often a substantial share of the entire school year—preparing for them. The work life of educators also focuses on test scores. Schools, and in many places individual teachers, are judged on the basis of their students' scores. Administrators and teachers worry greatly about scores, and they shape their behavior—and not just their instruction—to raise them. Teachers are routinely urged—not only by private firms trying to make money but often by their own principals—to resort to tricks that produce fraudulent gains in scores, and many do exactly that. Some simply cheat. I'll show you examples of both cheating and tricks in later chapters.

And this focus on testing profoundly colors many of the other reforms. Many charter schools focus their work and their marketing on raising test scores. The website of KIPP schools, for instance, states that "KIPP schools relentlessly focus on high student performance on standardized tests and other objective measures."[1] Similarly, much of the effort involved in the Common Core, and a great deal of the controversy about it, has focused on the new testing that has come with it.

This test-centered world has been in place long enough, in various forms, that many people think it is the normal state of affairs. It isn't. It is relatively new in the United States. It's also unique. That's not to say that high-stakes testing is rare or that the pressures it creates are more severe in the United States than anywhere else. That's not the case. In some East Asian countries, where a student's success depends to a great degree on a single exam, the pressure on students (and their parents) to do well on tests has reached an extreme that far exceeds what most students experience here. In South Korea, which may well be the most extreme in this respect—there is no way to gauge precisely—it has been estimated that fully 75 percent of all students attend one of the country's 100,000 *hagwons*, after-school private cramming schools. The pressure to do well is so intense that some observers blame it for the country's suicide rate, which is the highest among all OECD countries.[2] The situation is similar in Singapore, where the press has reported that 70 percent of parents of children *from preschool* though the secondary levels send them to "tuition classes," many of which are cram schools for the high-stakes tests.[3] Similarly, a dean from one of China's leading education colleges told me recently that if you observe instruction in tested subjects in the final grade of many high schools, you will see no instruction other than exercises that emulate the *gaokao*, the matriculation exam used for college admissions. The reason? Students who miss more than a few items will not be admitted to university.

Yet even these countries, in which high-stakes testing exerts more pressure on students than it does here, don't do what we do. They don't test students nearly as frequently as we do, and they don't give test scores such a large and direct role in evaluating schools and teachers. Singapore, for example, has an intensive and elaborate system for evaluating teachers that is intended primarily to help their development but also serves to weed out people who don't perform adequately. This system relies heavily on the judgment of both supervisors within a teacher's school and outsiders and makes almost no use of test scores (at least officially). Perhaps the most striking difference is that our government is the source of the testing pressure here, while in some of the East Asian countries the frenzy over tests is seen as arising from culture and tradition, and the education authorities see it as a serious problem and have been seeking to reduce it. For example, in 2016 Singapore's acting minister of education, Ng Chee Meng, gave a speech that included this as part of a call for a more holistic approach to education:

> Our students rank highly in international benchmarking studies. We are recognised for the high standards we have achieved.
>
> However, the focus of our education system should go beyond test scores. Currently, despite our very best efforts to move towards a holistic education, there is still a narrow emphasis on academics and paper qualifications. This is deeply ingrained in our culture, translated into expectations of our children, parents, and teachers. Eventually, this is perhaps even manifested in employer mindsets in workplaces.
>
> We need a better balance in our students' education journey. This means dialing back an excessive focus on academics. We need to free up time and space to nurture other dimensions that are just as important for our children's development. Let them not just study the flowers, but also stop to smell the flowers, and wonder at their beauty.[4]

It's hard to imagine an American state superintendent or secretary of education saying that we need to reduce the focus on test scores to allow students to wonder at the beauty of flowers.

And not all of the countries we might see as competitors have the East Asian culture of extreme pressure to do well on tests. Most European countries, for example, have a high-school matriculation exam, or set of exams, that govern admission to postsecondary education, such as the Baccalaureate in France, the Abitur in Germany and Finland, and the A-Levels in England. But Finland, in recent years the darling of the education world because of its very high performance on one of the international assessments in math, and Germany have no high-stakes testing in any other grades.

So before turning to the effects—some good but mostly bad—of these test-based reforms, it's worth taking stock of two things. How did we come to this pass? And what aspects of this system are the most important for understanding its failures?

○ ○ ○

It's almost hard to imagine now, but there was a time when standardized testing in the United States was for the most part a low-pressure enterprise. When I was in school in the 1950s and 1960s, the principal function of most standardized tests was to help teachers diagnose students' strengths and weaknesses, not to serve as a summary measure for accountability. In fact, at least one major testing company urged educators to administer their tests no later than October—when they would be useless as an accountability tool—because information early in the school year is much more helpful for improving instruction. The entire construction of many tests, from the writing of individual test items to the design of the score reports, reflected these diagnostic purposes. In most instances there was no "proficient" standard that was considered adequate. In fact, in most cases there were no performance standards at all, just descriptive reports of relative strengths and weaknesses. Some test vendors explicitly warned teachers and administrators that scores by themselves are not adequate for evaluating a program or a school.

This began to change a long time ago, but the shift was gradual, and it didn't fundamentally change education for some time. The transformation had started by the 1970s, most importantly with the adoption of "minimum competency" tests by many states. These were used primarily as a bar for high-school graduation, and because they were aimed entirely at low-performing students, they had little impact on the education experienced by many others.

A major impetus for additional testing was the publication in 1983 of *A Nation at Risk* by the National Commission on Excellence in Education, an advisory panel set up two years earlier by Terrell Bell, President Reagan's secretary of education. The report was so alarmist that it is worth excerpting part of the introduction here:

> Our Nation is at risk. Our once unchallenged preeminence in commerce, industry, science, and technological innovation is being overtaken by competitors throughout the world.... While we can take justifiable pride in what our schools and colleges have historically accomplished and contributed to the United States and the well-being of its people, the educational foundations of our society are presently being eroded by a rising tide of mediocrity that threatens our very future as a Nation and a people. What was unimaginable a generation ago has begun to occur—others are matching and surpassing our educational attainments.
>
> If an unfriendly foreign power had attempted to impose on America the mediocre educational performance that exists today, we might well have viewed it as an act of war.... We have, in effect, been committing an act of unthinking, unilateral educational disarmament.[5]

While the report urged confronting a variety of problems in American education—for example, the short school year, weaknesses in the teaching workforce, and undemanding curricula—the reform movement it spawned focused more than anything else on state-mandated testing. Chris Pipho, who was with an organization called the Education Commission of the States, wrote, "Nearly every large education reform effort of the past few years has either mandated a new form of testing or expanded uses of existing testing."[6] Gordon Ambach, a former commissioner of education of New York State who was at the time executive director of the Council of Chief State School Officers—the national association of state superintendents and commissioners—said that the nation had entered a period not only of measurement-driven instruction but also of "measurement-driven educational policy."[7] In addition to expanding the amount of testing and increasing its importance, the reforms of the 1980s brought another important change from the minimum-competency era: they shifted the focus away from holding students accountable for their scores to using students' scores to hold educators directly accountable.

In the testing world, the increasingly high-stakes uses of tests became known as "measurement-driven instruction." Most jargon is worth forgetting, but this term is important because it signaled a fundamental change in the purpose of testing. Achievement testing had always been intended as a tool to improve instruction. The reforms didn't change that. However, in the traditional approach the main purpose of scores was to give teachers information that would help them teach more effectively. Improved scores would *follow* greater mastery of the curriculum, just as better polling results would follow an effective campaign. "Measurement-driven instruction" reversed this: tests would now *lead.* Improving performance on the specific test was to be the explicit goal, and higher-quality instruction would be the consequence. This was the tail wagging the dog.

Another critical turning point occurred in the 1990s, when we entered the era of pay-and-punish: states began to mete out concrete sanctions and rewards, including money, for test scores. Although this marked a fundamental transformation of education, it happened with remarkable speed. By the end of the decade, thirty-three states imposed sanctions or rewards based on scores.[8] The states followed a variety of different approaches, but in hindsight, one can see in state programs portents of the federal initiatives NCLB and ESSA years before NCLB was enacted.

A particularly influential program was Kentucky's KIRIS (Kentucky Information Results Information System), first implemented in 1992. The KIRIS system reported performance on tests only in terms of a few performance standards—cut points on the distribution of scores—that placed all students into four large bins: Novice, Apprentice, Proficient, and Advanced. Variations in performance within any one of these bins were not reported and didn't count: for purposes of rewards and punishments, it made no difference whether students were at the bottom of the big Apprentice bin or at the top. Schools were required to bring all students up to the Proficient cut score within twenty years. (In practice, the system was a bit more complex. The parents of some college-bound students argued that this system would lead teachers to pay less attention to their kids, who were well above the Proficient standard and hence irrelevant to the critical "percent Proficient" measure. In response, the state gave schools extra credit for students in the Advanced bin, which would offset some students left at lower levels. The implementing regulations for ESSA issued at the end of 2016 explicitly allowed states to follow this approach.) Using what some people called "straight line" accountability, each school was given a biennial performance target established by drawing a straight line from its initial percentage of Proficient students to 100 percent. Schools that exceeded their targets by a sufficient amount were rewarded with money; those that fell far enough short were subject to punishment.

At the end of the decade, all of the states that rewarded and punished schools based their systems, like Kentucky's, on performance standards that placed students in a few huge categories. Most also required that a given percentage of students reach a set target within a specified time. They differed, however, in which performance standard had to be reached, how long schools had to do this, and what percentage had to reach it. The required percentages ranged from 50 to 100 percent.[9]

So NCLB didn't start the pay-and-punish system; it just made it national in scope and imposed a degree of uniformity across the fifty states. In many states it also ratcheted up the pressure to raise scores. It mandated that all states use the proficient standard as a target and that 100 percent of students reach that level. It imposed a short timeline for this: twelve years. It required that schools report the performance of several disadvantaged subgroups: economically disadvantaged students, racial/ethnic minorities, students with disabilities, students with limited proficiency in English, and migrants, and it mandated that 100 percent of each of these groups had to reach the proficient standard. It required that almost all students be tested the same way and evaluated against the same performance standards. And it replaced the straight-line approach by uniform statewide targets for percent proficient, called Adequate Yearly Progress (AYP). The use of uniform AYP targets required faster improvements in the early years for schools that scored relatively poorly. The law mandated an escalating series of sanctions for schools that failed to make AYP for each reporting group.

Some opponents of NCLB hoped for relief from the Obama administration, but they were quickly and sorely disappointed. Faced with deadlock on education issues in Congress, Secretary of Education Arne Duncan used his control over funding to increase even further the pressure to raise scores. The most important of Duncan's changes was inducing states to tie the evaluation of individual teachers, rather than schools, to test scores. This idea took root quickly and has been responsible for some of the most ludicrous uses of test scores, such as the evaluation of teachers based on the scores of other teachers' students I described in chapter 1.

NCLB was enacted with support of a remarkably broad coalition, but over time it became widely reviled. Even many of the people who supported it in principle agreed that it was not working well and was creating serious stresses and problems. Nonetheless, political gridlock kept NCLB in force until 2015, when Congress finally managed to enact its replacement, ESSA.

It's not yet entirely clear what changes ESSA will bring on the ground, in the daily lives of teachers and students. ESSA gives states some additional flexibility in terms of both testing and accountability—although far less than they had before NCLB was enacted—and we don't know yet how they will choose to use this limited autonomy. Moreover, ESSA requires federal approval of state assessment and accountability plans, and we don't fully know how the US Education Department will use that authority.

Still, the statute itself indicates that ESSA will be another, perhaps modestly less draconian, variation on the now all-too-familiar tune. It removes some elements of NCLB that proved particularly controversial, but it leaves the basic model of test-based accountability largely in place.

ESSA maintains many of the core elements of NCLB, although some in altered form. The testing requirements are unchanged, as is the core requirement that schools and districts be held accountable for improvements in scores. The states are required to set "ambitious long-term goals" for scores and report progress toward these annually. The requirement that almost all students be tested in the same way is retained. ESSA maintains the requirement that tests be reported in terms of performance standards and progress be measured in terms of the percentage of students who reach one of them.

Of the policies that ESSA does change, two are particularly important. First, ESSA explicitly acknowledges that scores alone are insufficient, but as I'll explain in the final chapters, it doesn't go nearly far enough in this direction. States are required to produce an accountability index that includes academic achievement on state tests, but they cannot use only scores. States must include graduation rates for high schools. Perhaps more important, they are required to include one additional measure of "school quality or student success." ESSA is vague about what this might be. It lists a number of possibilities—"student engagement," "educator engagement," "student access to and completion of advanced coursework," "postsecondary readiness," and "school climate and safety,"—but then adds "any other indicator the State chooses that meets the requirements of this clause." These are hardly substitutes. If it is important to foster student engagement, then it is no substitute to increase the percentage of students completing advanced coursework—or vice versa. And recall the requirement I noted in the previous chapter: if states elect to make use of this flexibility, they must give "much greater weight" to test-based indicators (in the case of high schools, in combination with graduation rates) than to any nontest indicator they choose.

The second big change in ESSA—more accurately, a series of changes—is that it reduces somewhat the control of the US Education Department, and it explicitly forbids the secretary of education from imposing a long list of specific requirements on states. The prohibition that has received the most attention was a reaction to Duncan's pressure to use scores to evaluate teachers: the secretary is not permitted to prescribe any system for evaluating teachers or principals. The federal formula for computing required gains is gone, and states are free to set their own targets. States have more flexibility in deciding how to intervene with schools shown by their indicators to be failing.

The bottom line is that ESSA doesn't allow states to depart substantially from test-based reform but does offer them the prerogative to broaden accountability modestly and to lessen somewhat the pressure to raise scores (subject, under the terms of the law, to federal approval). However, keep in mind that it was states, not the federal government, that set the nation firmly on the track of test-based accountability. I anticipate that the pressure will abate somewhat in some states, but there is nothing in ESSA to suggest that the daily life of teachers and students will no longer focus far too much on the drive to raise scores.

○ ○ ○

Readers who know the education world may object that I am oversimplifying: there have been many different testing and accountability approaches over the past few decades, and each has had its fans and detractors. We had minimum-competency testing, followed by somewhat harder tests administered in more grades. We had "standards-based reform," the argument for which was that test-based accountability would finally work if curricular standards, tests, and instruction were closely aligned. We had an early wave of enthusiasm for using performance assessments, in which students must respond to complex tasks and do more than choose a correct answer, premised on the idea that all would be well if we confronted students with "authentic," realistic tasks. And we had the "value-added" approach, the argument that the system would finally work well if we held schools accountable for student growth rather than their level of performance at the end of a grade. Then came the push by the Obama administration to hold individual teachers rather than entire schools accountable for scores. Then we had the Common Core State Standards, which accompanied a revived enthusiasm for performance assessment and the widespread but rhetorical claim that we are now holding people accountable for the "college and career readiness" of their students. Now, with ESSA, we have a limited return to state-level flexibility.

These were not trivial changes, and their effects on teachers and students were in some cases substantial. However, this continuing ferment about the best flavor of test-based accountability is for present purposes a distraction. The basic model has remained in place throughout: relying primarily on the pressure to raise test scores to improve schools. And none of these different variations on the theme escapes the fundamental conclusion that this approach has been for the most part a failure.

○ ○ ○

Many of those who pushed for these reforms had the best of motives. They were deeply concerned about the weak achievement of many American students, and they were convinced that test-based accountability held the key to improving schools and helping students. And many were motivated by a praiseworthy aim of reducing the glaring inequities in American education—the large and persistent gaps between rich and poor, minority and nonminority, and students with special needs and those without. This was the reason, for example, for setting a single performance target for all students, for mandating reporting by subgroups, and for holding schools accountable for the performance of each group separately. The belief that test-based accountability would help low-achieving students catch up is one reason why NCLB achieved an unusual degree of bipartisan support. George Bush's much-lauded phrase was that the program would end "the soft bigotry of low expectations," and the bill won the support of leading congressional liberals, including Ted Kennedy in the Senate and George Miller in the House, as well as many conservatives. Miller said to me at the time that the requirement to report performance for each subgroup would finally "shed some light in the corners." Critics have argued that some of the supporters had less praiseworthy motivations—in particular that they wanted to weaken public education to make way for alternatives such as school choice and charter schools. Perhaps so, but this doesn't alter the fact that much of the motivation for the reforms in general, and for some of the specific provisions that turned out to wreak the most havoc, was a sincere desire to improve public education.

Whatever their motives, the proponents were wrong. The reforms caused much more harm than good. Ironically, in some ways they inflicted the most harm on precisely the disadvantaged students the policies were intended to help.

○ ○ ○

But why did the reforms fail so badly? To many people—and certainly to many of the proponents—the reforms seem to be simple common sense. Measure what is important, reward and punish people based on how much of it they produce, and they'll produce more.

But this is too simple, too blunt a tool for managing an enterprise as complex and difficult as education. Over the coming chapters I'll explain in detail some of the specific reasons the reforms failed, but before delving into details, let's take stock of the big picture. What did this long series of reforms create?

To start, the system it imposed on schools rewards far too narrow a slice of educational practice and outcomes. To understand just how narrow, ask yourself what you would like to see when you walk into a classroom. When I watched my own kids' classrooms, I certainly did want the kinds of achievement that show up in standardized tests, but I wanted to see much more than that. I wanted to see good instruction—clear explanations, productive discussion between students and teachers, and a high level of student engagement. I wanted to see signs that students were motivated and enjoyed learning. I wanted to see a classroom atmosphere that encouraged students to work well together. And, of course, I wanted achievement in subjects that were *not* tested. The high school both of my kids attended had a superb music program that enrolled a sizable share of the students and brought them to a very high level of proficiency. I valued that. Your list may be different, but I'll wager that most of you have a list much longer than test scores in a few subjects.

The often unspoken premise of the reformers was that somehow all the rest of this stuff—other subjects, such as history, civics, art, and music, aspects of math and reading that are hard to measure with standardized tests, and "softer" things such as engaging instruction, love of learning, and ability to work in groups—would take care of itself. It didn't, and that shouldn't have surprised anyone.

The second reason for failure is that the system is very high pressure. Throughout the years of reform, its proponents steadily ratcheted up the pressure on educators and, sometimes indirectly, kids. In a few short years we went from jawboning educators to raise scores to firing them for failing to do so.

Narrowness and high pressure are a potent combination. This is why daily life in schools revolves around testing. And it creates strong incentives both to give short shrift to other important goals of education and to take shortcuts in raising scores, including bad test prep and even cheating.

A third critical failure of the reforms is that they left almost no room for human judgment. Teachers are not trusted to evaluate students or each other, principals are not trusted to evaluate teachers, and the judgment of professionals from outside the school has only a limited role. What the reformers trust is "objective" standardized measures. This was not accidental. Reformers have often argued—with good reason—that the previous systems for evaluating teachers were a bad joke. In most school systems, evaluation of tenured teachers was perfunctory, and almost all teachers were judged to be fine. Short of moral turpitude—embezzling, drinking on the job, sexual misconduct, and so on—most teachers were secure in their jobs regardless of how well or poorly they performed. Reformers wanted an evaluation system with teeth, something that would separate the wheat from the chaff, that would give weak performers real incentives to improve, and that would provide a defensible basis for terminating those who for whatever reason never reached an acceptable level of performance. Given past experience, they didn't trust others in the system to play that role. This is not a problem limited to schools; using human judgment in performance evaluations is particularly difficult in civil service systems, because the people doing the evaluating rarely face consequences for doing it poorly. In response, the reformers turned to objective measures, primarily standardized tests.

But teaching is far too complex a job to evaluate without any judgment, and many of the things we most value in schools aren't captured by tests. Perhaps that is why some of the high-performing systems in other countries rely on the judgment of professionals in evaluating teachers and schools. I've noted one example: Singapore. Another is the Netherlands, whose students are among the highest achieving in Europe on PISA (the Programme for International Student Assessment), one of the two most important international comparative assessments. The Dutch do use standardized testing to evaluate schools, but they test far less than we, do not use the scores directly to reward or punish educators, and rely a great deal on evaluations by professional school inspectors.

In contrast, the focus of reform in the United States has been to rely as much as possible on standardized measures and to minimize human judgment, even though the result was to leave a great deal of what is most important unmeasured—and therefore to give educators no incentive to focus on it. This is one of the most fundamental flaws of test-based accountability and one of the most significant reasons for its failures.

The uniform performance targets imposed by the reformers—motivated by their praiseworthy aim of reducing the inequities in American schooling—backfired and contributed to the failure of the reforms. These targets gradually became more stringent in two ways: encompassing more and more students and being set at higher levels of performance. NCLB mandated that the "Proficient" standard, and not a lower cut-score, be used as the target, and it requires that 99 percent of all students—even those with mild cognitive disabilities—be held to that target.

This was a dramatic change from past practice. Just as the reformers hoped, these changes made it impossible for schools to shunt low-performing groups aside and not worry about their learning—or at least their test scores. Unfortunately, they also created unrealistic goals in some settings, and that in turn led educators to respond in undesirable ways. You'll see some of the unintended consequences in later chapters.

A final reason for the failure of the reforms is rarely noted but may be as important as any of the others: the complete absence of any other incentives to balance the pressure to raise scores. Every single person in the education system is given the same incentives, that is, to raise scores, in many cases very rapidly. The teacher is no different in this respect from the building principal, the district superintendent, and even the state commissioner. Absolutely no one is given any incentive to monitor or control *how* these gains are achieved. In particular, no one has any incentive to look for bad test prep or other inappropriate behavior. As I will explain in the next chapter, this has a historical precedent: the Soviet industrial system, the system that produced consumer goods no one wanted to buy. It failed there, and it was doomed to fail in our schools. It is no accident that many of the types of inappropriate test prep by teachers that I will describe in coming chapters were actively encouraged by administrators, and it is no accident that some of the most publicized cheating scandals were actively supported by—and in at least one case deliberately started by—the people at the top.

4

CAMPBELL'S LAW

On September 18, 2015, a headline in the *New York Times* announced, "VW Is Said to Cheat on Diesel Emissions; U.S. Orders Big Recall."[1] The Environmental Protection Agency accused VW of installing "defeat devices" that turned off emissions-control technologies under normal driving conditions but not under the specific conditions that mirrored those used in government emissions tests. The result was that under normal conditions, the affected cars emitted as much as 40 times the allowable level of certain nitrogen oxides which contribute to asthma, other respiratory illnesses, and cardiovascular problems. The EPA ordered the recall of nearly half a million diesel cars marketed under the VW and Audi names. Within days, VW admitted that it had installed these defeat devices on eleven million cars sold worldwide. VW faces the possibility of enormous fines and has been sued by several states. The price of its stock immediately plummeted. The *Economist* wrote that "the damage to VW, the world's largest carmaker, is cataclysmic" and suggested that there could be major ramifications for the global auto industry and for the German export economy.[2]

VW's cheating was new only in its scale and brazenness. A remarkably similar instance of cheating had been exposed nearly two decades earlier. In 1998 the nation's seven largest truck manufacturers, including Caterpillar, Volvo, and Mack Trucks, settled a civil lawsuit filed by the EPA for faking the results of emissions testing by installing defeat devices on 1.3 million diesel truck engines. The result, by EPA's estimate, was the release of millions of tons of pollutants into the air. The seven companies were required to spend a billion dollars, including a civil penalty of $83.4 million—at the time the largest settlement ever for a violation of environmental protection regulations, but a pittance compared to the penalties VW faces, which as I am writing include $16 billion in civil penalties and a likely $2 billion criminal fine in the United States alone.[3] Nine years later the federal government forced an electronics company to stop selling defeat devices through its website and retailers.[4] And as the *Times* reported, this scandal was just another incident in a long history of cheating by the auto industry.[5]

The most important lesson of the VW scandal, however, is far bigger than the auto industry, and it has a great deal to do with the failure of education "reform." More than forty years ago, Don Campbell, one of the founders of the science of program evaluation, wrote: "The more any quantitative social indicator is used for social decision making, the more subject it will be to corruption pressures and the more apt it will be to distort and corrupt the social processes it is intended to monitor."[6] In other words, when you hold people accountable using a numerical measure—vehicle emissions, scores on a test, whatever—two things generally happen: they do things you don't want them to do, and the measure itself becomes inflated, painting too optimistic a view of whatever it is that the system is designed to improve. That's not to say that only bad things happen, or that having the accountability system is necessarily on balance worse than not having it. Some people will do what you want and perform better, and you may get more of the outcome—student learning, lower emissions—that the accountability system is designed to foster. Or you may not. In some cases the system fails entirely. That has happened in some schools, as we will see. However, whether the impact of accountability is *on balance* positive or negative, you will get some misbehavior and some corruption of the outcome for which people are accountable. People can be quite creative in devising their own "defeat devices," and I will devote a few chapters to explaining some common defeat devices used with educational testing. As a result of this corruption, performance won't be as good as the performance measure makes it seem. We should always ask, what is the mix of good and bad effects?

Campbell recognized that this problem would rear its head in educational testing: "Achievement tests may well be valuable indicators of . . . achievement under conditions of normal teaching aimed at general competence. But when test scores become the goal of the teaching process, they both lose their value as indicators of educational status and distort the educational process in undesirable ways." That is exactly what happened when high-stakes testing became the core of education "reform."

And Campbell was not the first to give this warning. Earlier I mentioned E. F. Lindquist, one of the most important early developers of standardized tests, who explained clearly why test scores by themselves aren't sufficient for evaluating schools or teachers. Lindquist also warned about Campbell's Law in educational testing, decades before Campbell's seminal article. In a 1951 publication, Lindquist wrote:

> The widespread and continued use of a test will, in itself, tend to reduce the correlation between the test series and the criterion series [the later behavior, outside of the testing situation, that is our real concern] for the population involved. Because of the nature and potency of the rewards and penalties associated in actual practice with high and low achievement test scores of students, the behavior measured by a widely used test tends in itself to become the real objective of instruction, to the neglect of the (different) behavior with which the ultimate objective is concerned.[7]

The result is score inflation.

The warnings continued. As test-based accountability developed in the United States, a number of specialists in educational measurement warned that high-stakes testing would produce inflated scores. By the 1980s those warning of what lay in store were coming from some very prominent people in the field: George Madaus at Boston College, who served as president of the National Council on Measurement in Education (NCME), the primary professional association in educational measurement; Lorrie Shepard at the University of Colorado, who has served as president of NCME, the American Educational Research Association (AERA, the primary association of education researchers), and the National Academy of Education; and Bob Linn at the University of Colorado, who served as president of both NCME and AERA and who is widely considered to have been one of the most important figures in measurement of the past half century. I first added my voice to the chorus in a publication in 1987.

Although the problem of Campbell's Law in education is not news, it's easier to understand—and for some people, easier to swallow—once one considers examples from outside of education. Since Campbell wrote this, the problem has been documented all sorts of settings other than schools and auto manufacturing. It has been found, for example, in the fast food industry, in policing (both inappropriate arrests and distorted arrest rates), postal delivery systems, airline on-time statistics (ever wondered why there are delays at one end or both and you still arrive "on time"?), and job training programs, to name a few. It's because the problem is ubiquitous that it is labeled "Campbell's *Law*" in the social sciences.*

There is particularly extensive documentation of Campbell's Law in two areas that have strong parallels to education reform: health care delivery and the Soviet system of incentives in manufacturing.

It has been common for some years to provide "report cards" on various aspects of medical practices and hospital outcomes. Just like test-based accountability, this is expected to give people information about the quality of services and to give doctors and administrators incentives to improve them. Critics have long voiced some of the same concerns that opponents of test-based accountability have expressed—that the measures can be misleading because they are incomplete, that the numbers are deceptive when one can't fully adjust for differences in patients' (read: students')

* For a fascinating if depressing overview of instances of Campbell's Law in many different fields, See Richard Rothstein, *Holding Accountability to Account: How Scholarship and Experience in Other Fields Inform Exploration of Performance Incentives in Education* (Nashville: National Center on Performance Incentives, Vanderbilt Peabody College, 2008), http://www.epi.org/files/2014/holding-accountability-to-account.pdf. I provided Rothstein with some examples for his monograph, and most of the examples in this chapter are described there.

conditions at intake, and that practitioners often find ways to game the system.

A particularly disturbing example arose some years ago, when New York State began publishing report cards with mortality rates for coronary artery bypass surgery. The rationale—the "model of change," as education policy makers like to say—was the simple one that motivated a lot of education "reform": publicize performance, and you will prod people to improve their practices. But Campbell warned that this rationale is not just simple; it's simplistic. Sure enough, Campbell's Law quickly made its appearance, in very disturbing ways. Two studies revealed that many cardiologists diverted care from some sicker patients because those patients harmed their ratings. Sicker patients, after all, are less likely to do well after treatment. You might think that doctors, who devote their careers to protecting the health of their patients, would be able to ignore these perverse incentives, but you would be wrong. Not long ago, a dozen years after these studies were published, a cardiologist wrote an op-ed in the *New York Times* describing his first experience with these report cards, which was consistent with the findings of that first study. He was then a new cardiology fellow, and he and his colleagues were evaluating a seriously ill elderly man with severe coronary blockages to decide whether to perform a bypass. The senior surgeon arrived and nixed the surgery *without even seeing the patient*. His explanation was that there was too much risk of a bad outcome, for which he would be penalized by the state agencies monitoring the report cards. What's more, surgeons had an additional incentive to avoid risky patients: it helped them produce good numbers they could then use to advertise themselves.[8]

That would be troubling enough, but the findings of one study were far more unsettling. The publication of report cards caused a substantial increase in the hospital readmission rates of certain categories of patients. Because their physicians had not provided them with treatments from which they would have benefited, they were more likely to become acutely ill again. Worse, the report cards produced a slight but statistically significant increase in mortality.[9] Not only did the program backfire and make people sicker; it actually killed some of them.

There are many other examples of pernicious side effects of well-intentioned accountability systems in health care. The Blair government in the United Kingdom implemented accountability policies in the National Health Service that are similar in principle to American education reform: they set many numerical targets for specific aspects of performance and used ratings on these measures both for public shaming and for concrete sanctions. Performance rapidly improved on these measures, and some of the improvement appears to have been real. Some of it, however, was anything but.

One of these measures was the percent of emergency room patients who are seen in less than four hours. This percent improved rapidly, but not always by legitimate means. Five different types of gaming were observed, the most remarkable of which was that some hospitals queued patients in ambulances parked outside until enough patients had been cleared away.[10] Another target required that patients be admitted to a hospital bed within twelve hours of admission to an emergency room. One solution: move the patients' gurneys into the hallway and classify gurneys in the hallways as "beds."

Some of these examples might seem like simple cheating, but health care also provides many examples of another response to accountability pressure that has an exact parallel in education: shifting effort from unmeasured—but important—activities to measured ones. One example from the United Kingdom arose because the accountability system counted waiting time for new outpatient ophthalmology appointments but did not take into account follow-up visits. One hospital improved its waiting time for new appointments by delaying or canceling follow-up appointments, which were not counted. A review found that twenty-five patients lost their vision over two years as a result.

Many of the examples of Campbell's Law in health care arise because there are simply too many important aspects of practice to measure. In response, the people designing accountability systems focus on a small number, which they may choose for any number of reasons. For example, in 2003 a US health-care provider, PacifiCare of California, set up a system that included incentives for five practices: screening for cervical and breast cancer, checking hemoglobin and A1C for diabetics, and childhood immunizations. Just like a test: the measured practices (the test items) would serve as a sample of all important aspects of practice (the domain). The effects were mixed. On the good side of the ledger, a few of the rewarded practices improved, although others showed no change. However, there was a catch. When researchers examined other some activities that were not rewarded, the news wasn't good. Some of these unrewarded practices were unchanged, but others, such as appropriate use of antibiotics and screening for chlamydia, actually deteriorated.[11] Faced with a limited amount of time, health-care workers shifted their efforts from important activities that were not measured to those that were—and for which they would be rewarded.

Were Pacificare patients better off? It's safe to guess that some were better off (patients whose cancer was caught earlier), while others were worse off (people with undiagnosed chlamydia). We don't know whether adding up all the wins and losses would indicate that the patient population as a whole was better or worse off, but we do know for certain that the measure used gave a misleading impression of improved medical practice.

A much simpler case of focusing work too narrowly because of performance incentives came to light in 2016, when the Insurance Institute for Highway Safety released new crash-test results. One of the IIHS tests, called the small overlap frontal tests, evaluates what happens when only 25 percent of a car's front end hits a fixed barrier at 40 miles per hour. Crashes of this sort are particularly dangerous, and simple frontal crash tests don't indicate how well cars protect occupants in such accidents. Therefore IIHS began doing the small overlap tests in 2012, and this resulted in rapid improvements in the scores automakers achieved. However, unbeknownst to many consumers—but of course not to auto manufacturers—IIHS conducted these tests only on the driver's side until mid-2016. In June of that year, IIHS released the first results of small overlap frontal tests on the passenger's side. The vehicles were seven small SUVs, all of which had earned the coveted "good" rating in earlier—left-hand-side—testing. Of the seven, only one received a good rating for the right-hand-side test. Three were rated as "acceptable," two as "marginal," and one as "poor," which is the lowest rating on the IIHS scale. Becky Mueller, the author of the IIHS report, offered this explanation: "Some manufacturers told us that in the short term they could make more driver's-side modifications to more vehicle models to improve safety rather than making improvements to both sides."[12] Unfortunately, this is no surprise.

A pinnacle of Campbell's Law was the Soviet manufacturing system. In the Soviet system, rewards and punishments were doled out based on a typically simple set of numerical targets set by central planning agencies. Readers who are old enough will probably recall examples of ludicrous responses to these incentives, because they were a staple of popular discussion of the Soviet system. Some of these may have been urban legends. For example, I remember being told as a kid about a factory that met its quota of shoes by producing only shoes for left feet. I doubt that is true. However, there are many examples that have been documented.

One well-documented example is a Soviet factory that was having difficulty meeting its quota for the number of shoes produced in a year because of supply constraints, so it produced only small sizes that required less material.[13] This wasn't anomalous. In another case, both a factory and the productivity of its individual workers were evaluated by the number of linear meters of cloth produced. The optimal bolt of cloth had a width of 142 centimeters, but to perform "well," the factory produced bolts with an average width of 106 centimeters, which weren't useful for some of the factories that needed cloth. In a number of industries (cement blocks, for example), the performance metric was simply the weight of production in tons. In response, some factories produced only heavier products. For example, one factory increased its output of roofing iron by 20 percent in weight but only 10 percent in terms of the area of roofing materials. There was no technical justification for the increase in the weight of the product per square meter; in fact, in many cases lighter would have been better because lighter materials require less support. Because the output of many factories was measured in terms of the count of items produced, factories produced low-quality consumer goods that could be made quickly and at low cost.

Most descriptions of this perverse system focus on the resulting bad decisions about the products, but it is equally important to ask what effects it had on innovation and risk taking, which are at the root of long-term improvement. The Soviet system created strong incentives to shun innovation and risk taking. Why? Because when one takes a risk, the gamble often doesn't pay off, so in the short term you are worse off—you have produced fewer shoes while experimenting with a new innovation. In the long run you are worse off for not innovating, but the short-term focus of the performance accountability system puts you at risk of never reaching the long term.

None of these examples mean that the systems failed. For all the gaming that has been documented in the US and British health care systems, both provide a high level of care on average. And while everyone makes fun of shoddy Soviet goods, the fact is that by some important measures the Soviet industrial system succeeded. Its primary goal was a rapid expansion of heavy industry, in part to support the production of military hardware. As the Germans learned in World War II and the United States learned during the Cold War and space race, the Soviet system, for all its flaws, did succeed in those respects. Sputnik worked, and Soviet military equipment was formidable, even though Soviet cars and shirts were garbage.

Nonetheless, these examples highlight two important lessons. The first is simply that you can take Campbell's Law to the bank. It's going to show up in any high-pressure accountability system that is based only on a few hard numbers. We need to look for it and try our best to minimize it and to tamp it down when it occurs. We haven't done either in education reform.

The second lesson is that we need to look at the *net* effects of reforms, balancing the negative effects against the positive. In some cases the net effects of accountability systems are positive, even strongly positive. Despite all the gaming, I'll bet (although I don't know this for a fact) that British patients are on average better off because the National Health Service holds hospitals accountable for emergency room waiting times. The moral of the story about ambulances parked in the driveway isn't to stop holding hospitals accountable for wait times; it is to do it with our eyes open and to be ready to fix the inevitable problems that arise.

○ ○ ○

So what do these examples have to do with education reform? A great deal. All of the examples above—yes, even the Soviet industrial system—have close parallels in the accountability system we have dropped into our schools.

In educational testing the corruption of measures about which Campbell warned takes the form of *score inflation*—increases in scores larger than improvements in learning justify. In some instances, as I will show in the next chapter, this inflation has been huge. Although this problem has been documented for more than a quarter of a century, it is still widely ignored, and the public is fed a steady diet of seriously misleading information about improvements in schools.

The corrupted practices Campbell noted take many forms in schools, paralleling the examples above. Many of them contribute to inflated test scores, while others haven't been shown to inflate scores but have nonetheless degraded rather than improved what goes on in classrooms.

Cheating. The testing parallel to the cheating by Volkswagen is, well, cheating. A modest number of cheating scandals have made the news—most notably, the scandal in Atlanta that resulted in prison sentences for some educators—but cheating appears to be far more common than these publicized cases suggest. I'll describe some examples in a later chapter. Moreover, I'll show that some common forms of test preparation that most people consider ethically acceptable, and that are used entirely openly, are really cheating.

Reallocation. The Volkswagen and Pacificare cases are analogous to another form of test preparation that needn't be cheating but can still inflate scores: capitalizing on the incompleteness of the measure used for accountability. In the Pacificare example, this was straightforward: a small sample of activities was used to represent the overall quality of a medical practice. In the case of diesel engines, the sampling is a bit more complex. Diesel engines have to function in a wide array of circumstances—idling, decelerating, maintaining a constant speed, accelerating lightly, accelerating hard, and so on. To gauge emissions, the EPA has used static tests—that is, tests in which the vehicle is actually not moving. Monitoring vehicles while in motion during normal use is much more expensive. Thus the EPA sampled one operating condition out of many. Volkswagen's cheating entailed designing software that generated good emissions figures under that one condition but not under others. In both cases, the response to accountability was to focus to a substantial degree on *improving the measure itself*, not on improving the underlying process the measure was intended to track.

The Volkswagen strategy has a precise counterpart in educational testing: focusing instruction on the small sample of material likely to appear on the specific test used in that particular system, at the expense of other important material that is either omitted or given little emphasis. I'll show this concretely in a later chapter.

Excluding people with bad numbers. The New York cardiology report card case also has a parallel in educational testing. One obvious analogy is making people ill; while we have no documented cases of deaths resulting from high-stakes testing, it certainly has been making many students and teachers sick. However, that's not the analogy I want to stress. The key value of this case is that it illustrates faking numbers by fiddling with the group—patients, students, whoever—from whom measurements are taken, in order to exclude some who would generate unfavorable numbers. We have ample documentation of this problem in testing as well—for example, allowing low-scoring students to be truant on the day of testing.

Lowered standards. The example of airline on-time statistics has analogues in testing as well. Since the key statistic in our current system is the proportion of students who score at least at the "Proficient" standard, states have an incentive to make sure that their Proficient standards are not too high. And as has been well documented, many have done precisely that.

There are other ways that people game test-based accountability systems. As I'll explain in a later chapter, a particularly important one is *coaching*, which entails focusing test prep on unimportant, often incidental characteristics of the test used for accountability. Coaching is particularly important because it can produce totally fraudulent score gains and often shades into outright cheating.

○ ○ ○

What's the takeaway? Test-based educational accountability can't avoid Campbell's Law, although some approaches may generate worse problems than others. That is not an argument against testing, against holding educators accountable, or even against using tests—in some way—in an educational accountability system. However it does show that we have an *obligation*—I'm using that word deliberately—to examine the negative effects carefully and weigh them against the positive impacts to see whether the system is, on balance, succeeding.

If we do examine the evidence honestly, the answer is that America's test-based accountability has been failing. In the chapters that follow, I'll discuss at some length both the positive and negative effects of the systems we have imposed on schools. I'll start with score inflation, about which we have had disturbing evidence for more than twenty-five years.

5

SCORE INFLATION

Test scores have been a big deal everywhere for years, but perhaps nowhere more than in New York City from 2002 until 2010, the years when Joel Klein was the chancellor of the city's school system. Klein made rewards and punishments based on standardized test scores the core of his system. Schools were given "report card" grades based on test scores. Some schools were closed because of scores, and others were given bonuses for them. Teachers were given "value-added" ratings based on their students' scores, and these were sent to principals. Near the end of his time, Klein instructed principals to use these ratings to determine which teachers received tenure. Those who didn't, of course, were likely to lose their jobs. Principals, in turn, were fired because of their schools' scores. In several grades, students' promotion to the next grade was made contingent on their test scores. "Quality reviewers" brought test-prep materials to low-scoring schools.

Scores soared. They rose rapidly statewide, but the statewide gains were substantially fueled by increases in New York City, which were much faster than the average improvement in much of the rest of the state.

The New York Department of Education claimed success, and many people bought it. The press seemed to be thrilled. The *New York Times* reported in 2008 that "reading and math scores for New York students in grades three through eight showed extraordinary gains . . . with particularly striking leaps in the large urban areas, including New York City."[1] In 2007 the Department of Education won the Broad Prize for Urban Education, a half-million-dollar award to an urban district that—supposedly—has made the greatest improvements in student achievement. Klein and his accountability policies became an exemplar, both within the United States and internationally. Other large districts—for example, Washington, DC, during the reign of Michelle Rhee—adopted similar test-centered "reforms."

There were clouds on the horizon, however, in the form of the National Assessment of Educational Progress (NAEP), a set of standardized tests that are widely considered a gold standard for evaluating educational trends. When scores on the NAEP were released in 2007, they showed that New York City's eighth-graders had made *no* progress whatsoever in mathematics on that test over the previous two years, despite their huge gains on the state test. The Klein administration had vociferous critics for many reasons, not just its pressure to raise scores, and the NAEP results added fuel to their concerns. The press became increasingly skeptical of the good news flowing from the district, and journalists quickly changed their tune. Some reporters didn't just worry about Campbell's Law and the possibility of exaggerated gains. They smelled blood, and some repeatedly called experts in testing—including me—to ask about possible malfeasance on the part of state officials. (I told them that they were right to worry about possible inflation but that I was aware of no malfeasance and would have been greatly surprised if there was any.)

This set the stage for the release of state-test and NAEP scores in 2009, which dropped the controversy into the laps of two newcomers: David Steiner, the new state commissioner of education, and Meryl Tisch, elected as the chancellor of the state Board of Regents that March.

It started as usual: another report of large gains on the state test, the third straight since the new tests were introduced in 2006. However, shortly afterward the federal Education Department gave Steiner, Tisch, and Klein embargoed information about the pending release of data on the state's 2009 performance on the NAEP. This is standard procedure; it gives the people in charge time to figure out what to say. This time the state did show score gains on the NAEP,

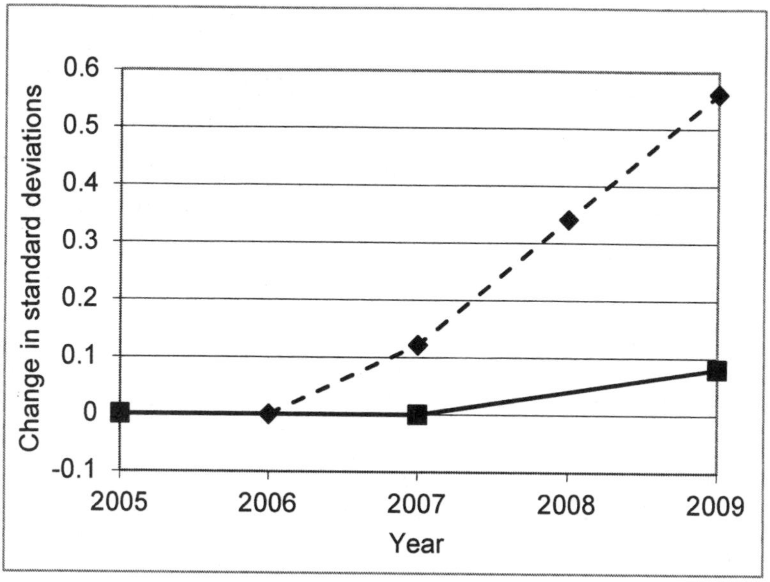

Figure 5.1. Eighth-grade math scores in New York State on the state's high-stakes test (dashed, diamonds) and the National Assessment of Educational Progress (solid, squares).

but they were a small fraction of the increase on the state test. For example, over the entire period the gains on NAEP in eighth-grade math were roughly one-sixth as large as the gains on the state test. The trends on the two tests are shown in figure 5.1.

The press jumped on this discrepancy. On October 15, 2006, the front page of the *New York Times* read "U.S. Math Tests Find Scant Gains Across New York."[2] Two days later, the *New York Post* wrote that "when state and national testing methods produce such starkly discrepant pictures, folks logically conclude that one—if not both—must be wrong."[3] In many cases, less rosy news from NAEP hasn't seriously derailed the flow of seemingly good news from testing programs, but Klein, Steiner, and Tisch had no such luck. The same article quoted Diane Ravitch as saying, "What this amounts to is a fraud. This is a documentation of persistent dumbing down by the State Education Department and lying to the public." The department had to confront this glaring and well-publicized disparity in trends, and they had to do it publicly.

Klein took the standard path and defended the scores on the state test: "This doesn't in any way undermine what we've accomplished here."[4] His argument was that the state test measured what the state considered important.

Steiner and Tisch followed a far more unusual course: they took it on the chin. They told the press that the NAEP results showed that there was something fundamentally wrong with the state's testing program. They expressed concern about score inflation and announced that they would modify the state's tests to combat it. They promptly gave instructions to the state's testing contractor to start altering their tests to make them both broader and somewhat less predictable. They also made a public commitment to allow outside evaluation of score inflation. (Full disclosure: my research group and I were beneficiaries of this, obtaining access to New York data.)

Who was right? By now you know, but it's worth unpacking the argument a bit more.

Let's start with a hypothetical example. Many New Jersey residents work in New York. Suppose I'm an employer and want to hire some entry-level workers who will need some math skills, say, to operate sophisticated machinery. I find that I have applicants who just graduated from the schools in both New York City and Hoboken, New Jersey. Would I want different math skills from the two groups? Would I sort them into two piles so that I could use the New York test to evaluate the math skills of the kids from New York and the New Jersey test—which samples differently from the math domain—to evaluate the Hoboken kids? Would I care which test they took?

Of course not. My only concern would be whether the applicants have the skills they need to do well at the jobs for which they are applying. The specific test they took would matter only if I had reason to believe that one of them better matched the skills I needed.

By the same token, in looking at New York City applicants, would I think, "Why should I care about the skills measured by NAEP? The New York test measures what New York thinks is important"? This would be sensible only if I believed that what is covered by NAEP is unimportant for my purposes. In other words, only if a lot of what is covered by NAEP is not part of what I mean if I say that kids are learning more math.

Is that plausible? A colleague of mine, Jen Jennings, made this concrete. The NAEP math test is made up of five main areas of content: numbers and operations (arithmetic and then some), measurement, geometry, data analysis and probability, and algebra. Jennings asked: did the small gains the state's students showed on NAEP appear in all five of these areas? She found virtually *no* progress in four of the five content areas. What gains the state did show were a result of improvements in algebra, which was heavily weighted on the state's own test. In other words, students improved only on the one part of the test for which they had been heavily prepped.

So if Klein were right, he would have to be able to tell parents, employers, and the public that when he announced improved achievement in mathematics, they should take that to mean *only* an improvement in algebra and *not* in numbers and operations, measurement, geometry, or data analysis and probability. Joel Klein is one very persuasive guy, but even he would not be able to make that argument stick.

So Steiner and Tisch were right. The state's test scores were badly inflated.

Don't think this was only a New York problem. Superintendents and commissioners generally aren't eager to have studies of possible score inflation in their systems. Trust me: asking one of them for access to their data in order to find out whether scores are inflated doesn't usually get a welcoming response. So there are far fewer audits of impressive score gains on high-stakes tests than there ought to be. Nonetheless, we have enough evidence, accumulated over more than twenty-five years, to know that inflation is common and that it is often very large. Numerous studies have found that score gains were exaggerated three- to sixfold, and there have been some instances in which very large gains in scores have been accompanied by no real gains in learning whatsoever. These studies confirmed what Don Campbell and E. F. Lindquist had predicted decades earlier and gave us hard data showing just how severe this problem had become.

The real puzzle wasn't whether New York's scores were inflated. The real puzzle was why we were still witnessing this argument as late as 2009.

○ ○ ○

Score inflation—not just its pervasiveness but also its severity—is so central to the failure of American education "reform" that a few more examples are in order. Several of the studies I will describe are old, which goes to show that we have seen—and ignored—these warning signs for a long time.

I'll start with the first empirical study of score inflation, which I carried out with several colleagues in the late 1980s. I'll tell you the story of this study because it illustrates another serious problem I'll come back to later: the unwillingness of many people who control public education to allow honest evaluations that risk findings they don't want.

High-stakes testing started gathering momentum in the 1970s, and a very small number of people in the field of educational measurement—I was among them—started warning early on that this was likely to produce inflated scores. However, as of the late 1980s there was still not a single study evaluating whether inflation occurred or how severe it was. With three colleagues, I set out to conduct one.

First, I had to find the funding the study would require. This wasn't easy, as score inflation wasn't on the radar screen of the education policy world, including foundations and other organizations that fund research.

Then came the far harder task: finding a state or district that would allow us to do the study. We started by submitting a proposal to a state education department that was actually looking for experts to evaluate its new high-stakes testing program. A few weeks later I got a call from someone I knew in the state education department. She knew we were qualified to do the study; to start, one of my colleagues was Bob Linn, quite possibly the single most esteemed person in educational measurement at the time, and very well known in the education policy community. However, she didn't like our plan to evaluate possible inflation. "Isn't that a validity question?" she asked. Of course it is, I replied. Scores were likely to go up, so a critical question would be whether these increases were giving the public valid information about students' achievement. She then said that the state's testing contractor would do the department's validity work. I explained that testing contractors don't evaluate score inflation and that they end their work before there has been a chance for score inflation to develop. "No," she answered, "you're not hearing me. Our testing contractor does our validity work." The state rejected our proposed study and then withdrew its request for proposals altogether. Back to square one.

Next stop: a large district in the same state. The administrators agreed to allow the study after we agreed not to identify the district. We designed the experiment, assigned classrooms to different testing conditions, wrote some tests ourselves, purchased materials for two commercial tests, and hired a testing firm to package, distribute, retrieve, and score the tests—a huge effort requiring lots of work and money. Shortly before the tests were to go out to schools, I was summoned back to the district. The superintendent wasted no time: he started the meeting by telling me that he was throwing us out because the study was politically too risky. I pointed out that in addition to not identifying the district, we had even agreed to partially obscure the descriptive information normally required in publications, such as enrollment counts and demographics, to hide the district's identity. He replied that this didn't offer him enough protection. He said that he expected the study would show up in a newspaper and that some teacher in his district would realize that he or she had been in the study. "Then I'll be in trouble with my legislature," he explained. End of discussion.

So we started over yet again. Eventually we found a large district in another state that allowed us to conduct the study, but only under restrictive conditions designed to protect the district from negative publicity. One of these constraints is unfortunately quite common: we were not allowed to identify the district or state. (Imagine getting permission to evaluate one drug in a given category, say, one anti-inflammatory medication, but only on the condition that you not tell the public which drug you evaluated. Or permission to subject cars to collision tests but not to disclose the makes and models of those that fail.) In addition, we were not even allowed to identify the specific tests used because that might provide a clue about the district's identity. For more than twenty-five years, the two most important of these tests have been known as Test B and Test C.

This wasn't an isolated case. I have had several other studies rejected or terminated because of political risk, and I know others have as well. In one state, when I proposed exploring a topic related to inflation, I was told "That's just not our priority now" and was then denied access to data that the state had provided to numerous other researchers, including a colleague of mine. Imagine if the same were true of drug companies. 'You want to investigate whether our nonsteroidal anti-inflammatory drugs have negative effects on cardiac health? Sorry, that's just not our priority now.' Nor is the problem restricted to score inflation. In one case a state superintendent was displeased by some of the responses teachers gave to a survey that some colleagues and I administered, and when I refused to censor the report, she barred me from any research of any kind in that state for years. She even told one of the state's most important foundations that she would not allow her department to cooperate with a study it was launching if I had any role in it. In another state, I had two studies of assessment accommodations for students with disabilities killed in midstream, and the person who stopped one of them told me frankly that the reason was that he didn't want to bear the political risk.

These specific cases reflect a more general and much more troubling pattern: by and large, states and districts allow access to data only if they want the particular study the researchers propose and aren't worried about the outcome. All of the education researchers I know who work with data from states or districts are familiar with the routine: explain in detail not only what data you need but what specific questions you will address with them, and then wait to see whether the proposed analysis passes muster. It is common to receive a memorandum of understanding that specifies—and limits—the questions that can be addressed. It is also the norm to be prohibited from sharing the data with others—unlike many other fields, in which the highest-quality journals will refuse to publish a study unless the authors make their data available for replication and additional analysis.

There are admirable exceptions to this stonewalling, and I would have been unable to carry out much of my own work without them. The exceptions, however, prove the rule. This reluctance to allow risky evaluation is deplorable, but I will put it aside for now and get on to the results of this study and some others.

○ ○ ○

If you are skeptical, you might ask: but how do we really know when scores are inflated? Joel Klein's argument—more precisely, the flaw in his argument—holds the key.

Most studies of score inflation follow a simple principle. Recall that tests are small samples of content drawn from big domains, like "eighth-grade mathematics." We want to draw conclusions about mastery of eighth-grade mathematics, not performance on the forty or fifty specific items that were placed on a test. So increases in scores are meaningful only if they signal similar increases in mastery of the domain. If they do generalize to the domain, *gains should appear on other tests that sample from the same domain.* If a poll is giving you useful results, you should find similar results in other similar polls. Not identical results, of course, but similar enough that they point to the same general conclusion. If not, one or the other has to be wrong. The same is true of tests.

Therefore, most studies of inflation compare gains on a high-stakes tests to those on another test that should provide similar information about student achievement. This second test, usually called an *audit test,* should be a credible test that is unaffected—or at least less affected—by score inflation. NAEP is the most commonly audit test for several reasons. It is considered a very high-quality test. NAEP scores are not susceptible to inflation because teachers aren't held accountable for scores and therefore have no incentive to engage in NAEP-focused test prep. And NAEP scores are there for the taking. In math and reading, NAEP is administered every two years, and the scores are available to anyone on the web. The comparison in figure 5.1 that Klein rejected—comparing improvements on NAEP to improvements on the state's test—is precisely the comparison most often used in studies of possible score inflation. However, sometimes researchers use other tests as audits or administer their own. The studies I will describe here all rely on a comparison with one or more audit tests—NAEP, a lower-stakes test administered by the district, or a low-stakes test administered by the researchers.

○ ○ ○

To start, we know that inflation can be severe. You've already seen one example: the inflation of New York State's eighth-grade math scores shown in figure 5.1. The average gain on the test the state used for accountability was roughly six times as large as the state's improvement on NAEP. This inflation was large in absolute terms as well. The scale used in figure 5.1, standard deviations (also known as effect sizes), is unfamiliar to most people, but it's standard in statistics and is useful in discussing score trends because it allows us to compare trends on tests that are reported on different scales. In some cases, effect sizes can be translated into more familiar percentiles, and I can do that here. The trend in state test scores indicates that the median student in 2009—that is, the kid who scored better than half of her peers—performed so well that she would have outscored 71 percent of comparable students only three years earlier, when the testing program had begun. In contrast, NAEP scores suggest that this typical student would have outscored only 53 percent of the state's students three years earlier.

The multiple of 6 in the New York data is on the high side, but it isn't the largest that has been found. In a few studies very large gains on the state test have been accompanied by *no improvement whatever* on an audit test. A particularly striking example—important for other reasons as well, to which I will return in a moment—was the trend in reading scores when Kentucky instituted its groundbreaking high-stakes KIRIS program in 1992. You may recall that KIRIS was one of the pioneering pay-and-punish systems and that it served in many ways as a template for NCLB. During the first two years of the program, the average score in fourth-grade reading increased by 0.75 of a standard deviation. That is, the average increased a third more than New York's math scores, but in only two years rather than three. This means that the typical student in 1992 would have outscored fully 77 percent of the state's students only two years earlier! It was obvious to me that this was exaggerated, but NAEP showed that it was even more inflated than I had thought. The state showed no gain whatever on the NAEP reading test.[5]

The first study of score inflation, the one I had so much difficulty carrying out, measured inflation in a form easier to understand: months of schooling. Both the test used by the district and the primary low-stakes test we administered were reported in "grade equivalents," an easily understood measure that unfortunately has fallen out of style. The grade equivalent (GE) is simply the typical score at any point in schooling, expressed in years and months (with ten months per academic year). These can be calculated for any group, but we used the national distribution of scores. For example, in this study, a GE of 3.7 indicated the score reached by the median student nationwide in March of third grade.

Four years before our study, the-district-I-cannot-name started using a commercially prepared test that I am not allowed to identify and therefore call Test C. Scores rose rapidly, and by 1986 the average math score in the spring of third grade was 4.3. That is, students appeared to be about half an academic year above the national average. Pretty good, given that a large proportion (I'm not allowed to tell you that proportion either) of the students in the district were poor and from historically low-scoring groups: African Americans and Latinos.

In 1987 the district switched to a different but very similar test (Test B), and the average score plummeted by half an academic year (figure 5.2). It took a scant three years to recover, putting the average score right back where it had been in the last year of Test C—fully half an academic year higher than when the new Test B was first used.

This sort of sawtooth pattern—scores rising over time, dropping when a new test is introduced, and then rising again—was familiar to testing experts, although not to the public. With some effort, one could come up with a charitable explanation. Perhaps the students

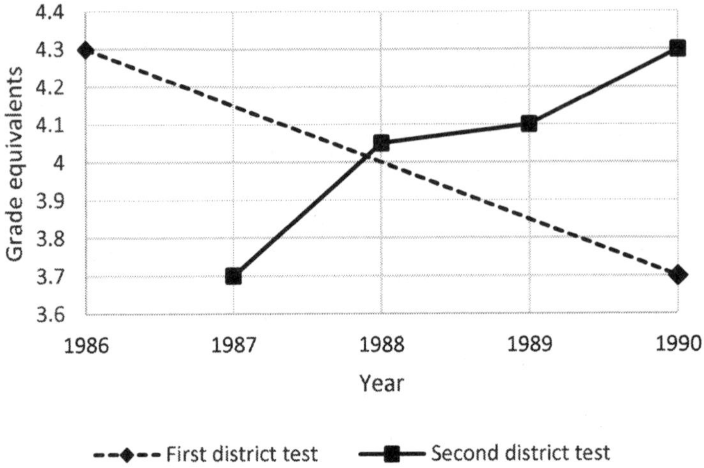

Figure 5.2. Third-grade math scores on two different tests.

maintained their mastery of the material on Test C while adding proficiency on material emphasized more on the new Test B.

Or maybe not.

Our main innovation was to administer *precisely the same test (Test C) that the district had used until four years earlier*. That's the diamond in the lower right of figure 5.2. Sure enough, as kids were improving on the material emphasized by Test B, they were losing (coincidentally, by an identical amount) mastery of material on Test C. Teachers were simply substituting an emphasis on the details of one test for details on the other.[6]

If you have an appropriately skeptical bent, you might suggest that maybe kids just weren't motivated for our test, which was administered two weeks after the district's own. We worried about this too, and we had a way to check whether our scores were biased downward by low motivation. There was no hint of this among third-grade kids or among fifth-grade girls, but it was clear that a small number of fifth-grade boys didn't take our test seriously. That's why we present only the third-grade results. The fifth-grade results were more extreme, but they were potentially misleading. (The reason is complex, but motivation isn't a serious threat to the design of most other studies of score inflation.)

I've shown this figure to thousands of people over the years, and I have often asked: which of the scores from the final year is the honest one to give to parents? Virtually everyone who has answered has said the lower one. The lower one is indeed the one people should trust, but the public almost never gets to see it. There is rarely an audit that would provide them the lower average. They see only the higher one. Inflation goes unnoticed, and everyone is misled to believe that education has rapidly improved.

Not all examples of score inflation are dramatic as these first ones, but even smaller amounts can be seriously misleading. For example, during the first years of Kentucky's KIRIS system, the state's tests showed dramatic gains in mathematics in the fourth and eighth grades. The state's NAEP scores confirmed that students' achievement had improved—but by far less. The average gains on KIRIS were roughly *four times* as large as those on NAEP.[7]

These are not isolated cases. While score inflation has not been apparent in every place studied, it appears often, and I am not aware of a single credible study of high-stakes testing in the United States that has failed to find inflation in at least some of the systems examined.

When news of score inflation began to register, a widespread response was to blame it on multiple-choice testing. This argument regained currency recently. You will frequently see claims that using some form of 'performance assessments'—tests in which students are required to write or do something, not just select an answer from among several choices—will take care of the problem of bad test prep and score inflation. We need "tests worth teaching to," I have been told more times than I can recall.

Sadly, it just isn't true.

Certainly some forms of test preparation are limited to multiple-choice tests—for example, the process of elimination (only multiple-choice items give you answer choices to eliminate) and plugging in answer choices (only multiple-choice items give you answer choices to plug in). And a number of the best-known studies of inflation have examined testing programs systems that were entirely or largely multiple choice.

However, all that is required for scores to become inflated is that the sampling used to create a test has to be *predictable*. This predictability can involve the content tested, the way that content is presented, the format of test items, or the way students' responses are scored. For inflation to occur, teachers or students need to capitalize on this predictability, focusing on the specifics of the test at the expense of the larger domain. (I show some examples of how this is done in chapter 7.)

There is no reason to expect formats other than multiple choice—short constructed-response items, elaborate performance assessments, or whatever—to be immune to these problems, and there's no evidence that they are. The one study we have that directly addressed this question—in fact, it was designed to answer it—was one of the studies of the Kentucky KIRIS program I described above. One of the innovations in KIRIS was to use other formats: constructed response (where students have to write answers), complex performance tasks, direct tests of writing, and portfolio assessments in both writing and math. Multiple-choice items were used very little in some years and not at all in others. You've seen two of the findings. In every case examined, KIRIS score were inflated, in most cases severely. The fourth-grade reading scores summarized above are one of the most severe instances of inflation found anywhere.

A second mistaken belief is that inflation arises only if the system imposes serious and concrete sanctions and rewards for scores. Wrong again. All that is needed is that teachers feel pressure to raise scores on a specific test. This was shown concretely by our first study of inflation. While the system in the-district-I-cannot-name was high stakes by the standards of the time, it was extremely lenient compared with what we now impose on schools. For the most part, scores did not lead to concrete consequences for either students or teachers. Students were not held back in grade because of low scores. Teachers and principals, at least if tenured, were not at risk of losing their jobs because of scores, and tenure was not based on scores. There were no cash awards to schools for scores and no school closures because of scores. Rather, the district employed what a spokesperson for another district with similar policies called "the strategy of applied anxiety." Scores were the core of the district's evaluation of schools, and teachers felt strong pressure to raise them. That was enough.

You may have noticed that all but one of the examples I have given show score inflation in mathematics. The problem of corrupted scores isn't limited to math; after all, it's just Campell's Law in educational garb, and Campbell's Law has shown up almost everywhere people have looked, not just in the education system. However, there are a number of reasons why most studies have focused on mathematics. Testing in math and reading is ubiquitous and has been the core of education accountability in most states since well before NCLB and ESSA. NAEP provides a ready audit test in math and reading in grades 4, 8, and 12, but NAEP tests in other subjects have been infrequent. Reading tests are as common and important as math tests, but they don't provide as many opportunities for inappropriate test prep as do tests in math or other content-rich subjects, such as history or the sciences. When teaching the many subjects that focus on specific content, one of the main ways teachers can game the system is focusing on the tested fraction of that content, at the expense of other content that is important but not emphasized by a particular test. Reading doesn't afford this opportunity. And a considerable share of reading skill is picked up out of school, starting with parents reading to young children and continuing with kids' reading out of school. In contrast, most students learn most of their math in school, affording more opportunity to game the test. It's therefore not surprising that some studies that have directly compared math and reading have shown that inflation is more common and tends to be more severe in math than in reading. However, the Kentucky findings above show that even reading scores can be severely inflated.

○ ○ ○

It would be bad enough if we simply had exaggerated score gains that were misleading the public and creating an illusion of improvement. The problem is worse than that.

What makes the problem so much worse is the fact that *inflation varies from place to place*. You might say, "Well, of course it does. Some teachers will cut corners more than others. Why should we be concerned about this?" There are at least two reasons to worry a great deal.

The first reason is that we are identifying the wrong teachers, schools, and systems as successes and failures. This is not just fundamentally unfair to teachers and their students. The entire logic of our reforms depends on rewarding the schools that do better and punishing those that don't. However, because in most contexts we can't separate score inflation from legitimate improvements, we are sometimes rewarding people who game the system more effectively, and we are punishing educators who do good work but appear to be doing *relatively* less well because they aren't taking as many shortcuts. On top of that, we are holding out as examples to be emulated programs that look good only because of bogus score gains and overlooking programs that really *are* good because the teachers using them are doing less to game the system. In other words, the system can propagate bad practice.

To illustrate this, I will show an example from a former student of mine who compared "value added" estimates for schools in Houston using two different tests: the state's high-stakes test (TAAS) and a lower-stakes commercial test administered by the district (the Stanford, or SAT-9). Value-added estimates using high-stakes tests are of course a key element of evaluating schools or individual teachers in many states. However, value-added estimates are rarely calculated with lower-stakes tests that are less likely to be inflated. To make sure that her results would not be a fluke, she did this comparison fully forty-eight times, using both reading and math, data from two different years, and different statistical approaches. Across these forty-eight comparisons, the consistency of the value-added estimates from the two tests ranged from mediocre to paltry. (For those readers familiar with statistics, the rank correlations ranged from 0.27 to 0.63.) In other words, if you used the lower-stakes test scores, you would rank many schools much differently than Houston did using high-stakes scores.

To illustrate this concretely, I'll show the median comparison in figure 5.3, which has value-added ratings based on fifth-grade math scores. Half the comparisons showed less consistency than this, and half more. To make sense of this graph, it is important

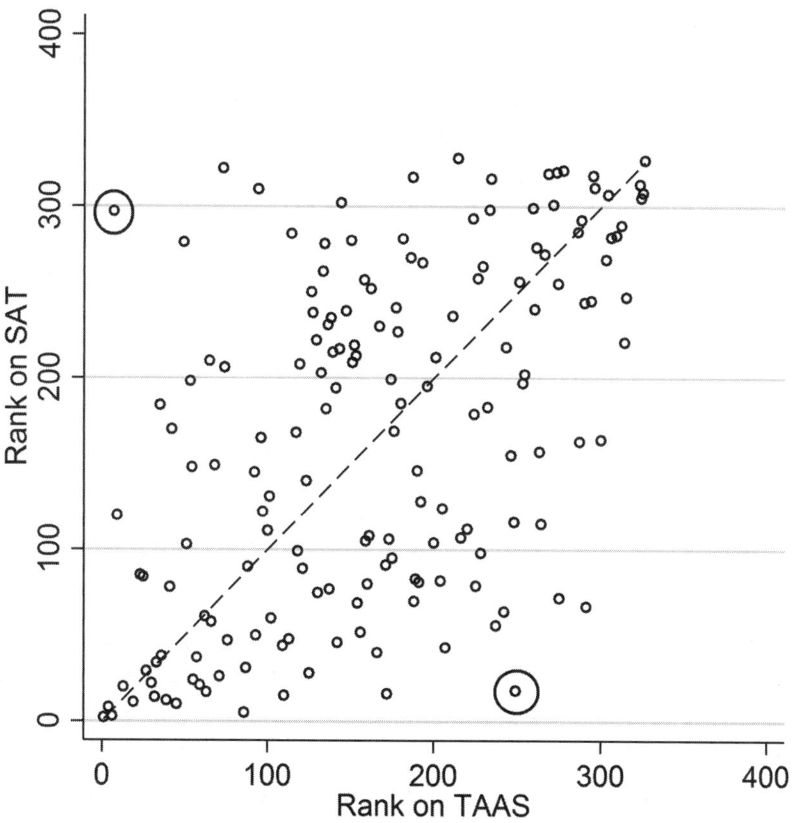

Figure 5.3. School ranks based on value-added estimates using the high-stakes TAAS and the lower-stakes SAT-9, grade 5 math.

to keep in mind that what I am showing is not how much scores went up in absolute terms. That is not an easy comparison to make with two different tests, and it is not the one that matters in most state accountability systems. Rather, I am simply *ranking* schools in terms of their value-added estimates. Arrayed along the bottom of the graph is schools' rank on the high-stakes TAAS test, while the vertical axis shows their ranks on the lower-stakes SAT-9. The schools along the dashed diagonal have approximately the same rank on both tests. Those above and to the left have higher ranks on the SAT-9, and those below the diagonal have higher ranks on the high-stakes TAAS.

So let's take two hypothetical schools. I'll call the first school Upright Elementary. The teachers in Upright refuse to do any test preparation. Instead they work diligently to improve their instruction, knowing that over the long run their students will learn more and do better on tests. They know that test prep can sometimes produce much faster gains, but they don't care. Let's call the second school Sham Elementary. The teachers at Sham have only one goal: to raise scores as fast as they can. They use any form of test prep they think will work, even if it squeezes out good instruction. Some even cheat. (Yes, people do cheat. In fact, Houston has engaged in practices that elsewhere were labeled as cheating. I'll come back to that in later chapters.)

Where would Upright and Sham appear in figure 5.3? To place them, you have to keep in mind that this figure shows ranks, so what we have to figure out is where they will appear *relative to other schools*.

Sham will make big gains on the TAAS, probably much bigger than those accomplished by Upright. However, it will accomplish this by sacrificing good instruction, so its gains on the SAT-9—or another audit test—will be relatively small compared with those of a comparable school that focused on instruction rather than test prep. Upright is the reverse: its teachers have sacrificed big gains on TAAS for the sake of real improvements that will show up on any similar test. So Sham will rank highly on TAAS and more poorly on the SAT-9. It could be the school I have circled on the lower right. Upright, however, will rank well on the SAT-9 and poorly on the TAAS, like the school I have circled in the upper left.

Sham gets rewarded, and Upright is sanctioned, which of course is the opposite of what we want. And keep in mind that this is the median case: in half of the comparisons, the consistency between the two tests was worse. In some cases, much worse.*

* Some readers may realize that there is an important technical issue underlying these comparisons. That is, even in the absence of score inflation, one would expect some inconsistency in school ratings across tests simply because the ratings are imprecise estimates, just like polls based on small samples. Of course, even if the scatter in figure 5.3 stemmed only from imprecision, that would be bad enough: it's not desirable to rate schools or teachers—and then punish and reward them—based on random noise. However, our ongoing work indicates that cause of the inconsistency in Houston was not just noise. It was also bias—inflation—in schools' TAAS scores.

The second reason to worry about variations in score inflation may trouble some people even more: a small but growing number of studies have found that score inflation is more severe among disadvantaged students, specifically racial and ethnic minorities and poor students. If score inflation is the measure of success—or failure—the reforms are most seriously failing precisely the groups they were supposed to help.

We can see one instance of this if we look more closely at the inflated New York State gains in eighth-grade math that I showed at the beginning of this chapter. During the first three years of the testing program, from 2006 to 2009, the average African American student gained one and a half times as much on the state test as the average white student. The scores of both groups increased dramatically, but the greater gains by African Americans took a big bite out of the average difference between them and white students. This gap shrank by more than a fourth in the space of only three years. At that rate, the entire gap between the two groups would disappear in only twelve years! Even more than the proponents of the system could have hoped for. However, it was a mirage. NAEP results showed that New York's white and African American students made nearly identical, very modest gains.

To those of us who are familiar with these sorts of data, the New York experience was no surprise. The first study that showed large racial differences in score inflation had been published decades earlier. Some of you may remember the "Texas miracle" of the 1990s: scores went up very rapidly on the state test, and the gap between white students and both African American and Latino students shrank dramatically. These gained George W. Bush national notice and played a prominent role in his election campaign. Both were illusory. NAEP showed both far smaller gains overall and very little narrowing of the gaps between whites and the other groups.[8]

A few years later the *New York Times* replicated this study, focusing just on Houston and using more recent data. The analysis by the *Times* reached the same conclusions as the earlier study. On the state's high-stakes test, overall gains were very large, and the achievement gap between white and minority students had nearly vanished. The *Times* wrote that claims of rapid gains in Houston "catapulted Houston's superintendent, Rod Paige, to Washington as education secretary and made Texas a model for the country."[9] However, the reporters found that overall gains were three times as large on the high-stakes test as on the Stanford audit test. And "the achievement gap between whites and minorities, which Houston authorities have argued has nearly disappeared on the Texas exam, remains huge on the Stanford test."[10] Like Joel Klein, Paige defended the district's scores, saying the two tests measured different things. All of the experts quoted by the *Times* disagreed.

Poor students, like minority students, also often show more inflation than others. For example, a study that examined reading scores across a number of states found that inflation was much more common among students eligible for free or reduced-price lunches than among other students.[11] Ongoing work by my own group has shown that context matters: it is not just the poverty of individual students that predicts the amount of inflation but also the concentration of poor students in a school. We found that poor children had, on average, more severely inflated scores than other kids in the same schools. Even after taking into account this difference in score inflation between poor and other students, schools with a higher proportion of poor students showed greater average inflation.

It's not surprising that disadvantaged students suffer more from score inflation. In fact, when my colleagues and I started my first study of inflation almost thirty years ago, we expected this. Low-performing schools often face severe barriers to improvement—for example, fewer resources, less experienced teaching staff, high rates of teacher turnover, higher rates of student transience, fewer high-performing students to serve as models, fewer parents who are able to provide supplementary supports, and less pressure for academic achievement from parents, among other things. Faced with these obstacles, teachers will have a stronger incentive to look for shortcuts for raising scores.

Ironically, one of the elements of school reform intended to help low-achieving students appears to have backfired, making these incentives worse. The key is that the performance targets are uniform and are coupled with real sanctions and rewards. When these targets require faster gains than teachers can produced by legitimate means, teachers have a strong incentive to search for whatever methods might raise scores quickly. The more severe score inflation shown by disadvantaged students is just one indication of this. You'll see more. There is ample evidence that test prep is more pervasive in the schools serving disadvantaged kids, and some signs that cheating is more common.

○ ○ ○

Up until now I've been writing about the inflation of students' scores, but people have also found ways to corrupt the scores of groups—schools and entire systems—that don't necessarily inflate the scores of individuals. Remember, the primary focus of accountability is educators, not students. What matters for rewards and punishments is the performance—or at least the apparent performance—of the school system, individual schools, and often individual teachers.

There are two ways of inflating group scores without necessarily corrupting the scores of individual students—focusing on "bubble kids" and manipulating the group of students tested. The second of these will take us directly to the topic of the next chapter: cheating.

First, bubble kids. In our system, the kids who matter most—in some cases, the only students who matter at all—are the ones who can be brought above that arbitrary "proficient" target or who are at risk of falling below it. These are the students many teachers call "bubble kids." They are the ones who count when schools and teachers are evaluated and when rewards and punishments are doled out, because those are all based on the percentage of kids who are "proficient." Kids who are far above the cut don't matter because they are unlikely to fall below it even if you don't pay them much attention. Kids who are far enough below the cut are a bad investment of time: the lower they are, the less likely they are to clear the hurdle, and the more effort it will take to get them there if they do. The big payoff is with kids who are close to the cut.

And this incentive works, although *works* might not be the ideal word. We have had evidence for years that many teachers devote disproportionate attention to bubble kids.[12]

When teachers focus on bubble kids, their scores go up. And if the teacher is giving these kids more or better instruction—not just more test prep—their scores *should* go up: they will have learned more. But while the teacher is focused on the bubble kids, what is happening to the nonbubble kids? Their performance can stagnate or even deteriorate with no effect on the magic percentage that is reported to the public and used for sanctions. If that happens, the scores for the teacher, school, or district are inflated even though the scores of the targeted kids are fine.

As it turns out, we are beginning to accumulate evidence that this scenario is too rosy: in some cases it appears that the scores of bubble students—and schools with a lot of them—undergo more inflation than others.

The second way to inflate the scores of groups is what I'll call *gaming*—manipulating who you test and don't test. This has been done in many ways—for example, reclassifying students as needing special education, excluding some poor or minority students, encouraging low-achieving students to be truant or to leave school, and changing grade assignments to keep low-scoring students out of a grade in which scores are most important.[13] When the students who would have been relatively low scoring are not tested, the scores of groups—teachers, schools, and school districts—will be inflated even if no students' scores are.

Gaming occasionally makes it into the press. Earlier I mentioned that the *New York Times* published an analysis using an audit test to document inflation in the "Texas miracle" in Houston. The reporters also investigated gaming as a source of score inflation. They found out that low-scoring students were encouraged to drop out and were then not listed as dropouts. Students were held back in the ninth grade and, in at least one case, promoted directly from there to the eleventh grade, thus skipping the state test.

NCLB and ESSA made this sort of gaming harder. For example, because schools are now responsible for the percentage of students with disabilities who are proficient, there is less incentive to reclassify students as disabled. (There still may be some incentive because under the law, schools can test students with disabilities in a number of different ways.) And both laws required testing 95 percent of each reporting group, which makes it more difficult to exclude low-scoring students from testing.

More difficult but hardly impossible. Perhaps the best example is the scandal in El Paso that hit the press—and the courts—years after the enactment of NCLB.

The El Paso case, which has many similarities to the practices the *Times* exposed in Houston years earlier, apparently began when the superintendent, Lorenzo Garcia, arranged to boost tenth-grade scores in one high school by excluding low-scoring students from testing, forcing some students out of school, and changing the grades on students' registration so that they would not be listed as sophomores and wouldn't take the tenth-grade test. Of the 381 students listed as freshmen in the school in 2007, fewer than half were listed as sophomores the following year. Scores improved dramatically. The fraud spread to other schools. Truant officers encouraged weak students to stay home during testing. Some were transferred to charter schools. At least seventy-seven students who were not allowed to reenroll as sophomores dropped out.[14]

As in the case of Houston, the resulting big gains gained attention statewide. Before the fraud was revealed, Garcia collected more than $56,000 in bonuses and was twice nominated for Texas superintendent of the year.

However, in the end Garcia's fame took a dramatic turn. In 2012 he pleaded guilty to several counts and was sentenced to three and a half years in federal prison for two crimes: his fraudulent manipulation of test scores and directing a $450,000 no-bid contract to a firm run by a former mistress.

Which brings us to cheating, which I'll examine in the next chapter.

6

CHEATING

In 2006 a young math teacher at Parks Middle School in Atlanta, Damany Lewis, went into a locked room where state tests were stored and removed a copy in order to provide teachers in the school with advance knowledge of the questions. He did this very carefully; worried that scissors would leave an obvious mark, he used a heated razor blade to peel back the tab that sealed the package. When providing the test items proved not to give scores as much of a boost as the school needed, his principal, Christopher Waller, told Lewis and a language arts teacher to go to the school's testing office and change wrong answers to correct ones. They did.[1]

This was a small step in the development of a large-scale testing scandal in the Atlanta district that came to a head only five years later. Stunning in its scope and audacity, this case received widespread national attention, with reports in the *New York Times*, the *Los Angeles Times*, the *Atlantic*, and the *Huffington Post*.[2] The scandal went all the way to the top, resulting in the indictment of, among others, the district's superintendent, Beverly Hall. It's likely that this scandal did more than anything else to bring the issue of cheating to the public eye.

Cheating—by teachers and administrators, not by students—is one of the simplest ways to inflate scores, and if you aren't caught, it's the most dependable. Thanks to increasingly frequent exposés in the press, a number of well-publicized criminal trials, and a few

My coauthor for this chapter is Aliya Pilchen, who as a student in a seminar at Harvard carefully documented most of the cases of cheating described here.

studies, we know that Atlanta was no anomaly: cheating has become a widespread scourge in our schools.

How Do People Cheat?

Documented cases of cheating are diverse, but the techniques the perpetrators have used fall into just a few broad categories. One that you will encounter particularly often in accounts in the media is one of Damany Lewis's methods: changing students' answer after the fact. His other approach, providing either teachers or students with test items in advance, also shows up frequently. The third type of cheating, which often pops up in cases involving a single teacher but has also been used in some larger-scale cheating incidents, is providing students with inappropriate assistance—even just giving them the answers—during the test itself. All of these produce fraudulent scores for individual kids as well as for teachers, schools, and districts. The El Paso case and a few others I'll describe here were different in that no one (as far as we know) intervened before, during, or after the test to alter students' answers. Instead, in these cases the method of choice was to exclude from testing students who were likely to score poorly, a technique that is often called "scrubbing" because it entails removing the worrisome students from enrollment rolls. Because in our system the aggregate scores for teachers or entire schools are the crux of the accountability pressure, scrubbing can be just as effective as other forms of cheating in generating bogus gains that will get educators off the hook.

The fact that the publicized cases are dominated by changing answers after the fact doesn't necessarily indicate that this is the most common form of cheating. However, changed answers on multiple-choice tests are one of the easiest indications of possible cheating to detect. The optical scanning machines used by testing companies are sufficiently sensitive that they can usually identify the smudges left behind when an answer is erased, and the software can identify which of the erasures change wrong answers to correct ones. A modest number of wrong-to-right erasures is expected; some kids will think better of a few answers and change them. Very large numbers of these erasures are another matter entirely, particularly if concentrated in specific schools. This is very unlikely to happen by chance—in some documented cases, extremely unlikely. Aberrant patterns in scores, such as gains that are statistically improbably large, are also easy to discern.

For this reason, revelations about cheating scandals often begin with reports of either large numbers of wrong-to-right erasures or implausibly large gains in scores. While improbable results aren't quite a smoking gun—"improbable" doesn't mean "impossible," and there is some chance, even if very small, that the results are legitimate—it raises a red flag and signals the need to investigate further. As you will see, that additional investigation often doesn't happen, for both innocent and not-so-innocent reasons.

The publicized cheating scandals also differ on another dimension: who the perpetrators were. Here again, I have to warn that the data are woefully incomplete. It's difficult enough to confirm that cheating has occurred. It's harder yet to confirm which people were complicit and in what ways they were. Still, we have enough information to know that the offenders vary from place to place. At one extreme we have the El Paso case, where the initiative for the cheating clearly came from the top—that is, from the district superintendent. At the other pole, I'll describe cases that appear to be the actions of individual teachers acting as lone wolves. Yet other cases lie between these extremes.

Cheating Scandals

A large number of cheating scandals have been exposed by the press in recent years, but three are particularly large in scope: Atlanta, Pennsylvania, and Washington, DC. All involved several of the cheating methods noted above, and in all three cases, implausible score gains and a large number of wrong-to-right erasures played a key role in exposing the fraud.

A small part of the Atlanta scandal first made the local press three years before it became national news. In 2008, two years after Damany Lewis cut up the package of tests, the *Atlanta Journal-Constitution* identified five schools in which students who had initially failed the state test made gains after summer school that were so large as to be statistically improbable.[3] In this case, the score increases found by the *Constitution* were more than four standard deviations above average. That number doesn't mean much to most people, so the *Constitution* quoted an expert who suggested that the gains were about as likely as a snowstorm in July. I'm not sure that helps much. Just how unlikely is a snowstorm in July, beyond "pretty damned unlikely"? So to be more specific, the probability of an event four standard deviations above the average is about 1 in 30,000.

This one report didn't have a dramatic effect, but it sparked continuing inquiries, and eventually the case snowballed. After the first *Constitution* article was published, a number of teachers contacted the reporters to describe incidents of cheating.[4] The following year the *Constitution* found nineteen schools in Georgia, twelve of which were in Atlanta, that had suspiciously large changes in scores.[5] By then the state had begun its own investigation. That investigation hinged in part on the actions of a single third-grade teacher, Jackie Parks, who admitted that she and six other teachers had changed students' answers and agreed to wear a wire to record other teachers.[6] The report, released in 2011, named 178 teachers and principals at forty-four schools who routinely cheated by changing students' answers on the state assessment. The report stated that cheating had been going on for over a decade.[7]

Beverly Hall, the superintendent of the Atlanta schools, championed "data-driven" instruction, which in this case meant unrelenting pressure to raise test scores. Her administration set very demanding—and, as she later admitted, arbitrary—targets for gains in scores that exceeded those required by NCLB, which was in effect at the time. All school employees, not just teaching staff, were given bonuses up to $2,000 if a school reached its target. Failure to reach the target could result in either demotion or termination, and over time she replaced 90 percent of the district's principals.[8]

Hall often spoke of the turnaround she had created in the city's schools with this strategy, and even more than Superintendent Garcia in El Paso, she was able to ride the score gains on state tests to both local and national fame. She awarded more than half a million dollars in bonuses before the cheating was widely acknowledged. During her tenure, two foundations, the GE Foundation and the Bill and Melinda Gates Foundation, gave the district grants totaling more than $40 million. In 2009, a year *after* the first *Constitution* article but two years before the lid blew off, Hall was named National Superintendent of the Year by the American Association of School Administrators, arguably the highest honor bestowed on a district superintendent. In response the city council declared September 8 to be "Beverly Hall Day," and the city held a ceremony in her honor.[9]

However, once the bad news was out, much of the blame fell on Hall's administration.[10] The press pointed out the extreme pressure the administration put on teachers and other educators to raise scores. The state's report maintained that her administration "created a culture of fear, intimidation, and retaliation" and had "punished whistle-blowers, hid or manipulated information, and illegally altered documents related to the tests" in order to cover up cheating.

While the *Constitution* deserves credit for the years of work that finally brought the Atlanta fraud to an end, the most telling portrait of the conditions that led some educators to cheat was an article by Rachel Aviv in the *New Yorker* that described conditions in the district as a whole but also focused intensively on one school that played a central role in the scandal, Parks Middle School.[11] This is the school where Damany Lewis and Christopher Waller worked. Aviv documented the way in which Waller choreographed an increasingly large and well-organized cheating ring. By 2008, as Waller later explained, the cheating had become a "well-oiled machine."[12]

Why did Lewis and others do this? At least in Lewis's case, it was not because he was comfortable cheating. Quite the contrary. He told Aviv later that when he first acceded to Waller's demand that he change answers, he couldn't even look at the second teacher with whom he did it: "I couldn't believe what we had been reduced to."[13]

Then why? In a nutshell, because their only other choice was to fail—not when compared with reasonable goals but when held to Hall's and NCLB's entirely arbitrary targets. Parks is located in a terribly depressed neighborhood. Half the homes are vacant.

Students call the neighborhood "Jack City" because of all the armed robberies. Very few of the students come from homes with two parents. Aviv reported that some students came to school in filthy clothing and that Lewis told students to drop dirty laundry in the back of his truck so that he could wash clothes for them. Some of the parents were dysfunctional because of drug use.[14]

During the years leading up to the cheating scandal, Parks had made real progress. A new principal renovated the school and worked on both refocusing students on academics and building a sense of community. Using funds that Hall's administration had obtained, the school implemented after-school and tutoring programs. However, this simply wasn't enough, given how fast scores had to rise to meet Hall's demands.

Lewis told Aviv that he had pushed his students harder than they had ever been pushed and that he was "not willing to let the state slap them in the face and say they're failures. I am going to do everything I can to prevent the why-try spirit." And at least some students did see the school's score gains as an indication that they were not failures. One told Aviv, "It was like our World Series, our Olympics. We had heard what everyone was saying: *Y'all aren't good enough*. Now we could finally go to school with our heads held high."[15]

Some skeptics may say that Lewis was being self-serving in offering altruistic motives for his cheating. After all, his job was on the line. And there is no doubt that fear of punishment, including the fear of losing one's job, did play a role in some educators' decisions. At one point Christopher Waller received a memo from the subsuperintendent responsible for Parks, Michael Pitts, that warned: "Please understand that no excuse can or will be accepted for any results that are less than 70% of school-based target acquisition." When Waller expressed doubts about meeting Parks's targets, Pitts told him, "The way principals keep their jobs in Atlanta is they make targets."[16]

Nonetheless, I see no reason to doubt Lewis when he claims that some of his motivations were altruistic, but this is in an important sense beside the point. The key issue is not the extent to which the motivations of one particular cheating teacher were altruistic or self-serving. The most important lesson from Parks School is that holding people accountable for reaching targets that they can't reach by legitimate means has led many educators to take desperate measures.

The criminal indictments resulting from the scandal show that prosecutors saw the cheating as systematic, not as the actions of lone-wolf teachers. A total of thirty-five educators were indicted, including Hall, other administrators, and teachers. Eleven were convicted under Georgia's Racketeer Influenced and Corrupt Organizations law, twenty-one reached plea agreements, and some were sentenced to prison.[17] Hall died of cancer before her case came to trial.

○ ○ ○

Another large scandal that started in 2009 was centered on Philadelphia but snared a substantial number of districts across Pennsylvania. An investigation undertaken at the request of the state's Department of Education found statistical irregularities in the scores of about sixty schools, roughly half of which were in Philadelphia. These included one school already suspected of cheating because of a large number of wrong-to-right erasures.

This report was not followed up at the time, despite comments by Andy Porter, then dean of the Graduate School of Education at the University of Pennsylvania, that the analysis was a reasonable way of detecting possible cheating.[18] However, the Philadelphia Public School Notebook, a nonprofit news organization, kept attention on the 2009 report, and the state Department of Education began a new investigation a few years later. The school district and state released a report in 2014 that identified 138 educators as having participated in or fostered cheating in one of several ways. The report showed that the perpetrators had used a variety of different methods. Half had either provided students with answers or changed incorrect answers, while the remainder were involved in other ways, such as failing to report violations of procedure.[19]

At the time I am writing this, the Pennsylvania Department of Education is continuing the investigation, and fifty-three districts around the state have been or are now being investigated. A grand jury was also convened. Eleven district administrators have been disciplined, and seven administrators and teachers have been criminally charged.[20]

As in Atlanta, the Philadelphia press—and the grand jury report—pointed to the pressures educators faced to raise scores in attempting to explain the cheating.[21] But in Philadelphia, unlike Atlanta, the school district eventually took an active role in investigating and documenting the cheating.

○ ○ ○

The most controversial case of possible large-scale cheating occurred in Washington, DC, beginning with the administration of Chancellor Michelle Rhee. Rhee was—and remained after leaving the DC schools—one of the nation's most prominent advocates of high-stakes testing as a tool for improving instruction, and like Hall, Rhee put her teachers and principals under extreme and unrelenting pressure to raise scores. Rhee had an unusual amount of power, as she was appointed as the city's first chancellor after the school board had been reduced to an advisory role. Rhee was able to implement a plan whereby teachers could receive bonuses of $20,000–$30,000 for good scores, while both teachers and principals could be fired for unacceptable scores. In a single day in 2010, Rhee fired 241 teachers, including 165 who had received low ratings based on scores.[22] By 2013 she had fired more than 600 teachers for low scores.[23]

Scores—of course—went up, and while Rhee's policies generated a strong backlash, they also propelled Rhee to national renown. My impression is that at that time, only Joel Klein in New York City had more national prominence as an advocate for using high-pressure testing to improve schools. As one indication of Rhee's reputation, when she resigned in 2010, Chester (Checker) Finn, one of the nation's most influential conservative commentators on education, wrote, "If Michelle Rhee should exit the schools chancellor's office, I'd recommend her to the Pentagon to take charge of the Iraq and Afghanistan situations. She keeps her eye on the ball, doesn't take no for an answer, recognizes and rewards talent, and purges the ranks of mediocrities."[24] After her resignation,

Rhee went on the *Oprah Winfrey Show*—another indication of the fame she had achieved—to say that she was declining all job offers and starting a new organization, Students First, to advocate her version of school reform. This organization, which she continued to lead for four years, rapidly became influential, and Rhee maintained a substantial presence in the media.

But in DC, as in Atlanta, there was trouble under the surface. For half a dozen years, controversy has continued about possible cheating during Rhee's control of the DC schools. Like the scandal in Atlanta, the DC case involves accusations of both widespread cheating and a deliberate cover-up. Unlike the Atlanta case, however, the scandal in DC has never been fully resolved.

The tale is long and byzantine, but it's worth sketching the main elements because it illustrates how difficult it can be to verify cheating and how resistant the system can be to a thorough and honest investigation. There are several reasons why cheating is not investigated carefully more often than it is, including the financial cost and a tendency to assume that no one is misbehaving unless the data shout that someone is. The DC case, however, is not of that sort. The warning signs were there, and prominent people demanded a serious investigation, but it seems that those in charge took steps to avoid one.

The issue arose in part because DC's test vendor at the time, CTB/McGraw-Hill, one of the nation's largest suppliers of tests, routinely checks for erasure patterns when its machines scan the answer sheets for multiple-choice questions. CTB's policy at the time was to flag classrooms with an extreme frequency of wrong-to-right erasures—more than four standard deviations above average (the same number that was the trigger in the Atlanta case). In 2008, one year into Rhee's tenure, CTB flagged ninety-six schools for high wrong-to-right erasure rates, including ten to which Rhee had awarded TEAM awards to recognize high performance. Deborah Gist, who headed the Office of the State Superintendent of Education (OSSE) in DC—an organization separate from and less powerful than the local education agency, the District of Columbia Public Schools (DCPS), that Rhee headed—asked for an investigation. It wasn't undertaken, and Gist dropped the request.[25]

The DC case was first revealed to the public in 2010, when *USA Today* published a report questioning score gains. The *USA Today* article focused primarily on one school, Noyes Elementary. Noyes was one of the district's great success stories. In the space of only two years, Noyes' students went from 10 percent "proficient" in mathematics to 58 percent. I'd have to take you through some math to show you why, but for people who are familiar with test data, gains of this magnitude are jaw-dropping. Or, to be more precise, they would be jaw-dropping if they were legitimate. Noyes garnered national as well as local recognition for its seemingly remarkable improvement. In 2009 it was one of only 264 schools nationwide named as a National Blue Ribbon School. Rhee, then chancellor of the DC schools, frequently cited Noyes as a sign of her success in transforming even the lowest-performing schools. *USA Today* reported,

> Wayne Ryan, the principal [of Noyes] from 2001 to 2010, and the school had been touted as models by district officials. They were the centerpiece of the school system's recruitment ads in 2008 and 2009, including at least two placed in *Principal* magazine.
>
> "Noyes is one of the shining stars of DCPS," one ad said. It praised Ryan for his "unapologetic focus on instruction" and asked would-be job applicants, "Are you the next Wayne Ryan?" [26]

If the *USA Today* article had identified possible cheating only at one school, it would be easier to write the problem off as a fluke. However, that wasn't the case. The article went on to point out improbable erasure rates in many other classrooms and cited three outside experts as saying that the erasures warranted investigation. The reporters also noted that the principals of some of the other schools in question had been given bonuses based on their scores.

A number of investigations over the next several years appeared to clear the district of large-scale cheating, although they did unearth a variety of irregularities and less extreme problems. However, critics of the district's administration have argued that all of these investigations have been seriously incomplete. In 2009

DCPS hired Caveon Consulting Services, a nationally recognized firm that specializes in detecting and preventing fraud in educational testing. However, the Caveon investigation was restricted to only a dozen schools, and John Fremer, the president of the company, explained that its investigation was limited at the request of the district to test security and procedures, not cheating as such.[27] The district hired Caveon again the next year, and the firm's report confirmed cheating in only a single school—Noyes. However, the acting chancellor who replaced Rhee—her former deputy, Kaya Henderson—had asked Caveon to look at only ten schools, not all of the schools CTB had flagged in 2010. Caveon's inquiry was also limited to just a small number of interviews at each school. The *Washington Post* reported that Fremer "said he was doing exactly what his client, DCPS, asked. Had it asked for more, he said, more could have been done.[28]

In 2011, in response to the *USA Today* article, DCPS asked the DC Office of the Inspector General to conduct an investigation. The inspector general's report, issued in 2012, focused primarily on Noyes. It found lapses in procedures but no evidence of teachers changing answers and evidence of only one teacher inappropriately offering students help during testing. On that basis, the inspector general declined to examine other schools.[29] A report of the US Department of Education inspector general released several months later also found no evidence of widespread cheating.[30] However, I have been unable to find anything that describes the scope of that investigation, and it is not included on the inspector general's website listing investigative reports.[31]

Concern might have withered away at that point if it were not for John Merrow, a well-known education journalist. Merrow suspected that the cheating allegations were warranted and continued digging. In a blog post in 2013, he revealed that he had obtained a memo indicating that Rhee's administration was aware of probable large-scale cheating as early as 2009.[32] The memo, dated January 2009 and marked "Sensitive Information—Treat as Confidential," makes it clear that the district was aware of problems with erasures affecting 171 teachers in seventy schools that had been identified by an analysis of CTB's erasure data by AIR, a major consulting firm with a large presence in education research. District officials arranged with an outside consultant, Sandy Sanford, to conduct an analysis of the erasure data, and the memo unearthed by Merrow was from him. In the memo, Sanford identified one school and documented just how extreme the erasures were, comparing them to the vastly lower erasure rates that are typical when cheating is not an issue. He raised the possibility that when numerous teachers in a school have excessive erasures, this might reflect coordination by a single person, presumably a building administrator. He noted that if the seventy schools were compromised, it would "be devastating with regard to our reported gains in 2008." Sanford recommended continuing the analysis and that in the meantime "we keep this erasure study on really close hold."[33]

Although Rhee issued a statement that she didn't recall receiving the report, Merrow was able to corroborate that the report was legitimate and that both Rhee and her deputy had discussed it at a number of meetings.[34]

This leaves matters up in the air. Clearly, there were a large number of wrong-to-right erasures involving many schools and perhaps many teachers. It's also now clear that Rhee's administration was well aware of this problem from the very first year of testing during her administration, but the district resisted a thorough investigation, and none was ever conducted.

The lack of a thorough investigation was not for want of calls for it. For example, after Merrow revealed the 2009 memo, Valerie Strauss, longtime education writer for the *Washington Post*, posted an article titled "Why Not Subpoena Everyone in DC Cheating Scandal—Rhee Included?" She noted that that Randi Weingarten, president of the American Federation of Teachers—the second largest teachers' union—had called for a full investigation in 2011 and had renewed her call in response to Merrow's release of the memo.[35]

Despite the continuing uncertainty about the extent of cheating in DC during the early years of Rhee's administration, we do have evidence of later cheating, although on a smaller scale than the early erasure data suggest. As a result of the controversy and the findings of irregularities by some of the limited investigations,

DCPS tightened up its testing procedures. Nonetheless, a 2013 report by the DC Office of the State Superintendent—perhaps coincidentally released one day after Merrow's blog post—stated that eighteen teachers had cheated on the district's high-stakes test the year before.[36]

A number of other large-scale cheating scandals have been exposed by the press, although they haven't gained as much notice. For example, the *Atlanta Constitution* reporters continued investigating possible cheating after they unearthed the Atlanta fraud. One product of their continuing inquiry was identifying suspicious patterns on the scores of forty-nine educators in eleven of the twenty-six schools in Dougherty County, a suburb of Atlanta.[37] In Los Angeles six charter schools were closed in 2011 after their directors were accused of ordering staff to provide students with questions and answers before the tests were administered.[38]

Suspicious patterns in test scores have been identified in many other locations where the additional investigation needed to confirm cheating wasn't carried out. For example, in 2012 the *Atlanta Journal-Constitution* found suspicious patterns of test scores in 196 districts around the country and in dozens of schools that had been recognized as National Blue Ribbon Schools.[39] In a suburb of Detroit, third- and fourth-grade reading and math scores at one school increased by an amount that the state determined was "highly unlikely due to chance alone."[40] In Florida a security system flagged more than seven thousand tests as suspicious due to similarities in results and a high number of erasures.[41]

The El Paso case I described in the previous chapter relied on an entirely different mechanism for cheating—removing low-scoring students from testing—but it bears an important resemblance to the Atlanta, Philadelphia, and DC cases: the scandal festered for years and came to light only because of a few determined people. The first indication of fraud emerged in 2009, when a former school board trustee, Dan Wever, became suspicious of the district's very rapid score gains and found indications of fraud in data from the Texas Education Agency website. He contacted both the Texas Education Agency and the US Department of Education, but neither followed up with an investigation. He then contacted a state senator, Eliot Shapleigh. Shapleigh had already heard anecdotes about forced transfers and removals from students, parents, and teachers, and in response to Wever's account, Shapleigh started his own investigation, talking with parents and even going door to door to find students who had been kicked out of school. In January 2010, with this additional information in hand, Shapleigh confronted Garcia. Garcia denied any wrongdoing and was temporarily vindicated after two state investigations that year were unable to find sufficient evidence to support Shapleigh's accusations of testing misconduct.[42] Two years after this process began, however, the fraud was finally documented by a district audit and an investigation undertaken by the FBI.

The El Paso and Houston cases are not the only documented instances of cheating by scrubbing. In 2012 the Lockland, Ohio, district dropped thirty-six of its six hundred students from its enrollment rolls before testing and added them back later. This and allegations of similar misconduct in two large districts, Toledo and Columbus, led the Ohio State Audit to launch a statewide investigation of scrubbing.[43] In 2001 more than five hundred high school students in Birmingham, Alabama, were encouraged to withdraw from school before the standardized tests in April but after the state had used enrollment numbers to calculate future funding and reimbursement levels.[44]

○ ○ ○

In recent years the press has also uncovered many smaller-scale cases of cheating. Some of these involved changing answers, as in Atlanta. In one case, after receiving an anonymous tip, the Nevada Education Department used erasure analyses to confirm that adults in a Las Vegas elementary school had violated testing protocols and changed student answers, but they were unable to identify the specific individuals who were involved.[45] State investigators in Maryland found evidence that educators at two schools in Baltimore had changed student answers on standardized tests in 2009 and 2010.[46] Middle-school students in Mobile, Alabama, discovered upon later reviewing their answer sheets that someone had changed their incorrect answers at some point between the first and last day of testing.[47] There have been similar findings of adults tampering with test scores in Oklahoma and Connecticut.[48]

Cheating by Individual Teachers

The press has documented a number of cases in which teachers or principals opened test booklets in advance. In some cases principals gave this information to teachers so that they could prepare students for the specifics of the test. In others, educators simply provided the illicit information to students directly. In 2010, for example, a teacher in Milford, Ohio, admitted to reviewing the test in advance and preparing a study guide for his students that included exact items from the test.[49] An internal investigation in East St. Louis revealed that a principal had asked teachers to look at exams to prepare students for particularly challenging items.[50] In 2007 a Florida teacher took an "accidental peek" at a test and realized that while he had taught students the definition of volume by multiplying length by width by height, the exam item involved the volume of a swimming pool and didn't use the word *height*. The next day he clarified the similarity between the height and depth to ensure that students understood how to respond to the item.[51]

There have been many documented cases of teachers cheating by providing inappropriate assistance to their students during testing. In some cases teachers have admitted telling students to change answers or providing correct ones—for example, in Houston; Cincinnati; Orlando; Woodbridge, New Jersey; Pontiac, Michigan; Prince William County, Virginia; Clarksdale, Mississippi; and twenty-three schools across California.[52] One indication that these teachers knew full well that they were cheating was the creative ways some of them tried to mask what they are doing—for example, using facial expressions, hand gestures, and preestablished code words to communicate that student answers were right or wrong, rather than simply telling students outright. One particularly creative teacher in Phoenix, Arizona, told a colleague she would pass out M&Ms during the test to help students arrive at the correct answer: a red M&M signaled that the answer was incorrect and the student should check his or her work, while a green M&M indicated that the answer was correct and the student could continue on to the next question.[53]

Students of mine who are former teachers have reported similar cheating strategies. For example, one reported that when she was about to administer the state test for her first time, some of her students asked if they would get M&Ms during the test. She found out that some math teachers in the school had given students a code matching the colors of the candy to the correct answer choice. They would walk around the room during the test, and when they found a student struggling with a question, they would give the student an M&M of the color that matched the correct answer choice. Special education students also reported to her that when the test was read to them—in subjects other than reading, this can be an acceptable accommodation for some students with disabilities—the proctor would read the correct answer more slowly and louder.

Educators have also admitted to leaving instructional posters displayed in classrooms and hallways, which could provide test answers and which violates standard testing procedures.[54]

How Common Has Cheating Become?

How common is cheating? There is simply no way to give a precise answer, but it is clearly widespread. A 2013 Government Accounting Office report concluded that "officials in 40 states reported allegations of cheating in the past two school years, and officials in 33 states confirmed at least one instance of cheating. Further, 32 states reported that they canceled, invalidated, or nullified test scores as a result of cheating."[55] In what may be the most cited academic study of cheating, Brian Jacob and Steven Levitt, using data from Chicago, estimated that "serious cases of teacher or administrator cheating on standardized tests occur in a minimum of 4–5 percent of elementary school classrooms annually." However, they noted that their method of estimating cheating, which relies on unexpected fluctuations in scores and unusual answer patterns, is likely to underestimate the true prevalence because it does not detect some methods of cheating.[56] Years ago, when Kentucky had implemented the KIRIS high-stakes testing program that was in many ways a precursor of NCLB and ESSA, some colleagues and

I surveyed teachers statewide. We assumed that we couldn't ask teachers about their own cheating, so instead we asked them how often various inappropriate testing practices occurred in their schools. Thirty-six percent said that test questions were occasionally or frequently rephrased during testing time. Twenty-one percent said the same of answering questions about test content or recommending revisions of students' answers. Seventeen percent said that hints were given occasionally or frequently. Nine percent said that answers were changed at least occasionally.[57] And while KIRIS was a high-pressure system, it didn't approach the pressure that teachers in districts like Atlanta or DC faced.

It's also clear that reports of cheating in the press, while increasingly frequent, represent just the very small tip of a very large iceberg. To start, think about how close the cheaters in the publicized cases came to getting away with it. Of course, we can't know what would have happened if the cast of characters had been different, but it certainly seems that the persistence of a single organization, or even a single individual, was essential in exposing the major scandals. In the Atlanta case, at the time the *Constitution* was working on its first article—which focused on a mere five schools, which could pass as an anomaly—Hall and the district were still riding high on the strength of their big gains in scores. What if the *Constitution* had not produced that first article, or if it had not persisted with its investigation the following year? In the El Paso fraud, two people played indispensable roles: Dan Wever, the former board trustee who uncovered suspicious statistics two years before the scandal really broke, and Eliot Shapleigh, the state senator who pushed the case for two years. In Philadelphia, the Philadelphia Public School Notebook, a nonprofit organization, played a critical role in keeping attention focused on possible cheating after the first indications surfaced. The controversy over possible cheating in DC might well have petered out had it not been for the persistence of a single journalist, John Merrow.

It's worth considering why we are so unlikely to ever find out how common cheating has become.

One reason is that despite a growing skepticism on the part of the press, much of the public, the education community, and the press remains gullible, willing to take the seeming good news of score increases—even extraordinarily rapid ones—at face value. Score increases *seem* to confirm that the reforms are delivering exactly what was promised: not only big improvements in learning overall but also, in places like Atlanta, very impressive gains for disadvantaged kids. This is a balloon that people are reluctant to pop. Remember that Beverly Hall was named Superintendent of the Year *after* the first *Constitution* article exposing fraud.

I remember a meeting some years ago with a group of a dozen superintendents of local districts who were interested in improving their accountability systems. I stressed the risk of inflated scores and tried to focus the discussion on things one might do to reduce the problem. One of the superintendents gave me what I took to be a condescending smile and said, "I don't have to worry about that in my district." When I asked why, he replied, "Because our score gains are too big to be a result of score inflation." He had the story exactly backwards: the speed of his district's gains was precisely why he *should* have been worried about inflation.

A second problem is simply the scale of the possible problem. There are currently over thirteen thousand school districts and almost one hundred thousand public schools in the United States. In how many of these districts is there a newspaper, an organization, or a a well-placed individual who will check for cheating? And how many schools can those few organizations and individuals investigate?

Finally, in some instances initial revelations have been followed by resistance to thorough investigation. It's for this reason that the DC and El Paso cases are so instructive.

The alternative to relying on random chance and the occasional persistence of a few individuals would be routine monitoring. As of now we have no routine auditing for score inflation and no systematic checking for bad test prep. For the most part, these are investigated only in the rare cases in which a researcher or a reporter takes the initiative and obtains access to data. Most states and districts spend very little for routine monitoring of potential cheating. For example, the *Atlanta Journal-Constitution*, once again taking the lead in investigating this problem, reported that "just

10 states budget for such inquiries, according to a recent survey of state education agencies by the *Journal-Constitution*. Those states set aside from $5,000 to $250,000 a year for investigations; [by way of contrast,] Georgia spent at least $2.2 million on cheating cases in Atlanta and Dougherty County. In many states, officials acknowledge they can afford rigorous inquiries only in the most blatant cases."[58] At least one state, California, dropped its routine test audits of randomly selected schools to save money (a total savings of $105,000).[59] And some just don't see a reason to look. The *Constitution* article quoted Gloria Turner, Alabama's director of student assessment, as saying, "We don't just go looking. We assume everything is going as it should."[60] The warning signs have been present for years, but policy makers haven't acted on them, leaving everyone else—educators, parents, and of course kids—to pay the price.

Apportioning Blame

Who is responsible for cheating? And who is punished?

In some cases, no one is held responsible and no one is punished. I pointed out in the last chapter that the fraud in El Paso, in which scores were inflated by making sure that some potentially low-scoring kids weren't tested, bears a striking resemblance to the cheating that the *New York Times* had exposed in Houston nearly a decade earlier. The El Paso superintendent went to prison. No one was punished in Houston.

But this prompts the larger and more uncomfortable question: Just who is responsible? Is it just the people who actually carry out the fraud or require it? Or are those who create the pressures to cheat also culpable, even if not criminally?

Shortly after the first convictions in the Atlanta case, this question was raised by Richard Rothstein, an economist who has written extensively about the perverse effects of high-stakes testing. He noted that the teachers who cheated were responding to extreme pressure from the district administration to raise scores, and he added: "What the trial did not explore was whether Dr. Hall [the superintendent] herself was reacting to a culture of fear, intimidation, and retaliation that her board, state education officials, and the Bush and Obama administrations had created. Just as her principals' jobs were in jeopardy if test scores didn't rise, her tenure, too, was dependent on ever rising test scores."[61]

Rothstein has a good point. In 2014 Secretary of Education Arne Duncan, whose policies did a great deal to worsen the pressure exerted by tests, admitted that "testing issues today are sucking the oxygen out of the room in a lot of schools."[62] To my knowledge, however, he didn't concede that his own policies were a substantial part of the problem or suggest backing down from them.

Rothstein also raised an even more uncomfortable question: given the consequences the district imposed for failing to raise scores, was cheating the most unethical option teachers had? He wrote:

> Certainly, educators can refuse to cheat, and take the fall for unavoidable failure in other ways: they can see their schools closed, their colleagues fired, their students' confidence and love of learning destroyed. That would have been the legal thing to do, but not necessarily the ethical thing to do. As one indicted teacher told the judge before the trial, "I truly believed that I was helping these children stay in school just one more year," something from which they would have benefited far more than being drilled incessantly on test-taking strategies so they could pass tests legally.

This, of course, was precisely Damany Lewis's argument. He found cheating to be repugnant, but less so than the consequences for kids that the system would impose in its absence.

I'm not going to propose an answer. However, this raises a more general point: what is a reasonable dividing line between ethical and unethical responses to high-stakes testing? Not everything legal is ethical. And the press coverage of the scandals has mostly missed a critically important part of the story: the dividing line between cheating and unethical test prep is very hazy. I'll come back to this after describing some forms of test prep in the next chapter.

7

TEST PREP

A few years ago, a student from another country told me that when she was taking prep classes to prepare for the tests required for application to most US universities, an instructor told her that on tests sold by the Educational Testing Service, it is usually safe to eliminate any politically incorrect answer choices. Would this actually help a student score well? I have no idea. However, it is a good illustration of the lengths to which people will go to help students score well on tests without bothering to teach them the knowledge and skills the tests are supposed to measure.

There is no doubt that test-based accountability has resulted in a huge commitment of time and effort to test preparation. I can't be more precise, in part because people don't agree on the dividing line between test prep and regular instruction. In fact, one of the most pernicious effects of reform has to been to blur—and in some cases entirely obscure—the distinction between test prep and teaching. But observe schools or talk to teachers or parents, and it's clear that test prep now absorbs a good bit of available time.

Arguments about "test preparation" or "teaching to the test" often go nowhere because people use these terms in all sorts of ways and can point to both good and bad examples. Proponents think of teachers using tests to figure out what students can't do well and then teaching them to do it. Opponents provide appalling examples of teaching test-taking tricks or drilling kids endlessly on things they expect to see on the test.

Both are right—up to a point.

Of course there is good test preparation. One of the legitimate purposes of tests is to help teachers learn what aspects of their teaching need to be changed or strengthened, which ultimately benefits their students. I'll give an example from my own teaching. In addition to writing papers, students in my introductory class on testing take two exams, each with ten or a dozen constructed-response questions—that is, questions to which they write free-form answers. A widely misunderstood rule of test construction is what you could call the Goldilocks principle: if you want to differentiate among students based on how much they have learned, the tasks on a test should not be too hard or too easy. If they are, they tell you nothing about who has learned more and who less. However, that is not the only purpose of my exams. I also want to make sure that nearly everyone in the class has mastered some key concepts, and I certainly wouldn't want the students—who are wise to the Goldilocks rule—to skip these essential ideas when reviewing. So I allocate a few of the ten or twelve items to questions that I expect almost everyone to get at least approximately right.

One year I included a question that I expected almost all of the students to answer acceptably. I was shocked to find that only about 20 percent did.

I couldn't pin this on the students. My class is known to be tough, and the students who enroll despite this are mostly capable and hardworking. That left only me to blame. So I overhauled how I taught that material the following year. I did this not to get better responses to similar questions in the future but to try to explain the material better. That time it worked.

Studies have shown that testing can also encourage desired types of teaching. When states started directly testing writing—that is, giving tests for which students had to write, rather than just tests that used multiple-choice and other formats to show whether they had certain skills related to writing—many teachers increased the time they devoted to teaching writing. In the late 1980s and early 1990s, Vermont experimented with portfolio assessments. These entailed collecting and rating work students did in the course of instruction rather than sitting them down at a set time to take a test. My group had the privilege of being the independent evaluator of that effort. The assessment had numerous technical problems that undermined its usefulness for some of its intended purposes. For example, the state wanted to compare the performance of schools, but we advised them that the portfolios were scored so inconsistently that such comparisons would be useless and misleading. However, the portfolio assessment did encourage some of the desired changes in instruction. For example, many math teachers incorporated more complex problem-solving into their instruction, which was one of the goals of the testing program.

If most teachers responded to our current test-based accountability system in ways like that, I wouldn't be writing this book. But by and large, that is not what has happened. High-stakes testing has generated a vast amount of test prep that bears no resemblance whatever to these positive examples. At its best, bad test prep wastes precious time. Often it does much more harm, corrupting instruction and producing the fraudulent gains I discussed earlier. And some of this test prep, even when carried out openly, shades into cheating.

Three Types of Bad Test Prep

The only way to make sense of the wide variety of test prep strategies—and to understand why some are so destructive—is to look at a few concrete examples. And it is helpful to distinguish between three different types of bad test prep because their implications—for example, their effects on score inflation and on the quality of instruction—can be quite different.

REALLOCATION BETWEEN SUBJECTS

To start, what would you expect would happen if you put great pressure on teachers to raise their scores on tests of a few subjects but ignored everything else? This is not rocket science: you would expect them to cut back on things that don't count and shift resources to the tested subjects. It's just Campbell's Law. And they do. We've known for decades that they often cut back on subjects like social studies, art, and music. In the early years of the Texas accountability system, one of the first high-pressure testing systems in the country, some teachers reported that they reduced—sometimes very substantially—the amount of time devoted to teaching science, which was not tested, in order to make additional time for prepping kids in math and reading.[1] Over the last few decades, a substantial number of studies in other locations have shown that schools have cut back or eliminated instruction in numerous untested subjects other than science, including social studies, music, art, and physical education.[2] Some educators have also curtailed nonacademic but important activities, such as recess.[3] (Anyone who thinks that recess is unimportant hasn't taught in an elementary school.) A few states have tried to address this by testing a larger number of subjects, but by and large, the problem has been allowed to fester for decades.

A student of mine who is a former fifth-grade teacher in Texas described what this looked like in her school:

> Art and music rooms are now "Math Labs" where multiple choice math packets have been substituted for drums and paintbrushes. For the lowest performing students, Physical Education has been turned into remedial instruction on computers. The playgrounds are empty. Enrichment and recess have been removed from the typical elementary school day. Science and Social Studies went from being marginalized in the curriculum to being completely eliminated. The teacher who is on the payroll as the science teacher now pulls out small intervention groups to give them remedial instruction for the exams.

In the trade, this response to testing goes by the ugly term *between-subjects reallocation*. Mea culpa: I coined it. In this case, however, the jargon is useful. As one would expect, teachers are simply reallocating their instructional resources, especially time, to better match the content of the tests. However, the fact that in this case they are reallocating *between subjects*—between tested and untested subjects—is critically important.

Reallocation between subjects avoids the pitfalls that are the main focus of this chapter. In itself, it doesn't degrade instruction or inflate scores in tested subjects. Other types of test prep do.

Nonetheless, reallocation between subjects is very troubling, for two related reasons. The first is obvious: some of what is being cut back is important for students and ultimately for all of us. Students who don't learn social studies and science, for example, are poorly equipped to be informed citizens and will be less competent in many lines of work.

The second problem created by reallocation between subjects is that it can create a misleadingly positive impression of the impact of test-based accountability. I'll explain in a later chapter that the one unambiguous positive effect of test-based accountability has been an increase in the mathematics performance of younger students. Advocates tout this as evidence that their policies have led to better instruction, but to some extent, better performance in math is simply reflecting time taken away from social studies, science, and other subjects. By reallocating instructional time between subjects, teachers have reallocated student learning.

REALLOCATION WITHIN A SUBJECT

This brings me to the second kind of test prep, reallocating time and other resources *within* tested subjects, focusing on content that is emphasized by the test. Let's start with a chart from a PowerPoint file that the Quincy, Massachusetts, school district used to keep on its website for the benefit of the district's teachers. The first page showed three secondary-school math texts. When you selected a text, you got a separate screen for each chapter. Figure 7.1 shows the screen for chapter 4 of the Algebra I text, with each row denoting a different section in the chapter. The underlined numbers were live links to all of the publicly released test items that assessed that part of the chapter, over a period of four years. There were four items testing content from this chapter: two testing material from section 4.2 and one each from sections 4.4 and 4.5. Over the four years, there were no test items assessing material from the other sections of chapter 4.

Why would teachers want this chart, and why would the district want to give it to them? Because it is an extremely efficient way to raise scores on the state's test. With just a quick look at this

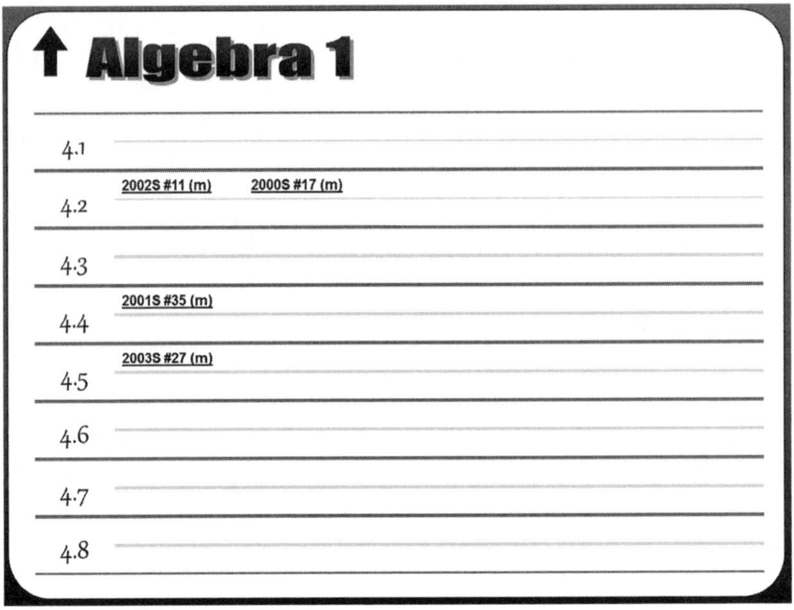

Figure 7.1. One page from a PowerPoint file showing material covered by the Massachusetts mathematics test.

PowerPoint presentation, you can see in a only a minute or two that chapter 4, "Graphing Linear Equations and Functions," is tested much less than many of the other chapters. In a matter of seconds you can see that it is probably safe to skip five of the eight sections in this chapter without penalty on the test, which frees up time for the three sections that hold the paydirt. In addition, clicking on the links to see the actual test items used in the past would show you *how* the state tested that content, but let's leave that aside for a moment.

You might say, So what? Perhaps sections 4.2, 4.4. and 4.5 are more important than other sections of chapter 4. And in fact, in many instances, tests do give more emphasis to more important content. But sometimes not. Sometimes it appears that differences in emphasis are accidental results of sampling, just as a pollster might happen to phone you and not me. Consider these two eighth-grade English / language arts standards that were in place until recently in New York:

- Interpret characters, plot, setting, theme, and dialogue using evidence from the text.
- Evaluate the validity and accuracy of information, ideas, themes, opinion, and experiences in texts to identify multiple levels of meaning.

Which is more important? It's hard to see why the second is less important, and indeed, it happens to bear a striking similarity to a major focus of the Common Core standards that replaced these standards. Yet over a five-year period, the test gave heavy emphasis to the first (12 percent of the possible raw score points on the entire test) but very little weight to the second (a mere 2 percent).

However, the truly critical point isn't the importance of the material that's emphasized by the test; it's the importance of the content that is deemphasized or omitted altogether and that teachers spend less time on as a result. Recall that until mid-2016, the Insurance Institute for Highway Safety conducted one of its crash tests, the small overlap frontal test, only on the driver's side. Why was that a problem? Not because the safety of drivers is unimportant but because passengers also want to survive. Many consumers—I was one of them when I purchased a car nine months before the news about right-side crash tests hit the news—naively assumed that the published results indicated the degree of protection of *both* passengers, but when IIHS started releasing passenger-side results, it turned out that some manufacturers had been teaching to the test, and passengers were at much greater risk. Knowing that only the driver's side would be tested, car manufacturers made that side much safer but didn't bother doing the same for the passenger's side because it wasn't being tested. Scores on the safety tests—if you take them, as I did, as an indication of the safety of the entire car—were inflated. The analogy applies to polls as well. A test is like a poll, a small sample that ideally allows you to draw conclusions about something much bigger, such as an electorate. Given the small size of most samples, a poll may happen not to survey people from some locations—say, Tulsa or Newark. Would a candidate conclude that she is safe to ignore voters in Tulsa or

Newark? Obviously not, because even though they weren't polled, they vote.

A test is no different. It's a small sample that allows you to draw conclusions about a much bigger domain of achievement. So "important" in this case means "important for the conclusions people base on test scores." Are five of the eight sections of the chapter in figure 7.1 irrelevant to what people have in mind when they use an algebra test score to gauge the competence of a student? Often the answer is no: the omitted content is important, but it was omitted only for want of space and time. In fact, if you hired someone else to write your test, that omitted content might well be tested.

For more than two decades, teachers have been reporting in studies that they cut back on important material, including content explicitly included in their curriculum, because it doesn't help them on the test. One of my favorite examples was a math teacher in Boston who said to my team after completing a pilot survey, "Why would I teach irregular polygons?" She didn't mean that irregular polygons are unimportant; she meant that to the best of her recollection, irregular polygons didn't appear on the state test for the grades she taught. (We looked. She was almost right. We did find a single irregular polygon. However, it was symmetrical, and she probably mistook it for regular.)

Most people with experience in schools, however, don't need expensive survey research to document that important content is pushed aside because of a test. They see it and hear about it all the time.

When confronted with reallocation, people often argue that when this happens, students do learn something real. They are sometimes right. In the case of the Quincy PowerPoint file, if teachers spent all of their time on sections 4.2, 4.4, and 4.5, and if they taught those sections well, students would at least learn that content.

The problem is that while they have learned *something* of value, their scores can be deceptive because of what they *haven't* learned in order to make more time for the material that's tested. The problem arises when this omitted content is important for the conclusions that people base on students' scores—including their parents, teachers who will have the students in later years, future employers, and the public that receives the results in the newspaper. We would want to believe that kids whose scores increased learned more algebra, which happens to include the other sections of chapter 4. An employer who needs basic algebra skills is not likely to be thinking about the difference between sections 4.1 ("coordinates and scatterplots"), which wasn't tested, and 4.2 ("graphing linear equations"), which was. But students often learn much less about those untested sections than the increase in scores would suggest because those sections are now starved for instructional time.

Many districts and states, like Quincy, provide information to help their teachers reallocate. It's so widespread that there is a common term for the material that teachers are told to focus on because it is emphasized by the test: *power standards*. Let's be blunt: states and districts are helping to undermine their own tests. I'll come back to this at the end of the book because it is one of the most important failures of our system: no one above the teacher has any incentive to worry about *how* teachers raise scores. If there is a way to boost scores, administrators have every incentive to push it, even if the gains it produces are bogus. Some resist this temptation. Others don't. Those in charge of state and local education agencies are as desperate for rapid gains in scores as anyone else.

COACHING

While reallocation can undermine instruction and inflate scores, it isn't the worst sort of test prep. There are other types of test prep that at their worst teach students nothing of value whatsoever. These are really just a sleight of hand. My group calls these *coaching*. The key to coaching is the question I put aside before: *how* content is tested. Coaching focuses on unimportant details of the particular test, such as the format of the test items, other aspects of the presentation of material (is the question posed verbally, algebraically, or with a graph? what kind of graph?), and how students' responses are scored. These details also include small, incidental aspects of content, things that aren't of any substantive importance but that can affect how students respond. Coaching entails focusing test prep on these details, rather than on the underlying content that matters.

To make this clearer, I'll use the terminology Audrey Qualls, who taught educational measurement at the University of Iowa, once used in explaining this to a group of educators. If students really know the material, she explained, they should be able to use it successfully when confronted with "unfamiliar particulars." In the real world—in employment, for example, or even in later schooling—they are unlikely to encounter this material in precisely the form it happens to take on a specific test. If their "success" in answering a test item depends on the particulars of the specific test—for example, a particular kind of graph, a particular form of equation, a particular rule for scoring answers—then they don't really know the material in any useful sense.

Not all of the "tricks" students are taught to prepare them for tests are coaching in this sense, and some are beneficial. A good example appears in a test prep book that Princeton Review used to sell to prepare kids for the tenth-grade MCAS, which Massachusetts students have to pass to graduate from high school. The book suggests: "Many of the multiple-choice questions you'll see are long word problems. It's easy to get confused if you try to solve the question all at once. The best way to approach these questions is by taking 'bite-sized pieces.'"[4]

Why isn't this coaching? Because it is not tailored to any specific details of a particular test. It's also a sensible strategy that can be applied to a wide variety of complex problems. I use it myself both in solving problems and in teaching the mathematics that underlies testing. It's just good sense. If students learn to "chunk" problems effectively, it will help them in real life, not just on one particular test or on standardized tests in general.

Some coaching seems not to do anything much at all other than waste instructional time. For example, one study examined what happened after the Chicago Public Schools began requiring that all students take the ACT college admissions test. Teachers predictably began spending considerable time coaching, but for the most part it didn't work: scores didn't go up. The test prep didn't produce either real gains in learning or score inflation. The study found that "improvements from the PLAN (an earlier test) to the ACT are *smaller* the more time teachers spend on test preparation in their classes and the more they use test preparation materials" (my emphasis).[5]

Many coaching strategies, however, can be effective ways of producing fraudulent score gains. I'll give a few examples here. These depend on specific details in a given test, so I will walk you through the relevant particulars. These few are just a taste and don't do justice to the rich diversity of harmful coaching strategies.

I started the chapter with one strategy that shows up almost anywhere that multiple-choice testing is used: process of elimination (POE). I'm guessing that almost everyone who reads this will have encountered POE, the technique of eliminating incorrect answer choices rather than selecting the right one based on your knowledge of the material. The rationale, as explained in the Princeton Review test prep book I cited earlier, is simple: "Why is POE a good idea? Because it's often easier to identify the wrong answers than to find the correct one."[6] Having spent some time writing multiple-choice items, I understand why. It is very hard to write good "distractors," as the incorrect answer choices are called in the trade.

The problem with POE is that some of the students who find the correct answer by eliminating incorrect ones would be unable to generate the correct answer if they weren't given alternatives from which to select—for example, if they were simply given the question and had to write an answer, as students do on my class exams. And once they leave school and enter the real world, that's what they will usually encounter. They won't be given answer choices. They will be expected to come up with the correct answer themselves.

Plugging in also capitalizes on the multiple-choice format and is frequently used in preparing for mathematics tests. This is a particularly prized technique in dealing with equations. Ideally, a test item would evaluate whether a student can solve the given equation. However, even if students haven't learned how to do so, they can often find the answer by plugging in each of the answer choices to see which one fits. The problem is the same as with POE: in the real world, no one is going to give students answer choices to plug in.

POE and plugging in, however, are generic strategies and don't really give the full flavor of coaching. To get a good feel for coaching, it's necessary to look in more detail at a few examples that are focused on *specific* tests.

"Pythagorean Triples," or How Not to Build a Roof

Secondary-school mathematics tests often include an item about the Pythagorean Theorem: the square of the length of the hypotenuse of a right triangle is equal to the sum of the squares of the lengths of the two legs, $c^2 = a^2 + b^2$. This may seem like a bit of esoterica to some readers, the sort of thing you quickly forgot after graduating from high school, but in fact it has a great many practical applications. If you hire someone to build you a roof, you had better hope that she knows the Pythagorean Theorem.

The goal of coaching is to prepare students to answer items about the Pythagorean Theorem as quickly as possible, without worrying about whether they have actually learned it. How can we do this? Because of an incidental characteristic of many of the test items used for this purpose, it's easy.

To show you how, I'll again turn to the test-prep materials Princeton Review used to sell for the tenth-grade Massachusetts MCAS mathematics test. It offers two test-preparation strategies for these items.[7] The first presents the formula, with a diagram and a few sentences repeating the rule. It offers no explanation that would help students understand the rule; it is just a reminder to help them memorize it. As one former student of mine, a career educator, put it, this is "garden-variety lousy teaching," no different from what one might find in many classrooms even if there were no test at the end of the year. It's not coaching, because it doesn't capitalize on details of the test. But even though it is boring instruction, it can work: if the person you hire to build a roof happens to have been a student who memorized it and managed to retain it, you are in the clear.

The second method Princeton Review provided, however, is a perfect example of coaching. This method tells the student that there are two "popular" or "common" Pythagorean ratios, 3:4:5 and 5:12:13, and that one of these or a multiple of it will solve any problem they encounter in the MCAS. Just where are these particular ratios "common"? Not in the construction of roofs or an almost any other real-world context. They are common *on tests*, because without a calculator almost no students can calculate square roots. This puts the people writing test items in a bind. If you give students a test item in which the leg lengths are 4 and 6, almost no one (other than those who guess right) will be able to give you the hypotenuse. However, you will have no idea *why* students got the question wrong. Some of them will get it wrong because they don't know the Pythagorean Theorem. But some who *do* know the theorem will get as far as $4^2 + 6^2 = 52$ but will then stumble because they can't figure out $\sqrt{52}$ without a calculator. You won't know whether it is safe to hire one of them to build your roof.

The solution for the item writers is to use squares that students know. Most students know that $5 \times 5 = 25$, which makes it safe to use a triangle with legs of 3 and 4 and a hypotenuse of 5. If a student get a 3:4:5 problem wrong, the chances are pretty good—not perfect but good—that he doesn't know the Pythagorean Theorem. Therefore the 3:4:5 Pythagorean triple is very "popular" with item writers. (In my experience, 5:12:13 is less common, presumably because most students don't know off the top of their heads that $13^2 = 169$).

Enter the Princeton Review, which helpfully clues students in to this entirely incidental characteristic of the items they will confront. Don't bother memorizing the complicated theorem; just memorize the triples, which is easier and faster. Most of the students will get the item right, and everyone can go home happy. Well, almost everyone. Just don't hire one of them to build your roof.

You might ask if teachers really use this technique. They do.

Memorizing Arbitrary Symbols

Another particularly depressing example also comes from secondary-school mathematics. One of the first things students learn in algebra is simple linear equations with two variables. These equations are ubiquitous in the real world. My electric company charges me a fixed connection fee every month and then another amount for each kilowatt hour I consume. That is a simple linear equation with two variables: the number of kilowatt hours I consume and the total they bill me. In most cases, if you ignore wait times, taxi fares also reflect a linear equation with two variables, distance traveled and total fare. We in United States still use the Fahrenheit temperature scale, while virtually everyone else uses the metric system and the Celsius (Centigrade) scale. (The United States Metric Board, established to encourage a switch to the metric system, was abolished by President Reagan in 1982.) So if we want to know how hot or cold it is outside when traveling, we have to translate Celsius temperatures to Fahrenheit using the linear equation $F = 32 + 1.8C$, where *F* is the arbitrary symbol for degrees Fahrenheit and *C* denotes degrees Celsius. Because these linear equations are found everywhere in the real world, they are a primary focus of introductory algebra instruction, and students who don't understand them can't be labeled—at least not honestly—as proficient in basic algebra.

To show the extremity of this particular instance of coaching, I have to use the correct terminology. I'll illustrate this with taxi fares in Washington, DC, which I have plotted in figure 7.2. There is an initial charge of $3.25, which is the fare before you start the drive. This is called the *intercept*—the value of the outcome (in this case, the fare) when the value of the input (distance) is zero. Once the cab starts moving, the fare increases by $2.16 per mile. This is the *slope*: the rate at which the outcome changes for each unit increase in input—that is, per mile traveled. The greater the charge per mile, the steeper the slope of the line. The two variables are the distance and the fare. The intercept isn't a variable; it's a constant $3.25 regardless of how far you go.

To write a linear equation of this sort, you need symbols for the variables and for the intercept. These can be anything whatsoever. Understanding that the symbols are arbitrary is a fundamental skill in introductory algebra. If students understand basic linear equations and can apply that knowledge to the taxi-fare example, they should recognize the slope, not because it is represented by a particular symbol but because it is multiplied by the input variable—in this case, distance in miles.

However, many introductory texts—and not coincidentally, many tests administered in the secondary grades—happen to use the form $y = mx + b$, where m is the slope and b is the intercept. There is ab-

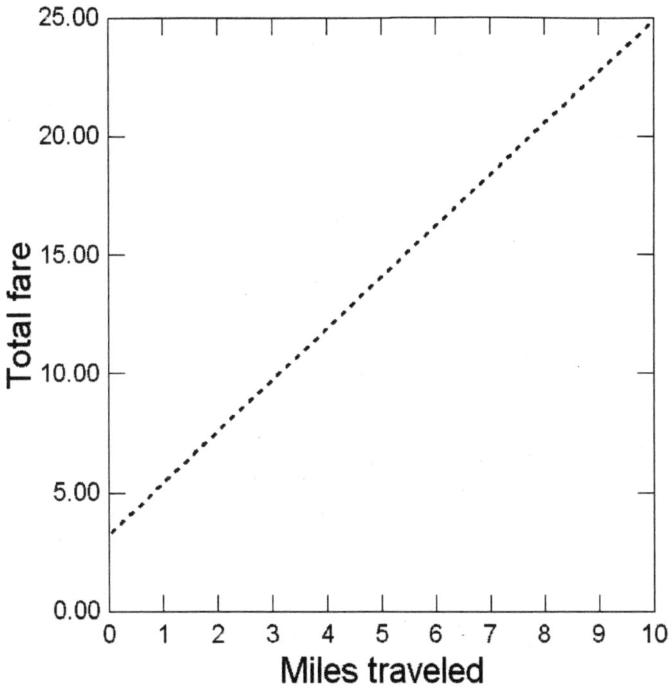

Figure 7.2. Taxi rates in Washington, DC. The initial charge (the intercept) is \$3.25. The charge per mile traveled (the slope) is \$2.16.

solutely no reason to prefer this form. I noted in an earlier chapter that two things are needed for score inflation: the test has to be predictable in some way, and teachers need to capitalize on that predictability. The fact that the test consistently and predictably uses the $y = mx + b$ format makes it very easy to coach—and to generate fake gains in the process.

One former teacher explained to one of my classes how all of the teachers in her school coached students for these items. Teachers had assiduously collected all the words that they had seen associated with each element of the equation in previous tests. For example, the words corresponding to m included *slope,* and those corresponding to b included *intercept.* They put together lists of these words and had their students memorize them. Students were told that when they started their math tests, they should write $y = mx + b$ at the top of the first page and then jot down under each symbol—even the equals sign!—the list of words they had memorized, including these:

- under y: *dependent, range, output, money*
- under =: *is*
- under m: *slope, rate of change*
- under x: *independent, domain, input, time*
- under b: *y-intercept, initial, constant, starting point*

With this list, students can simply map from words to symbols, or vice versa, without having any real understanding of what they are doing.

To see why this matters, let's say that a test author instead used the form $y = a + bx$, which happens to be—again, for no reason other than convention—a form the students will see far more often if they later go to college. (In my own classes, the *only* times I have used the $y = mx + b$ format is in explaining this example of coaching.) If the test used the more common $y = a + bx$ form, students who had been coached to answer test items using the list from my student's school would most likely get the question wrong. They had been taught to memorize that b signifies the intercept, but in this far more common form it denotes the slope. Their "success" on items that use $y = mx + b$ would be entirely bogus.

These last two examples illustrate an important point: while some coaching strategies depend on the multiple-choice format, many don't. POE obviously does; without the multiple-choice format, there are no options to eliminate. But neither the Pythagorean triples example nor the list of words for $y = mx + b$ depends on using any particular item format.

Why is this last point important? Because for thirty years, many people have blamed multiple-choice testing for the problems of test prep and score inflation, and they promise to make the test-based reform system work right simply by avoiding it and using other kinds of tasks. We've had hard evidence for decades that this promise is baseless, but that hasn't deterred some influential people from making the claim. The core problem isn't a particular format. It's the predictability and limited scope of standardized tests.

When Does Test Prep Become Cheating?

Is some of this test prep dishonest or unethical? Is it really cheating?

Most people don't think so. Educators use these types of test prep openly. Private firms sell materials showing how to use them, and more significantly, many states, districts, and school administrators distribute them. The types of test prep I have described here aren't mentioned when cheating cases hit the press. Most of those scandals have entailed changing answers, giving help during the test, or distributing test items before the test, all of which people agree constitute cheating. Some involved gaming the system by removing potentially low-scoring kids from the group tested, although, as you have seen, that hasn't always been treated as cheating. In reporting these scandals, the press never mentioned gaming the system with the likes of Pythagorean triples.

But let's step back. Where should we draw the line between undesirable test prep and cheating?

The effects of some test prep are not always clear. This is true of a lot of within-subject reallocation. In some cases, reallocation will improve instruction—if the material teachers begin to emphasize in response to the test is particularly important and the material they deemphasize is less so. We know that some teachers do drop important material, but we don't know the mix of good and bad reallocation. Moreover, even when it turns out that reallocation is undesirable, that won't always be apparent to teachers. So let's leave reallocation aside, at least when it is done with good intent.

But what about the cases where teachers omit material they *know* is important for students' success? What about when they know that the omitted material is part of what stakeholders—parents, employers, and others—expect scores to reflect? In those cases the teacher's reallocation will *necessarily* mislead the people using the test scores.

Coaching is a starker case because it is clear that many forms of coaching can produce *only* fraudulent gains. One doesn't need to imagine what parents and employers think scores mean. If we help students "succeed" on a Pythagorean Theorem question by teaching students to look for the Pythagorean triple 3:4:5 rather than by teaching them the actual theorem, they don't in fact know the theorem, and they won't be able to use it in later education, in the workforce, or in daily life. The same is true if they "solve" a problem involving a linear equation by memorizing that *b* stands for the intercept.

This poses an uncomfortable question: Should test prep techniques that produce fraudulent gains be considered cheating? How is using a type of test prep that can only yield fake improvements different from Volkswagen's using software that could only produce bogus emissions-test results?

In some cases there is one very important difference: Volkswagen's *aim* was to deceive, and some of those creating fake gains by means of test prep don't have that intent. Many people in education don't understand testing well, and some—we have no way to know how many—won't realize that a given technique generates only bogus gains. For example, it's likely that many teachers who drop material not emphasized by the test never think about how this will mislead the people who use their students' scores.

This stands in marked contrast to the behaviors commonly considered cheating. When teachers change students' answers on a test or use M&Ms to signal the right answers, it's clear that they know that they are producing fraudulent "success." Remember the care that Damany Lewis took to ensure that no one would notice that the packages from which he took test booklets had been opened.

However, a lack of knowledge about testing doesn't seem to be the only reason that some educators believe their borderline-cheating test prep is acceptable. Some years ago I was asked to spend an afternoon introducing key issues in testing to about 125 district administrators who had come to Harvard for a professional education institute. Toward the end of the session, I gave them a packet of real examples of test prep activities. All of the examples were bad in one respect: they were boring as sin. However, some were OK in another, important way: if students actually remembered what they were shown, they would have skills or knowledge that they could put to use somewhere else, say, in later education or employment. The other examples lacked even this redeeming value; they were simply ways to jack up scores on the specific test used for accountability, and they would provide students with no skills or knowledge that would be useful outside of the context of taking that particular test, or one very similar to it. The first Pythagorean Theorem example above would fall into the "potentially OK" category. The second, the Pythagorean triples, would—or should—fall into the "completely unacceptable" category. (The packet included both of these strategies.) The task I gave the administrators was to classify the examples as good or bad, considering only whether they would produce gains limited to the test. I told them to ignore whether they were good or bad instruction in any other respect.

Their reaction took me completely by surprise. A minority—perhaps a third of them—immediately got the point and had no difficulty with the task. In discussing it, some said things like "If you think this is bad, you should see what goes on in some of our schools." Most of them, however, labeled virtually everything as "good." For example, process of elimination was just fine with most of them. I responded by asking what would happen if they relied on POE and the test authors then switched to a constructed-response format in which there were no choices to eliminate. The answer was obvious: kids would get the new items wrong. Some justified POE anyway, saying that the strategy itself represented a "valuable skill" even though it had nothing to do with the skill that the item purported to measure. More telling was the emotional tenor of the room. Many of the participants became visibly angry. As I expected, a few weeks later I was sent the worst teaching evaluations I have ever received.

What was going on? I think the answer lies in the famous quote by Upton Sinclair: "It is difficult to get a man to understand something, when his salary depends upon his not understanding it." As Richard Rothstein pointed out in his response to the Atlanta cheating scandal, because of our current "reforms" many educators have their backs to the walls. They are desperate for score gains, not only because their own jobs and schools are often on the line but also because the progress of their students is sometimes at stake. So, I walked in, secure in my position and facing none of this pressure myself, and explained to them why some of the techniques they rely on produce bogus improvements. Many of them simply didn't want to hear it.

Psychologists have a term for this: *dissonance reduction. Cognitive dissonance* refers to the discomfort people feel when they hold two contradictory beliefs or values. To reduce this stress, people will sometimes revise what they think to reduce the contradiction. This was a room full of educators, after all, people who had devoted their working lives to doing right by kids. Using test prep that generates fake score gains isn't doing right by kids. Finding ways to classify test prep as "good," even if they were a real stretch, warded off some of this additional stress.

However, the fact that we don't know which educators have the intent to deceive doesn't make bad test prep acceptable. It's still deception. It just confronts us with the murky distinction between intentional and unintentional deception.

Corrupting the Idea of Good Teaching

Not only is bad test prep pervasive. It has begun to undermine the very notion of good instruction.

This has happened in part just because of the passage of time. High-stakes testing and undesirable test prep have been in place for so long that many young teachers have spent their entire careers immersed in them. As some young teachers have told me, they simply have a hard time envisioning what instruction would look like without it.

It would be a serious mistake, however, to think that the corruption of the notion of good instruction stemmed only from the lack of opportunity to observe better teaching. Some of those who train new teachers have actively encouraged it.

For several years I have ended a class on educational testing by giving students exactly the same exercise that so angered many of the administrators I just described. This particular course always enrolls quite a number of former teachers. Being *former* teachers, they were no longer painted into a corner by a need to raise test scores, and perhaps for that reason, only a few have become defensive. They generally reach a fair degree of agreement about which of the test prep examples are good and bad, although a few have remained more charitable about this than I would be.

The first year I did this in class, one former teacher said, "This exercise would make no sense to many young teachers." I asked why. Because, she replied, I was asking them to distinguish between good instruction and bad test preparation, but what she and her classmates were busily labeling as bad test preparation was precisely the sort of thing *that she had been told explicitly is good instruction.* She had taught a class labeled MCAS Preparation for students who had previously failed the math test that Massachusetts requires for high-school graduation. She recounted that at the beginning of the year, one of the administrators told her that her job was to "go into that room and come out in the spring with two or three additional test items." That is, her job was to get kids who failed by just a few items the first time over the hurdle when they took it a second time. One of her tools for doing this, by the way, was teaching Pythagorean triples. When I asked her if she used that trick, she replied, "Of course I do!" She added that because many of the items have the same content—calculating the length of a ramp—you can gamble a bit and simplify the task further, telling students to use the triples anytime they are asked to calculate the length of a ramp, without even mentioning the Pythagorean Theorem.

You might hope that this can be discounted as an extreme case because she taught a class dedicated specifically to getting marginally scoring students to pass a critical test. However, other former teachers immediately spoke up in agreement. One, for example, said that her administrators didn't talk to her about teaching her subject; rather, they talked to her about raising scores in it. And it wasn't just that group. I continue to hear the same thing from former teachers.

They were telling me that I was missing the boat by seeing test prep as something that competes for time with good instruction. In their experience, raising scores *had become the end goal, the mark of a "good" teacher.* To an alarming degree, they had been taught that test prep and good instruction are the same thing. No longer would teachers have to balance test prep against their larger instructional goals. And the test prep I was having them classify as "bad" was just one of the tools they were expected to use. If a technique increases scores but isn't what people typically call cheating, why not use it, if raising scores is itself the end goal?

It's hard to overstate the importance of their observation. For the present, it indicates that one of the few checks against inappropriate test prep—teachers' own understanding of the differences between prep and good instruction—has been eroded. For the longer term, it suggests that simply lessening the pressure to raise scores may not be sufficient to undo the harm that test-based accountability has done. Mistrained teachers may perpetuate it on their own.

The ideal of good teaching is not easy to pin down, and I am not aware of systematic data evaluating what new teachers are told about test prep. However, signs of the shift my students were describing are easy to find in popular books that many new teachers encounter in their training, in the schools they first enter, or both.*

One of the rationales given to new teachers for focusing on score gains is that high-stakes tests serve a gatekeeping function, and therefore training kids to do well on tests opens doors for them. For example, in *Teaching as Leadership*—a book distributed to many Teach for America trainees—Steven Farr argues that teaching kids to be successful on a high-stakes test "allows teachers to connect big goals to pathways of opportunity in their students' future."[8] This theme is echoed by Paul Bambrick-Santoyo in *Leverage Leadership* and by Doug Lemov in *Teach like a Champion*, both of which are widely read by new teachers.[9] For example, in explaining why he used scores on state assessments to identify successful teachers, Lemov argued that student success as measured by state assessments is predictive not just of [students'] success in getting into college but of their succeeding there."[10]

Let's use Lemov's specific example to unpack this.

To start, Lemov has his facts wrong: test scores predict success in college only modestly, and they have very little predictive power after one takes high school grades into account. Decades of studies have shown this to be true of college admissions tests, and a few

* I'm indebted to Luke Dorfman, who as a participant in a seminar at Harvard reviewed the books I cite in this section.

more recent studies have shown that scores on states' high-stakes tests don't predict better.[11]

However, the critical issue isn't Lemov's factual error; it's his fundamental misunderstanding of the link between better test scores and later success of any sort (other than taking another similar test). Whether raising scores will improve students' later success—in contrast to their probability of admission—depends on *how* one raises scores. Increasing scores by teaching well can increase students' later success. Having them memorize a couple of Pythagorean triples or the rule that *b* is the intercept in a linear equation will increase their scores but won't help them a whit later. That is the fundamental distinction that my students said had been obscured in their training.

In the early days of test-based accountability, some observers worried that educators were coming to confuse the test with the curriculum—or as one put it to me, "The test *becomes* the curriculum." They saw this as one of the most significant drawbacks of test-based accountability.

Some of today's teacher educators, however, make a virtue of this mistake. The often tell new teachers that tests, rather than standards or a curriculum, *should* define what they teach. For example, Lemov argued that "if it's 'on the test,' it's also probably part of the school's curriculum or perhaps your state standards. . . . It's just possible that the (also smart) people who put it there had a good rationale for putting it there."[12] (Probably? Perhaps? Possible? Shouldn't they look?) Bambrick-Santoyo was more direct: "Standards are meaningless until you define how to assess them."[13] And "instead of standards defining the sort of assessments used, the assessments used define the standard that will be reached." And again: "Assessments are not the end of the teaching and learning process; they're the starting point."[14]

They are advising new teachers to put the cart before the horse.

Why does this matter so much? To start, it encourages reallocation—that is, focusing instruction on the tested sample rather than the domain or the curriculum that it is supposed to represent. Farr provided a clear example, a history teacher in New York named Mr. Delhagen, who asked himself, "What academic achievement should define success for my students?"[15] Farr described how Mr. Delhagen answered that question: "After studying one copy of the [New York State Regents] exam, he recalls that his reaction was, 'Whoa! This covers everything from the Neolithic revolution to 9/11. This is a bus tour!' To help make sense of that massive breadth of history, Mr. Delhagen got his hands on fifteen past global history exams and made a spreadsheet to analyze the key ideas and themes of the course."[16]

The problem, of course, is that this assumes, falsely, that anything that isn't sampled for that particular test isn't important for the conclusion based on scores—that is, that the omitted material isn't part of what students are expected to learn.

The bad advice given to new teachers, however, doesn't stop with reallocation. It includes coaching as well. A particularly egregious example is a suggestion that Bambrick-Santoyo made about the assessments teachers write for their own classes. He wrote: 'Once the specific sorts of questions that are employed by the end-goal test are noted, schools should work to create or select interim assessments that are aligned to the specific demands of the end-goal examination. This alignment should not be limited to content *but should also follow the format, length and any other replicable characteristic of the end-goal test*" (emphasis added).[17] He is advising teachers not only to reallocate but also to coach based on incidental characteristics of the accountability test. Set up your classroom to minimize students' exposure to anything unfamiliar. Forget Audrey Qualls's "unfamiliar particulars."

This is a perfect recipe for score inflation—and for setting students up to fail in the real world. It is mistaking the poll sample for the electorate. What we want is for students to gain the ability to apply knowledge and skills to problems they actually encounter—not to ensure their proficiency in applying them only to test items that look exactly like the ones they will confront in the main test at the end of the year.

And What about Equity?

As if all of this were not depressing enough, there is yet another disturbing part of the story. Inappropriate test preparation, like score inflation, is more severe in some places than in others. Teachers of high-achieving students have less reason to indulge in bad preparation for high-stakes tests because the majority of their students will score adequately without it—in particular, above the "proficient" cut score that counts for accountability purposes. So one would expect that test preparation would be a more severe problem in schools serving high concentrations of disadvantaged students, and it is. Once again, disadvantaged kids are getting the short end of the stick. Ironically, some aspects of the reforms that were intended to help disadvantaged students appear to have contributed to this demoralizing result. A big part of the problem, as I'll explain in the next chapter, is how performance targets have been set.

8

MAKING UP UNREALISTIC TARGETS

For decades, one of the primary—and most praiseworthy—goals of test-based reforms has been to reduce the glaring inequities in the American education system. In the early days of the minimum-competency testing movement, the focus was just bringing up the bottom a bit, but by the 1990s the goal had become much more ambitious, and "all children can learn to high levels" became a mantra in the education community. Policies put in place since then have made this expectation both more concrete and more extreme. Today's mantra is "college and career readiness," which in practice means treating the two as the same. And in a limited way, these efforts paid off. They have riveted attention on kids and groups that show relatively low achievement, and they have made it far harder for the educational system to ignore the performance of these students.

By the most important criterion, however, these policies have failed: they haven't actually done much to reduce inequities in performance. If you track scores on the tests used for accountability, it often *seems* as though we have made big strides to reduce gaps in achievement, but as you've seen, when we have had other data to check, this progress has turned out to be a mirage—just a sign of greater score inflation among low-scoring kids.

Part of the blame for this failure lies with the crude and unrealistic methods used to confront inequity. In a nutshell, the core of the approach has been simply to set an arbitrary performance target (the "Proficient" standard) and declare that all schools must make all students reach it in an equally arbitrary amount of time. No one checked to make sure the targets were practical. The myriad factors that cause some students to do poorly in school—both the weaknesses of many of the schools they attend and the disadvantages some students bring to school—were given remarkably little attention. Somehow teachers would just pull this off.

To see why this approach is unworkable, I have to explain how performance standards are set, how achievement targets are established using these standards, and just what it means that "all" students will be proficient. I'll then turn to why this matters so much: it creates perverse incentives for educators.

Making Up Targets

If one doesn't look too closely, reporting what percentage of students are "proficient" seems clear enough. Someone somehow determined what level of achievement we should expect at any given grade—that's what we will call "proficient"—and we're just counting how many kids have reached that point. This seeming simplicity and clarity is why almost all public discussion of test scores is now cast in terms of the percentage reaching either the proficient standard or, occasionally, another cut score. By and large people trust the performance standards, although there are periodically arguments about whether some of them are too lenient.

The trust most people have in performance standards is essential, because the entire educational system now revolves around them. The percentage of kids who reach the standard is the key number determining which teachers and schools will be rewarded or punished. For the most part, the press reports differences among schools and progress over time only in terms of this single statistic. If there are problems with the standards, the whole edifice is threatened. And the labels have a lot of heft. It is no trivial matter to tell a parent or a student that she is "not proficient" in meeting the expectations for her grade. It would carry less weight if we simply said, "You haven't reached standard 3."

This trust in performance standards, however, is misplaced.

For the few people who look at the readily available documentation, the process of setting these all-important standards looks impressive and scientific, even intimidating. These reports are full of scholarly jargon, such as "modified Angoff," "response probability," and "impact data." The process typically involves many steps and often more than one panel of judges, and the description can run on at some length. Typically a great deal of care is put into hewing to a prescribed way of conducting the process, and the entirety is carefully documented. This doesn't make engaging reading, and it isn't easily understood by laypeople. It's hardly surprising that most people don't delve deeper and assume that all this work and expertise is providing them with a trustworthy measure that means just what it says.

But in fact, despite all the care that goes into creating them, these standards are anything but solid. They are arbitrary, and the "percent proficient" is a very slippery number. To the old saw that "there are two things one never wants to see made: laws and sausages," I would add performance standards. For a number of years I have made this concrete for my students by requiring them to try to set standards using a simplified version of one of the most common methods. They are simply amazed, because most of them, if they had given it any thought before, assumed that the standards could be trusted. Most don't think so once they have gotten a closer look.

There are lots of different methods for setting performance standards, and most are quite complex. I won't drag you though a detailed (and boring) description of various methods. However, I'll give you a quick description of a few of the most commonly used methods. Aficionados would say that my descriptions are far too cursory to do this work justice. They'd be right, but none of the many details I'll omit have any bearing on the basic conclusions I want to stress.

Let's start with the "bookmark" method, which is currently the most commonly used approach in the United States. This method does not involve *any* examination of the actual performance of real students. It hinges entirely on people's guesses about how *imaginary* students would perform on individual test items. To be clear, these aren't just random guesses; a number of elaborate steps are taken to help guide people's judgments. However, for all that, they remain guesses.

To start, panels of judges are given a written definition of what a standard like "Proficient" is supposed to mean. These often entail a brief and general definition, coupled with a more detailed description. For example, Nebraska's definition of "meeting the standards" in sixth-grade reading is this: "Overall student performance in reading reflects *satisfactory* performance on the standards and *sufficient* understanding of the content at sixth grade. A student scoring at the Meets the Standards level *generally* utilizes a variety of reading skills and strategies to comprehend and interpret narrative and informational text at grade level" (italics in the original). This definition is accompanied by a list of ten things a student meeting this definition generally does, including the following three:

- Applies a variety of word-identification strategies (word structure, context, semantic relationships) to understand unfamiliar grade-level vocabulary.
- Identifies and analyzes how story elements (e.g., plot, setting, characterization, theme, point of view) impact text.
- Answers literal, inferential, critical, and interpretive questions with accuracy and identifies supporting information in the text.[1]

A short digression: the emphasized word *generally* is very important. One of the problems in setting standards is that students are inconsistent in their performance. Of the students who answer one question correctly, some will answer another question of similar difficulty incorrectly. Dealing with this sort of random variation comes naturally to statisticians and measurement experts but not to most people, and studies have found that panelists setting standards often overestimate the consistency of students' performance. That in turn can influence where they place the standards.

But back to the main story. The bookmark panelists then have to imagine one hundred marginally proficient students—that is, students who just barely exceed this standard. Real students don't come into play at this stage. The panel is then provided the test items, ordered from easiest to hardest. They are given an arbitrary (notice how often I am using that word) "response probability," which is the probability that one of these imaginary students would get any given item right. Often, for no reason other than convention, this response probability is set at 0.67. Finally, each panelist is asked to go through the items, moving from easiest to hardest, and stop at the one item that 67 percent of the imaginary students would answer correctly. That item pegs the Proficient standard.

If that sounds like an extraordinarily tough thing to ask of people, it is. First, panelists are required to imagine—accurately—these marginally proficient students on the basis of descriptions that, as you have seen, are open to a variety of interpretations. Then they have to guess—again, accurately—how these imaginary students would perform on every test item. I give my students NAEP's definition of *proficient* and have them try to guess the proportion of proficient students that would get a few NAEP items correct. Even though many of them are former teachers—and therefore have more of a feeling for what students can actually do than most people would—their guesses are typically all over the map. Usually, by the second or third item the entire class is reduced to laughter. That's before they realize the implication, which is hardly a laughing matter: the standards they had previously trusted, and on which the entire edifice of current education policy and practice rests, are anything but solid.

There is another, perhaps even more important, reason why performance standards can't be trusted: there are many different methods one can use, and there is rarely a really persuasive reason to select one over the other. For example, another common approach, the Angoff method, which was the dominant method for some time, is like the bookmark in requiring panelists to imagine marginally proficient students, but in this approach they are not given the order of difficulty of the items or a response probability. Instead panelists have to guess the percentage of imaginary marginally proficient students who would correctly answer every item in the test. Other methods entail examining and rating actual student work, rather than guessing the performance of imaginary students on individual items. Yet other methods hinge on predictions of later performance—for example, in college. There are yet others.

This wouldn't matter if these different methods gave you at least roughly similar results, but they often don't. The percentage of kids deemed to be "proficient" sometimes varies dramatically from one method to another. This inconsistency was copiously documented almost thirty years ago, and the news hasn't gotten any better. One more recent study, for example, compared three methods applied to tests in six different subjects. In the best case, the most lenient method labeled twice as many students "proficient" as did the most rigorous. And that was the *least* inconsistency in a total of eighteen comparisons. In the worst case, the percentage of students pegged as "proficient" was *almost 11 times* as large with one method as with another![2]

Worse, you don't even need to switch methods to get inconsistent results. Studies have shown that a variety of things that should not affect the placement of the standards often do—such as the response probability given to panelists, the mix of item difficulties, and the mix of item formats. Remember that the process is supposed to identify the kids who are proficient. A student who is proficient doesn't suddenly become less than proficient if you give different instructions to a panel of standard-setters, or if you happen to throw in a few more or less difficult items.

The "percent proficient" doesn't mean a great deal when one can move that number dramatically just by changing which of the many arcane methods one uses. Imagine a superintendent announcing to the press that "this year, 72 percent of our students were labeled proficient when we used Method A, but only 7 percent were when we used Method B." I'd love to be in the room to hear the response. The discrepancy among methods is usually not *this* great, but it is often more than big enough to undermine the conclusions the public is given.

○ ○ ○

A primary motivation for setting a Proficient standard is to prod schools to improve, but information about how quickly teachers actually can improve student learning doesn't play much, if any, of a role in setting performance standards. When panels set standards, they are not given information about practical rates of improvement, and for the most part they are not asked to consider them. They are just asked to try to figure out what level of performance constitutes "proficiency." It is common to give them information partway through the process about the percentage of kids who would be proficient if their initial standards were accepted, and in some cases this information is considered after the fact by policy makers, who might further adjust the standards to obtain a more acceptable failure rate. However, all of that information is about how students perform at the time the standards are set, not about reasonable rates of improvement.

Given this, it shouldn't be a surprise when panels of judges set standards either too low or impractically high. And those mistakes matter. Standards that are too low won't create incentives for improvement and may mislead kids and their parents about how prepared they are for later education and work. Excessively stringent standards can create incentives for inappropriate behavior and can needlessly demoralize students.

However, setting the standards themselves is just the beginning. What gives the performance standards real bite is their translation into concrete targets for educators, which depends on more than the rigor of the standard itself. We have to say just who has to reach the threshold. We have to say how quickly performance has to increase—not only overall but for different types of kids and schools. A less obvious but equally important question is how much variation in performance is acceptable. It's in the answers to questions like these that a lot of the mischief lies.

A sensible way to set targets would be to look for evidence suggesting how rapidly teachers can raise achievement by legitimate means—that is, by improving instruction, not by using bad test prep, gaming the system, or simply cheating. By analogy, suppose you were charged with improving the mortality rate of elderly hospital patients who have contracted pneumonia. Would you simply make up a target mortality rate and set a timeline for every hospital, regardless of circumstances, to reach it? Or would you look for relevant data, such as the mortality rates in the best hospitals, to help you set sensible targets?

There is no shortage of data that could help us set realistic targets for schools. One obvious place to start would be with the abundant historical information we have about trends in performance on tests that haven't been corrupted by test prep, score inflation, and cheating, some of which extends back more than half a century. We've seen periods of substantial deterioration and considerable improvement, and these provide some indication of what is practical. Years ago I asked H. D. Hoover, a prominent expert in educational testing and a mentor of mine, what he would set as a target. The number he gave me was 0.03 to 0.04 standard deviations per year. The larger of these numbers means that the median student in any year—the student who scores better than half of her peers—would have outscored 51.6 percent of her peers the year before. (The changes for low- and high-scoring students would be smaller.) When I asked him how he decided this, he chided me, saying that he had taken it from one of my own publications. I had shown that during the 1960s and 1970s, when virtually all tests showed a substantial decline in performance, the typical drop was about that size. It's harder to make scores go up than to make them go down, he reasoned, so why not use the size of the decline to set targets?

However, the targets in our test-based accountability systems have often required unremitting improvements, year after year, many times as large as any large-scale change we have seen.

There are other reasonable options for setting targets. Bob Linn, whom I mentioned earlier as perhaps the most esteemed person in educational measurement at the time, suggested that we could look at particularly effective educational interventions to set an upper bound on what run-of-the-mill schools might be able to do. We could look at data from other countries to get an idea how much performance varies in systems that are not plagued by inequities as serious as those in the United States. We could take into account the many factors other than school quality that influence how well students do.

On the other hand, you could just make up targets out of whole cloth. And for the most part, that is exactly what the reformers have done.

At the outset, the expectations set by reformers were modest. Minimum-competency tests set a low bar, requiring no improvement at all for most students, and many states had exceptions for some students who scored too poorly, such as special diplomas for kids with special needs—for example, some students with disabilities. Reformers correctly recognized that this did nothing to improve the instruction received by most students, so over time they made two changes: the bar was raised, and the proportion of students who had to exceed it was increased. By the 1990s, "all children can learn to a high level" had become a mantra in the education policy world. Commendable in principle, but the devil is in the details.

The Proficient standard was the preferred way to define "high level," but explaining "all" proved not to be a trivial task. There are obviously some students who can't pass a reasonably high performance standard—for example, certain students with severe disabilities. One of the innovations of NCLB was to make sure that "all students" was not merely a rhetorical device by defining precisely what it meant.

NCLB's definition of "all students" really did mean "almost all." To see how extreme the NCLB definition of "all" is, you have to delve into the implementing regulations in the *Federal Register*, which specify how various provisions of the statute will be implemented in practice. Normally the *Register* is a good remedy for insomnia, but in this case it makes for very interesting reading. Among other things, the regulations specify that *even students with mild cognitive disabilities* (in the first iteration, the *Register* used the old-fashioned phrase "mild mental retardation") should be held to the same level of proficiency as other students. Only students with a cognitive disability more severe than "mild" could be assessed relative to a lower standard. The *Register* cited two prevalence studies estimating that roughly three-fourths of 1 percent of all students have cognitive disabilities more severe than "mild," and to allow for some geographic variation in prevalence, the regulations set a limit of 1 percent of all students in a district who could be assessed using a lower standard. Additional students assessed against a lower standard would simply be counted as not proficient.[3] Not to belabor the obvious, but students with mild cognitive disabilities are by definition students who do poorly on cognitive tasks—one of which is taking tests.

How demanding—how realistic—is this? It depends on where one pegs "proficient." States have differed a great deal in this respect; some have imposed demanding standards, while others have been very lenient. But for illustration, let's use NAEP's Proficient standard. For years many reformers have pointed to the NAEP standard as a reasonable one and have excoriated states that set their Proficient bars at a lower level. For example, an advocacy group called the Collaborative for Student Success now runs a well-publicized website titled Honesty Gap that rates states as "honest" if their Proficient standard is as harsh as NAEP's. It explains that a lower standard "is the result of a lack of political courage from some policymakers that do not want to be truthful with parents that our students are not prepared for college or the workforce."[4]

What do we know about how realistic it is to demand that schools bring even students with mild cognitive disabilities up to the NAEP Proficient standard? Some years ago Bob Linn attempted to answer this by linking NAEP to the Trends in International Mathematics and Science Study (TIMSS), one of the most important international comparative assessments. Bob estimated that roughly one third of the students in Japan and Korea, two of the highest-performing countries in the world, would fail to reach the NAEP proficient standard in eighth-grade mathematics.[5]

So if states were to be "honest" and set targets as difficult as NAEP's, NCLB would have required teachers to bring our students with mild cognitive disabilities—students who score below 97 or 98 percent of their classmates—to a level that a third of the students in the highest-scoring countries in the world can't reach. And that within the space of twelve years. Is it any wonder that people looked for ways to cut corners?

We don't know yet what this will look like in the state plans eventually approved under ESSA, but ESSA does mirror NCLB in allowing alternate achievement standards only for students "with the most significant cognitive disabilities."

Don't misunderstand: I am not arguing that we should let schools off the hook with respect to the performance of kids with disabilities. As a former special education teacher, I strongly endorse the push to hold schools accountable for the performance of kids with special needs. I'm making a much more general point. Students labeled as having cognitive disabilities are just a particularly clear example of the fact that kids differ, and they differ a lot. The same problem applies, for example, to kids without disabilities who happen to be at the tenth percentile—that is, who score below 90 percent of their peers. If we are going to impose demanding "world-class" standards that will require improvement by most students, how are these low-scoring kids going to make the grade?

○ ○ ○

The pressure to dramatically improve the performance of low-scoring kids was not felt uniformly. One aspect of the great inequity of the American educational system is that disadvantaged kids tend to be clustered in the same schools. The causes are complex, but the result is simple: some schools have far lower average scores—and, particularly important in this system, more kids who aren't "proficient"—than others.

Therefore, if one requires that all students must hit the proficient target by a certain date, these low-scoring schools will face far more demanding targets for gains than other schools do. This was not an accidental byproduct of the notion that "all children can learn to a high level." It was a deliberate and prominent part of many of the test-based accountability reforms. The rationale was straightforward: to reduce inequality by imposing high standards on low-performing schools. Critics have argued that some proponents wanted low-scoring schools to fail because they thought that would help break what they saw as monopoly control by local districts and teacher unions. That may be true of some of the advocates, but there is no doubt that many did believe that this would be an effective way to reduce inequality.

Unfortunately, in this case as well, it seems that no one asked for evidence that these ambitious targets for gains were realistic. The specific targets were often an automatic consequence of where the Proficient standard was placed and the length of time schools were given to bring all students to that standard, which are both arbitrary. Sometimes the people in charge went beyond this and set even more stringent targets, again without evidence that the goals were realistic. Recall that Beverley Hall, the superintendent in Atlanta, conceded that the demanding targets she had set—which quite a number of her principals and teachers cheated to reach—were arbitrary.

Despite the arbitrariness of each stage of building performance targets, the resulting goals are typically endorsed without any effort to evaluate whether teachers have any acceptable way to reach them. Years ago I asked the deputy commissioner of a state department of education how they justified their requirement that their low-scoring schools produce truly massive and rapid gains in scores. I asked, "Aren't teachers in schools serving low-achieving students facing problems that would make it much harder to produce large gains in scores?"

I knew this man well. He was principled, deeply committed to improving education in general and the schooling of disadvantaged students in particular. I know he had no ulterior motive in demanding so much more of low-scoring students. He was also smart and had thought at great length about his state's reforms. However, he didn't have much of an answer to my question. He simply said that good teachers will compensate for the disadvantages some kids bring to school.

He didn't say *how* they would do this. Now, of course, we know something about how: many of them cut corners. That's why we have found both more test prep and more severe score inflation in schools serving disadvantaged kids.

Pretending That All Kids Are the Same

This brings me to a particularly touchy pair of questions: How much variation among kids should we expect? Just how much can we shrink this variation?

Short of cheating or inflating scores in other ways, there are only two ways to bring very low-scoring students to a high standard: dramatically increase everyone's scores or dramatically increase just the performance of kids at the bottom. The latter, of course, would mean making the variation among students far smaller. In my experience, advocates of test-based reform weren't explicit about which of these they expected. I recall a discussion with a state commissioner in the 1990s, during the heyday of "all children can learn to a high level." This commissioner was top-shelf: smart, very open to competing ideas and criticism, and eager to get input from people who knew things he didn't. I had seen him criticize subordinates for not voicing their disagreements with him, saying that it did him no good to have people just tell him he was right. He was planning on imposing much higher standards for graduation, and I asked him which of these two responses he expected. I gave him graphs to illustrate each of them. His first response was perhaps the most telling: he fell silent for a bit and then said, "I've never really thought about it that way." His second response: he wanted a combination of the two options.

Nonetheless, it is clear that the implicit assumption undergirding the reforms is that we can dramatically reduce the variability of achievement. How else can we bring even kids with mild cognitive disabilities to a "high" level of performance?

Unfortunately, all evidence indicates that this optimism is unfounded. We can undoubtedly reduce variations in performance appreciably, if we summoned the political will and committed the resources to do so—which would require a lot more than simply imposing requirements that educators reach arbitrary targets for test scores. However, there are limits on how much we can shrink it.

One of the clearest indications of this is decades of international comparative assessments, such as TIMSS. These make it clear that despite the glaring inequities in American education, the variability of scores in the United States is not atypically large. Some countries show somewhat less variation, while others show more. Even in some nations with much more equitable educational systems, the variability of students' scores is not all that different from that in the United States. To make this concrete, I'll compare the variation in US performance to that in two other countries, using eighth-grade math scores in the 2007 TIMSS. For one comparison I'll use the Netherlands, which scores a bit above the United States in TIMSS and far higher than the United States—very near the top internationally—on PISA (the Programme for International Student Assessment), the other most important international comparative assessment. The Netherlands also has the least variation in math scores of any country participating in TIMSS in 2007. For the other I will use Singapore, which is always among the top performers in math in international comparisons. Singapore is an interesting case because it has a single school system, and teachers are assigned by the national ministry to maintain a fair distribution.

You can see the results in figure 8.1: the three distributions are not very different. I have stylized the distributions a bit by drawing them as simple normal distributions—the infamous bell curve. A tabulation of individual scores would look much like this but more irregular, and it's easier to see the comparison when the curves are tidied up in this way. The dotted line represents the Netherlands. You can see that the range of scores is a bit more compressed than in the other two countries. That forces more kids into the middle of the score range. That is why the middle peak is taller in the Netherlands: a greater proportion of the student population is in that middle range. The solid line in the center is the United States, while the dashed line on the outside represents Singapore. You can see that while the Netherlands and Singapore differ somewhat from each other, neither differs all that much from the United States, which has a middling spread of scores. (For those familiar with this metric, the standard deviations are 61, 75, and 84.)

How can it be that even though our educational system is highly inequitable in ways that really matter—the quality of teachers, the quality of texts and other resources, the availability of advanced course, and peer effects, among other things—the performance of American students isn't unusually variable?

The answer is that as important as they are, differences among schools don't explain the bulk of the variation we see in student performance. That's not to say that the impact of inequitable schooling is insignificant. Anything but. Differences in school quality have

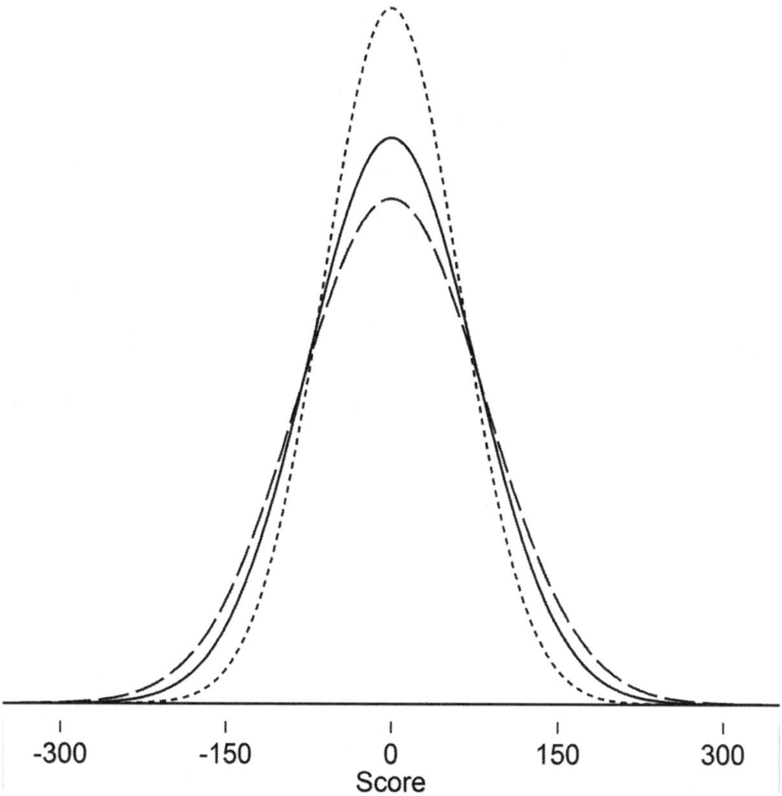

Figure 8.1. Variations in grade 8 mathematics in TIMSS, 2007: Singapore (dashed), US (solid), and the Netherlands (dotted). The scale is score differences from each country's average.

large effects, and I agree with many of the reformers that these shouldn't be tolerated. Nonetheless, variations in schooling are only one factor among many.

The simple fact of the matter is that whatever we do, we will be faced with a very large variation in performance. It may end up modestly smaller than it is at present, but it will remain very big.

To a remarkable degree, the reformers ignored this problem. In practice, if not in intent, they acted as if changing schools would largely eliminate variations in student achievement, ignoring the impact of factors that have nothing to do with the behavior of educators—for example, the behavior of parents, students' health and nutrition, and many characteristics of the communities in which students grow up. It's hard to know why. Perhaps some didn't understand the importance of the many noneducational causes of variation, despite the vast amount of research that has demonstrated this over a span of many decades. Perhaps some thought that schools could somehow compensate. Perhaps some were—rightly—so upset by inequities in schooling that they were willing to overlook this problem and take some collateral damage.

Whatever the reasons, this decision backfired. The result was, in many cases, unrealistic expectations that teachers simply couldn't meet by any legitimate means. I'll give you just one example, this a personal anecdote. I mentioned that years ago I was a special education teacher. One of my jobs was to teach remedial reading to a group of fifth- and sixth-grade students who were years behind grade level. I don't recall the details all these years later, but it is clear that at least some of them were dyslexic. Having already experienced years of failure in reading, most of them hated reading instruction. And I just wasn't very good at this kind of teaching. But let's say I had been a superb reading teacher and had doubled the rate at which they acquired reading skills. By any reasonable standard, that would have been an accomplishment worth celebrating. But by the standards of NCLB, and presumably ESSA, I would have been a failure, because even that remarkable progress would not have made them "proficient" in many states. What would I have done if I had been faced with a demand that I make them "proficient," and very rapidly at that?

We now know what many educators did. Faced with unrealistic targets, some cut corners or simply cheated. And perhaps because the system, in its zeal to address inequities, made the targets most unrealistic for educators serving disadvantaged kids, those kids—ironically—got the worst of it: the most test prep, the most score inflation, and apparently the most cheating. And yet inflated scores allowed policy makers to declare victory, and the public received a steady diet of encouraging but bogus news about rapid improvements in the achievement gap.

○ ○ ○

In short, setting unrealistic targets has been a major cause of the failures of education reform.

The question is what we will do in response. How do we crack down on the unconscionable inequities in schooling and pressure low-performing schools to improve without sabotaging our own efforts by pretending that all kids are the same? Continuing on the same path won't work. However, designing a good alternative is one of the single most difficult problems in education policy.

The failure of recent reforms is not a reason to give up on setting ambitious standards for improvement. Rather, I am simply arguing that to be effective—to maximize the desired effects while minimizing the inevitable undesirable side effects—targets for improvement should be realistic, within the range that teachers can reach by legitimate means.

I am also certainly not arguing against requiring improvements specifically for low-scoring kids and groups or against narrowing the gaps between them and higher-performing students. But to be effective in doing this, we again need to be realistic—not only in setting overall targets but in dealing with the diverse backgrounds and needs of students. As Bob Linn pointed out years ago, high standards for all is not the same as one common standard.[6] Not all doses of a medicine are beneficial, and not all demands for changes in performance are reasonable or helpful.

And the more ambitious the goals are, the more resources we will have to devote to them, to better enable schools to meet the targets with real improvements. Certainly we will need supports and training for teachers, but we may also need to commit resources outside of regular schooling as well—for example, high-quality (read: expensive) preschools.

I'll return to this in later chapters.

9

EVALUATING TEACHERS

Shortly after Arne Duncan became secretary of education in 2009, I was invited to a meeting to discuss testing and accountability with him and his senior staff. It was already apparent that he intended to carry on the Bush administration's focus on test-based accountability, and I tried to alert him and his staff to the pitfalls. I stressed that however valuable tests may be for helping to evaluate schools and teachers, they can never be sufficient because they fail to measure so many of the important goals of education. Worse, emphasizing them at the expense of other important goals had created some very serious negative effects. At one point, one of Duncan's staff members challenged me in a clearly annoyed tone of voice: "What is all this 'other important stuff' you keep talking about?"

I answered that the starting point for any good accountability system has to be deciding what we most want schools to do, including what we want to see when we walk into a classroom. We need to design the accountability system to reward these. To make this concrete, I gave him the following example from a fourth-grade class in Montgomery County, Maryland, taught by a young teacher named Norka Padilla.

While my son was in third grade, I told the principal of his school that I wanted to observe all of the fourth-grade teachers in the school to see which would make the best match for him. I had taught fourth-graders years before, and I had a clear notion of what I wanted to see. The district didn't encourage parental involvement in placement decisions, and the principal tried to put me off by telling me that all of them were good. But I persisted, and eventually he gave up and gave me permission. All were indeed good teachers, but it quickly became clear to me that Norka was exceptional.

When I observed classrooms, I always tried to watch at least one math lesson. In my experience, math is often poorly taught, and students come to see it as a chore—often a pointless one at that. I wanted my kids to see that math is useful and interesting, and ideally, I wanted them to enjoy it as well.

The first time I was in Norka's classroom, she started her math lesson by announcing, "It's time for math log." Math log, it turned out, was a single problem to which she devoted about fifteen minutes before every regular math lesson. Students could work on the problem together, but they wrote logs individually describing their work.

My first day in the class, the math log problem was this: "Which is stronger, a rectangle or a triangle?" This generated some buzz, and hands quickly went up. "What do you mean by 'stronger'?" some students wanted to know. That was already a good sign: the students were engaged and thinking critically.

Norka replied, "That's a good question, because you could define it a number of ways. I will define it this way. Suppose I gave you weights and asked you to pile weights on top of a rectangle and a triangle. Which would hold more weight before it collapsed? That's what I mean by stronger."

The buzz resumed, and fairly quickly, students had their answers. Most of them said that a rectangle would be stronger. Norka didn't agree or disagree. Instead her response was to pass out rectangles and triangles constructed from strips of cardboard, held with cotter pins in the vertices. She asked students to play with the shapes and see if they were right.

The buzz was louder this time. After a short while, Norka asked, "Who was wrong?" Hands shot up.

Norka then asked, "Would anyone like to try to explain their mistake?" This took a bit of time, but in due course hands started going up.

I was awed. Those of you who haven't taught may not quite see why. Norka had the entire class productively engaged, and they appeared be enjoying themselves. She had them exploring and reasoning about mathematics. That's accomplishment enough. She had brought them to the point where many of them seemed comfortable admitting their errors. She ended by giving them—fourth-graders, remember—a very difficult task of verbalizing their reasoning and their errors, and they were willing to give it a go. None of this is easy to do. The contrast between this and many other math classes I have seen, which stress procedures more than the reasoning behind them and are therefore both unchallenging and dull, was like night and day.

The next day I called the principal and told him that he should place my son into Norka's class. In that district, demanding a placement was even further off the charts than asking to observe classrooms, so it required a good bit of stubbornness on my part, but eventually the principal tired of me and agreed. The next year confirmed my one day of observation; simply put, Norka was one of the best elementary-school teachers I have encountered. Three years later I called the principal again and insisted that my daughter be assigned to Norka. He consented, and that year was just as impressive.

I told Duncan and his staff that this is a fine example of "other important stuff"—making math interesting and even fun, keeping kids engaged, getting students to reason about math rather than simply practicing procedures, teaching kids to communicate about their work, and helping students to focus more on learning than on simply being right. This is precisely the sort of thing I hope to see when I walk into a classroom. And I want it for *all* kids, not just my own.

I asked Duncan whether the accountability system he had in mind would encourage other teachers to try to teach like Norka. For that matter, would it even be neutral in this respect? If it wouldn't encourage activities like math log, would it at least not discourage them?

As I recall, no one in the room offered any response. The answer to both questions, of course, is no. In our test-based accountability system, a teacher has to throw self-interest to the wind to do things like math log. There are two reasons for this. First, many good activities of this sort fall outside of the range most standardized tests can sample well. Second, while good instruction in general will improve students' mastery and therefore should increase scores, it won't increase scores on a *specific* test as much as instruction—and test prep—aimed squarely at that particular test. In other words, teaching to the test can increase test scores more rapidly than high-quality teaching not focused narrowly on the specific test used for accountability. For the teachers who confront the demand that they raise scores quickly and by a large amount, the choice is clear, and it isn't math log. And the decision is unfortunately all the clearer for teachers who need to make particularly large gains—that is, teachers with disadvantaged students.

Not all teachers make the wrong choice, of course; some opt to pay the price that test-based accountability imposes on them. In 2012 Michael Winerip wrote in the *New York Times* about two New York City teachers who were rated near the bottom of the district's teacher evaluation scale because of their test scores (more specifically, their "value-added" estimates, which I'll return to in a moment). From his brief portrayal, they appear to have been good teachers, but they didn't want to devote time to test prep. They and their principal knew that the cost of forgoing test prep was often lower scores. For example, Winerip wrote of one of the teachers:

> Ms. Sangree might have scored higher than 11 in English by doing more test prep. There is a standard test-prep formula for writing an essay: Topic sentence; three sentences that give examples to support the thesis, one from literature, one from current events, and one from personal experience; concluding sentence.
>
> Instead, her class has spent weeks working on research papers about the Mayans. Rowan Groom explained to a visitor how she was doing her paper on Mayan clothing.
>
> "First we collected facts from books and National Geographic and Web sites and notes when we visited the Museum of Natural History," she said. "Next we sorted our facts into topics."
>
> They were ready to write. "First you do a first draft and then you revise and edit and we talk about our thoughts with our friends,

in the meeting area. Then we go into our revised draft and we edit some more, and after that we go across the hall to computer lab and type it up."

The state test does not require students to write a research paper.[1]

Which would you rather see when you walk into a classroom: kids working on a research paper like this one or kids practicing the standard test-prep formula? The research-paper assignment is very much like math log: precisely the type of engaging and demanding instruction I want to see in all classrooms. If you want scores to go up quickly, however, that simply isn't a prudent use of time. You have already seen some of what the test-based reforms have encouraged teachers to do instead.

○ ○ ○

The failures of test-based accountability shouldn't blind us to the serious and extraordinarily difficult problem the reformers were trying to confront. It was abundantly clear that in most districts there was no effective accountability for teachers after they were granted tenure, which in most locations requires only a few years of teaching. As both a public school teacher and a parent of students in public schools, I encountered the lack of meaningful accountability time and time again. Teachers who weren't competent, or who for some other reason didn't do what they should—or did do what they shouldn't—were allowed to continue teaching and often didn't even face any intervention.

In response to this deplorable lack of accountability, the reformers wanted a real evaluation system, one that would have teeth and focus on important outcomes. They wanted a system that would encourage teachers to improve and to weed out those who shouldn't teach. I want that too.

Designing an effective way of evaluating teachers, however, is far more challenging than the reformers appear to have recognized. First, the pervasiveness of Campbell's Law shows how difficult it is to design a performance incentive system that works more or less as intended. Worse, teaching as a profession has many characteristics that make evaluating performance particularly difficult. To start, it's hard to agree on what constitutes good teaching, and indeed there isn't always one answer to this question. Different teachers may find very different approaches successful, depending on the characteristics of their students, the context, and their own strengths and weaknesses. I rely heavily on graphics to explain concepts, and I spend countless hours creating and editing them. I rely on humor to loosen my students up, and I improvise freely in response to questions. Are these the right things to do? They work for me, but they might not for others.

Years ago, a colleague of mine at RAND, Brian Stecher, pointed out that in medicine, performance evaluations—as problematic as they are in that field—are helped by the presence of diagnostic categories and research-based standards of practice. Taken together, these provide a guide to practice and allow doctors to target interventions very differently for different types of patients. We can identify who is diabetic and who isn't, and we know some of the things that are essential to good practice in caring for people who are diabetic, such as carefully controlling diet and monitoring insulin levels. When a patient is identified as having an allergy that can cause anaphylactic shock, a competent doctor will train her to self-administer epinephrine, but she won't spend her time giving the patient instruction on how to monitor her insulin levels.

In contrast to medicine, education has relatively few diagnostic categories that have implications for standards of practice. There are some—for example, dyslexia—but not many. This makes it harder to evaluate the quality of teaching.

At least two additional problems hobble efforts to hold teachers accountable. As I'll explain below, test-based evaluations of teachers are highly unstable and vary, often dramatically, from time to time. Some of the alternatives to test scores, such as observations of teaching practice, suffer the same problem. And evaluations that include subjective judgment—widely used both in the private sector and in educational systems in other countries—face a particular obstacle in civil service systems, including public schools.

In the private sector, a manager charged with evaluating subordinates often "has money on the table," as Derek Neal, an economist who has studied incentive systems in education, has phrased it. The evaluator's own evaluation depends on the performance of his or her group. It's therefore not in her self-interest to give a positive evaluation to a weak employee, say, because she likes him or because she wants to avoid the conflict inherent in a negative evaluation. By the same token, it is not in her self-interest to give a negative evaluation to a productive employee for irrelevant personal reasons. For example, a sales manager would be shooting herself in the foot by giving a negative evaluation to a highly successful salesperson whom she happens to dislike. This is often not true in public employment, which is one of the reasons for employment protections in civil service systems.

For all its many problems, the test-based accountability system greatly reduces the problem of questionable subjective evaluations—but not as successfully as proponents argue. It relies on largely objective measures. Many test items are scored with no subjective judgment at all, and in most instances those that can't be scored without judgment—for example, essays and some other items that require substantial responses from students—are scored in ways that minimize the impact of subjectivity. Moreover, the reforms gave those doing the evaluations an incentive to focus on educators' output rather than irrelevant personal details. However, as you have seen, "objective" doesn't necessarily mean "trustworthy," because teachers can inflate scores.

Thus the reformers addressed the problem, but in what turned out to be a simplistic and unworkable way. In a later chapter I'll suggest more sensible ways to approach the challenge of evaluating educators, including some more reasonable ways of using test scores. In this chapter, however, I want to set the stage for that by explaining some of the problems that have arisen in using scores to evaluate educators. You've already seen some of them: the perverse incentives it created, which in turn have led to bad test prep, cheating, and inflated test scores. Here I'll focus not on incentives and their effects but rather on the limitations of the measures themselves—that is, why test scores provide such a problematic measure of educators' performance.

The Incompleteness of Tests

I was thinking too narrowly in that meeting with Arne Duncan. What I had in mind was the incompleteness of standardized tests *as measures of one tested subject.* There are important aspects of the mastery of mathematics, for example, that we can't capture well—or at all—with current tests. And there are important aspects of mathematics instruction, such as keeping students engaged and fostering their curiosity and eagerness to learn, that aren't reflected adequately by any measures of student achievement. I'll come back to this in a later chapter, when I discuss the importance of monitoring educators' practices as well as student outcomes.

What I was not considering in that meeting was another way in which testing is incomplete: the problem of subjects and grades for which districts and states have no appropriate tests. It didn't occur to me in that discussion just how unreasonable the responses to this problem would be.

Remember another elementary-school teacher I described at the beginning of this book, Kim Cook, who taught first grade in Alachua County, Florida. Like other states struggling to comply with Duncan's policies, Florida had statewide tests for only a small proportion of teachers. The state's truly astonishing solution, you'll recall, was simply to take scores from teachers who had scores from an appropriate test and use them to "evaluate" teachers who didn't. Florida had no tests before grade 3, so in Kim's case her district used the scores from fourth- and fifth-grade students *in another school.* And Florida was not unique. Tennessee's teacher-evaluation legislation specified that 35 percent of the evaluation of teachers who had their own growth score on the Tennessee Value-Added Assessment System (TVAAS) system should be based on that score. That left all the others whose students didn't produce scores that TVAAS could use—teachers in untested grades or subjects. For them, the Tennessee statute takes the Florida approach: use other teachers' test scores. For teachers who don't have their own rating, 25 percent of the evaluation should be based on their school's average TVAAS rating.[2]

An alternative response to the pressure to evaluate teachers with test scores was to scramble to find or develop some kind of test that could be used to evaluate the teachers for whom the state had none—for example, those who teach music, art, physical education, and some advanced science and math courses, as well as those in untested grades. In some cases, states left it to local districts to sort out the mess. Keep in mind that in most states the large majority of school districts are small. In New York and New England, for example, districts are township- or city-based, not county-wide, so outside of major cities, most districts are very small. These small districts have no capacity to develop good tests or even to screen commercially available tests for quality. I had a number of conversations with the chief state school officer of one of the states that opted for this find-a-test strategy and left the selection to local districts. Early on, he lamented the lack of assessment expertise in the majority of the districts that had to find or develop tests to evaluate these teachers. A year later, when I asked how things had progressed, he wryly answered, "I had no idea just how much bad testing money can buy." However, he didn't change the policy, which was an essential piece of the plan the state had given the US Department of Education in an application for funding under the Race to the Top program that Arne Duncan had instituted.

Both of these responses show just how unmoored from common sense test-based evaluation of schools and teachers reform has become. It's utterly irrational to "evaluate" teachers based on scores earned by students of other teachers, particularly teachers in other schools or who teach other subjects. Imagine, for example, that your own evaluation were based on the performance of employees in another branch of your employer's firm. Most of us would find this both ludicrous and intolerable. Even basing the "evaluation" on other people teaching the same students at the same time is a stretch. The students in my classes are typically taking three or four other classes at the same time as mine, and in some cases one of those classes is about related material—for example, a basic statistics class. Does the quality of instruction in that statistics class influence how well students do in my class? Of course. But that influence pales by comparison to the impact of what I do, and when a student in my class fails to learn something important in my curriculum, the blame should lie with me, not with one of my colleagues. And most of my colleagues are teaching things far less related to my own work—just as the math and science teachers with test scores are teaching things very distant from music, art, and history. This is so obvious that it wouldn't be worth mentioning it were it not for the fact that some of the reformers have ignored it and have punished and even fired teachers for the quality of other people's work.

And searching desperately for a test to use for this purpose isn't much better. Until one has a suitable test in hand, it defies logic to use tests to evaluate teachers. It's reasonable—although as you are seeing, anything but straightforward—to use a test to *help* evaluate an educator or a school if one has a test that measures a good share of what we expect the teacher or school to produce in that subject. To go backwards, however, and search for a test that measures *something* of value in a subject, just so we can say we are using tests to evaluate teachers, is unreasonable and, frankly, irresponsible. And in some of these subjects, it is not clear that we can design tests suitable for this purpose, at least over the short and moderate term. Perhaps I will be proved wrong on this last point, but until I have been, we shouldn't be using the tests to evaluate teachers' performance.

Let's consider one example: music teachers. My kids both learned to play more than one instrument, and they attended a public high school with a truly outstanding music program that was widely recognized in the community as one of the school's greatest strengths. The program engaged a large number of students, and the more selective groups routinely won regional as well as local competitions. The kids worked hard at it, and they loved it. How would you evaluate the music director and his program? I know what other parents and I used, including the students' engagement and enthusiasm and the quality of the work they produced, as evidenced by both what we heard at concerts and the awards the groups won every single year. It never once crossed my mind to ask for standardized test scores. I could easily design a standardized test that would capture bits of what students learned—for example, music theory—and those could be put to good use, but they wouldn't begin to give an accurate evaluation of the director's exceptional work. It would be just silly—and potentially destructive—to make his evaluation dependent on a standardized test selected not because it purports to measure what we would need measured but because we "needed" a test to evaluate music teachers.

Taking Test Scores Out of Context

Our test-based accountability system takes test scores out of context. That was a deliberate goal of the reformers; they wanted measures that someone sitting in a state capital could interpret without ever looking at the school from which they were obtained. However, that's one of the main reasons the reforms have failed. Test scores taken out of context often don't tell you what you need to know.

Consider the case of Joyce Irvine, who from 2004 until 2010 was the principal of Wheeler Elementary School in Burlington, Vermont. Wheeler serves a highly disadvantaged population; in 2010 thirty-seven of the thirty-nine fifth-grade students were either refugees or special-education students. During her time at Wheeler, Irvine added a number of enrichment programs, including a summer school, and converted the school into an arts magnet. She worked very hard—often eighty hours per week—and both her hard work and her success were recognized by her colleagues and her superiors. Her final evaluation began, "Joyce has successfully completed a phenomenal year," and the superintendent called her "a leader among her colleagues."

In 2010 she was fired from her job as principal and assigned to a lower-paying administrative position. The reason: low test scores. Under one of Arne Duncan's policies, to qualify for funds from the federal economic stimulus program, the district had to replace the school with a charter school (the state had none), remove the principal and half the staff, or remove the principal and "transform" the school. Irvine had to go. As she said, "Joyce Irvine versus millions. You can buy a lot of help for children with that money."[3]

Was it reasonable to be concerned because Wheeler's scores were low? Of course. Signaling potential problems is one of the most important functions tests can serve. Was it reasonable to assume that Wheeler's low scores reflected a lack of competence or effort on the part of its principal? Of course not. The fundamental mistake this illustrates is taking scores out of context. The system didn't require that the district consider whether the school produced a reasonable level of achievement or had produced an acceptable rate of improvement *given the circumstances it faced.* In fact, it made that sort of judgment irrelevant. Poor scores are taken to be sufficient to indicate that the school's staff is failing, and for the most part the circumstances confronting the school *can't* be taken into account. It's much like insisting that doctors treat patients based on one symptom without considering which of its many possible causes is the relevant one.

Because the quality of education is confounded with context, good educators teaching under difficult circumstances are punished. By the same token, weak teachers assigned to schools with high-achieving students get a pass.

Trying to Use Tests to Explain, Not Just Describe

The Wheeler School example illustrates another problem with using test scores to evaluate educators: mistakenly attributing scores—high or low—to the actions of educators, despite the many other factors that influence student achievement. Used properly—in particular, used in ways that limit score inflation—tests are very useful for describing what students know. On their own, however, tests simply aren't sufficient to explain *why* they know it. This was explained clearly by the early designers of standardized tests, but their warnings are no longer heeded.

Of course the actions of educators do affect scores, but so do many other factors both inside and outside of school, such as their parents' education. This has been well documented at least since the publication more than fifty years ago of the "Coleman Report," *Equality of Educational Opportunity*, a huge study commissioned by the US Office of Education, which found that student background and parental education had a bigger impact than schooling on student achievement.[4] While the debate about the precise relative contributions of schooling and background still rage in the research world, there is no doubt that factors other than schooling are enormously important. This is part of the explanation for the huge variation in student performance we find anywhere we look. And, of course, it is one of the many reasons that the one-size-fits-all approach to reform has backfired so badly.

Test scores would justify a conclusion about the effectiveness of educators only if one could somehow separate the impact of the other factors that influence scores. One can do that—albeit not completely—either by observing the school or by means of some statistical techniques (or both). That brings me to "value-added modeling."

Using "Value-Added Modeling" to Evaluate Teachers

Even though some parts of our accountability system totally ignore factors other than the actions of educators that influence scores—the policy that forced Burlington to can Joyce Irvine is an example—policy makers haven't been entirely blind to this issue. Their primary response has been to rely on various types of "value-added modeling," frequently dubbed VAM.

Other than VAM, most of the test-based accountability systems reformers have imposed have taken one of two approaches. One, the NCLB approach, simply compares the performance of one cohort of kids—say this year's fourth-graders—to an arbitrary standard, the "Proficient" cut score. Each year every school has a target, a percentage of kids in that cohort who should reach or exceed the Proficient standard. The second approach, exemplified by the Kentucky system I described earlier, bases accountability on the change between successive cohorts. If the percentage proficient in this year's fourth-graders exceeds last year's percentage (or the percentage two years previously, in Kentucky's case) as much as your arbitrary target demands, you're golden. If the percentage proficient doesn't improve enough, you may be punished.

VAMs are an entirely different approach. The original idea behind VAM was that we can track the scores of individual students over time to estimate how much each one improved in a given subject. Using earlier scores, we can predict how each student is likely to score at the end of his or her current grade. Sometimes these predictions are based solely on students' earlier scores, while in other systems they take into account some background factors as well. Schools don't have a lot of background information about students, but the variables included in the VAM model can include gender, receipt of free or reduced-price lunch, limited proficiency in English, or disability status. Either way, each student's *deviation* from her predicted score for the current grade is assumed to measure the impact of a teacher's work. The estimate of a teacher's value added is obtained by adding these deviations from prediction for all her students. If a teacher's students do better than predicted, that is taken to show that she is effective, but if they do worse, she is ineffective. Hence these deviations are taken to indicate the "value" the teacher has added to his students' trajectories.

While this seems conceptually simple, it is devilishly hard in practice, raising very difficult problems of both measurement and statistical modeling. Moreover, while VAM began with this approach, it has spawned many others, some quite different from this first one, and the differences among them are technically complex. For simplicity, I'll stick with this original approach.

The movement to use VAMs had two major motivations. The first is that it is simply more logical to hold teachers or schools accountable for how much students have improved over the year they taught them, rather than for the achievement they have accumulated over their entire lives to that date. If a student starts at a new school in fifth grade but came in at a second-grade reading level, it's not fair to punish the new school for his low test scores, and by the same token, it's not fair to credit a teacher for the high scores of a student who enters school that year already performing very well. The second motivation is that it helps separate the effects of teaching from all of the other things that influence test scores.

However, while VAMs *help* to separate the impact of teaching from everything else, they don't solve the problem entirely. The explanation is technical. In the typical VAM approach we start by predicting students' scores with a model that includes earlier scores and perhaps background factors. The estimate of VAM is obtained by adding up the discrepancies from those predictions—that is, by looking at variations in performance *that we have not predicted using the variables in the model.* This variation that we can't predict could be a result of *anything* that isn't included in the statistical model—including, but by no means limited to, the impact of the teacher. Using VAMs to evaluate teachers requires that one *assume* that this unpredicted variation among teachers is attributable to teachers, but that needn't be entirely true. It might be, for example, that the teacher was given a particularly challenging or particularly easy cohort of kids this year. Or that there were a lot of illnesses that disrupted the class. Or that a new principal arrived, and order either improved or deteriorated or a result. Or that curricular changes altered the fit of the curriculum to the test. The list of other things that can contribute is endless.

In 2014 the American Statistical Association (ASA), the primary professional organization of statisticians in the United States, issued the *ASA Statement on Using Value-Added Models for Educational Assessment.* The ASA summary of this point was straightforward: "VAMs typically measure correlation, not causation: Effects—positive or negative—attributed to a teacher may actually be caused by other factors that are not captured in the model."[5] That is, if a VAM is used to estimate your "effectiveness" as a teacher, that estimate will sometimes blame or credit you for things that have nothing to do with your teaching.

So can't we solve this by including students' background characteristics in the model, as some systems do, to take their effects out of the remaining variation in scores? Not entirely. First, the factors that obscure the effects of teaching are not limited to students' backgrounds; they also include other attributes of a school and community, such as school size, the amount of extracurricular tutoring students receive, the characteristics of students' peers, teachers' colleagues, and the school administration. Second, we generally have only very limited information about students' backgrounds. Finally, controlling for students' background can ironically do more harm than good. We know that in many settings, advantaged kids get better teachers (as mine did when I insisted they have Norka Padilla as their math teacher). When this is the case, we would want the evaluation system to pick it up. However, controlling for students' background will also remove the differences in teacher quality that are associated with them.

This is not to say that VAM entirely fails to reflect the impact of teachers' work. Done well—and if score inflation is held to a minimum—it does. The problem is twofold. Like any other metric based on test scores, it leaves a great deal unmeasured. And for the portion it does measure, it doesn't dependably separate the effects of a teacher's work from many other influences, both within the school and outside of it. And, of course, it only works at all in subjects that students study year after year. You can't measure growth from year to year in subjects like chemistry that most students study only for one year.

Rating Teachers with the Wrong Test

Suppose you and I both teach science in the same grade and we are equally effective teachers. I am asked to teach a class that focuses on topics A, B, C, and D. You are asked to focus your instruction on topics C, D, E, and F. At the end of the year, our students are given a test that focuses on A, B, C, and D.

You lose. Your students' test scores will appear to show that you're "ineffective," even though in fact we are equally good, because you didn't teach A and B. No matter how important E and F were for your students—even if they were the core of what you were expected to teach—the time you put into them was simply wasted for purposes of your evaluation.

My example is contrived, but it's not far-fetched. This sort of thing happens frequently, although often not in so extreme a fashion. It often affects educators who teach material that is advanced for their grade level, and it can be particularly severe when VAMs are used to evaluate educators. A good example appeared in a 2012 blog post by Aaron Pallas, a sociologist at Columbia University, titled "Meet the 'Worst' 8th Grade Math Teacher in NYC." He described the case of Carolyn Abbott, a seventh-grade teacher in Anderson School, who was literally rated as the worst eighth-grade math teacher in New York City, which used VAMs to evaluate teachers. To put this in some context, when Abbott taught the cohort of kids at issue in the seventh grade, they scored at the ninety-eighth percentile of the city's students. The next year, when she had them as eighth-graders, they scored at the eighty-ninth percentile. Still very near the top, but below the prediction from the VAM model, which was the ninety-seventh percentile. And as I explained, deviations from the predicted scores are interpreted as "effectiveness." The difference between the ninety-seventh and eighty-ninth percentiles put Abbott at the bottom of the district's rankings. This put her application for tenure in jeopardy.

The reason was poor alignment of the test with the material Abbott was supposed to teach. Anderson is an unusually advanced school, and much of its teaching is literally years above grade level. Pallas noted that much of the content assessed in the eighth-grade test is taught to Anderson students in the fifth or sixth grade. Abbott explained that she didn't teach the curriculum her eighth-graders were tested on. Instead, she primarily taught the more advanced algebra that shows up on the state's high-school Regents Integrated Algebra test. Because she was evaluated using the wrong test—and because scores are taken out of context—she couldn't be "effective" no matter how well she taught.[6]

Teachers' Ratings Are Inconsistent across Tests

Carolyn Abbott's case, where the district was using a test that was simply the wrong one for her students, is a particularly severe instance of a more general problem: the rating of teachers (and principals and schools) often differs disconcertingly from one test to another. You've already seen one reason for this in an earlier chapter: educators in some schools may inflate scores on the accountability test more than those in other schools, causing them to rank differently on the high-stakes test than on a lower-stakes test. However, even if we leave inflation aside, this inconsistency can be large and has to be addressed if tests are to be used sensibly in evaluations.

The contrived example above shows why: tests, as you know, are samples of tasks, and they give more weight to some content than to others. Different tests don't include identical samples of material, and they often give different emphasis to the material they have in common. As a result, any given test is likely to align better with the intended curricula of some teachers than that of others. And those differences in alignment are misrepresented as differences in effectiveness.

One of the most important studies of this problem was carried out by J. R. Lockwood and colleagues at RAND, who tracked the growth of students in mathematics from fifth through eighth grades on one of the most widely used achievement tests. They calculated value-added estimates for teachers using the two subscales that test offered: procedures and problem solving. Because the procedures and problem-solving scores came from the same test, there was no difference between them in accountability pressure.

They found very little consistency in teacher ratings across the two parts of the test. Their most disquieting finding was that "the variation within teachers across achievement measures is *larger* than the variation across teachers" (emphasis added).[7] To make this technical statement concrete, imagine that you rated a group of teachers twice, once using each of these two math tests. Lockwood found that the difference in ratings between the two tests for the average teacher was greater than the difference between two randomly chosen teachers. This makes it hard to claim that one teacher is "better" than the other; to do that you would need to specify which of the two parts of the math test you are considering.

Lockwood's study is in one sense an extreme case; it's unlikely that any district or state would choose between tests that assess only mathematical procedures or just problem solving. Moreover, the study reflects only a relatively small sample in one district. Nonetheless, the warning is clear: estimates of teacher effectiveness can be highly sensitive to how the test samples from the domain.

Teachers' Test Scores Are Unstable over Time

Most teachers don't change dramatically from year to year. Norka Padilla was a superb teacher when I observed her; she was a superb teacher the next year, when my son was in her class, and she remained a superb teacher three years after that, when my daughter was one of her students. Certainly teachers' work can improve or deteriorate over time, but barring unusual events, these changes tend to be gradual. One doesn't often see huge annual fluctuations in teachers' effectiveness.

The test scores of their students are quite another matter. These *are* generally very unstable over time.

At this point, a technical distinction becomes important: the difference between *reliability* and *bias*. In common parlance, *reliable* has many meanings, including "trustworthy," but to explain the inconsistencies in scores over time, I have to stick with the narrower and more specific technical usage. To make this distinction concrete, imagine that you go to a store to try out bathroom scales. And suppose that you also just came from your doctor's office and know what your weight is. Suppose now that you step on and off one scale several times and that it always gives you the same answer: it tells you that you weigh three pounds more than you really do. Demoralizing. So you try a second scale. The second one is inconsistent, varying a pound or so from one time to the next, but you notice that the readings seem to vary around the correct weight you were given in your doctor's office, with some readings too high and others too low. Let's say that if you averaged all the readings it gave you, the average from the second scale would be right on the money. In other words, the first one is *systematically* wrong, while the second one is inconsistent but not systematically wrong.

In technical parlance, the first—the systematic error—is *bias*. The inconsistency of the second bathroom scale is called *error* or *unreliability*. Reliability means only consistency, and error—for example, from sampling in polls—is inconsistency. It's not systematic, and it's therefore not bias. Where this departs from common speech is that the first bathroom scale, even though it gives you the wrong answer, is considered reliable, because it reliably—that is, consistently—gives you the same answer. It just happens to be the wrong answer. And the second is unreliable because it is inconsistent, even though it would give you the right answer if you were neurotic enough to weigh yourself a dozen times each morning and average the readings.

At this point I am simply noting that teachers' average test scores are unreliable—that is, inconsistent over time. I am not saying that they are biased. They sometimes are—for example, when teachers inflate scores—but that is a different part of the story. The inconsistency in teachers' scores means that some of the scores happen to be wrong—some will be too high, some too low—even though over the long run they could average out just fine.

There are many reasons for the inconsistency in teachers' average scores, but the most important is that they have different kids in their classes each year. Each cohort is just a sample of kids, and there are good samples and bad ones. In my classes we call this the Leo effect. Years ago a researcher I know asked some elementary-school teachers why a substantial drop in test scores in their small school had moved up one grade per year: third grade one year, fourth grade the next, and so on. "That's Leo," one of the teachers quickly suggested. Leo was an extremely disruptive kid, and the drop in scores tracked his progression from one grade to the next.

Some years ago this instability was shown in detail by a colleague of mine, Tom Kane. Figure 9.1 is an adaptation of one of his graphs. Each dot represents the change in average scores for one school from 1999 to 2000 for a representative sample of California schools. Along the horizontal axis of this figure is number of fourth-grade students in the school. Along the vertical axis is the change in average mathematics score. The numbers on the axis reflect the reporting scale for the California test at that time, and for most people it won't be clear just how big these changes really are, but they are very large. To make this concrete, a change of twenty points would move a kid from the fiftieth percentile to the eighty-eighth percentile. So what this shows is that except in very large schools, average scores fluctuate—both up and down—a great deal from year to year. As one would expect, the smaller the schools, the greater the fluctuation—just as polls with few respondents have larger margins of error than polls with a lot of respondents. This is an indication that the fluctuation arises in large part because of the sampling of students, not because of variations in the quality of education.

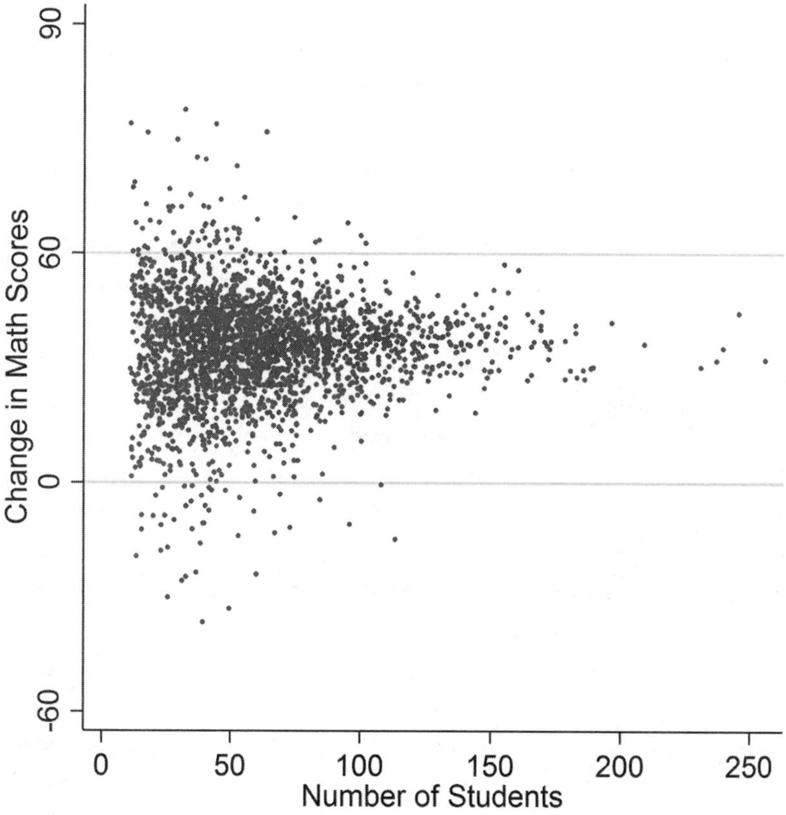

Figure 9.1. One-year changes in average fourth-grade math scores for California schools, by school enrollment.

This graph would look worse for individual teachers. Most elementary-school teachers have fewer than thity students, and in some locations—for example, many rural schools—far fewer. So when we evaluate individual teachers, many of them would be at the far left of figure 9.1, with huge fluctuations from one year to the next—not because their effectiveness varies that much but because their students do.

Figure 9.1 is based on students' scores without any adjustment to remove the confounding effects of background factors, such as parental education. The fluctuation would be even worse if the impact of those factors were removed. The reason is that most of the background variables that strongly influence scores are quite stable over time. Schools that serve advantaged communities in one year typically still do the next. They will tend to score better than schools serving disadvantaged kids year after year. So if you tinker with scores in an attempt to remove the effect of background factors, you will be removing things that *increase* the stability of scores. You'll make the problem of unreliability even worse.

For this reason, it isn't surprising that VAM estimates are highly unreliable. I noted earlier that VAM partially removes the effects of background variables. These background variables are generally stable; most kids who are eligible for free lunch one year don't become wealthy the next. So if you remove the differences between kids who do and don't get free lunch, you are removing one of the things that help make students' scores stable from one year to the next.

Despite the ongoing vehement arguments between opponents and supporters of using VAM, they generally agree that the estimates are very unstable over time. There are many different estimates of this instability, some of which are technically complex, but a simple way to show its severity is to rank teachers in one year using a VAM and see how they are ranked the next. It's worth walking through a concrete example. I'll use one from a widely cited study led by Dan McCaffrey, a former colleague of mine and one of the nation's most respected experts on VAM. Dan and his colleagues estimated value added for teachers in five large districts in Florida over a period of five years. Using five different districts was a way to ensure that their results were not a fluke. They put teachers into quintiles for each year—that is, the bottom 20 percent, the next 20 percent, et cetera. They then asked: if you look at the teachers who were rated either as least or most effective in one year—that is, in the bottom or top quartile—where do they end up the next year? How many of the least effective teachers remain ineffective? I have put their findings for the bottom 20 percent of elementary-school teachers in table 9.1, and to simplify things I have included only the districts that showed the most and least consistency.

Let's start with the best case, the district in which ratings were most consistent over time: only 41 percent of teachers who were ranked in the bottom 20 percent in any given year remained there

Table 9.1. Value-added ratings of teachers the year after being rated as in the bottom 20 percent.

	Bottom 20%	Second 20%	Third 20%	Fourth 20%	Top 20%
Best case	41	25	16	9	10
Worst case	31	18	18	18	16

Source: Daniel F. McCaffrey et al., "The Intertemporal Variability of Teacher Effect Estimates," *Education Finance and Policy* 4, no. 4 (2009): 572–606, table 4.

the following year. In fact, only about two-thirds of these teachers even remained in the bottom 40 percent. The rest were rated higher than that the following year, and 10 percent were rated as being in the top 20 percent. The worst case showed much less consistency: teachers ranked as in the bottom 20 percent in the first year were as likely to be rated in the top 60 percent as in the bottom 40 percent, and they were half as likely to be rated in the top 20 percent as in the bottom 20 percent. So are these teachers ineffective or not? The results for the top-rated elementary-school teachers were similar in terms of consistency, and the ratings of middle-school teachers were only slightly better.[8]

○ ○ ○

This is a daunting list of problems, and it has led some critics of the reforms to argue that we should entirely abandon holding educators accountable for scores. They can point to other systems that don't impose accountability using externally imposed tests, such as Finland. However, I think that is too simple a response. It's not obvious that the Finnish model would work as well in the United States, which differs in many critically important ways, including the selection of teachers and student demographics. In addition, in some subjects and grades, standardized tests, *if used sensibly*, provide valuable information about some of the most important goals of education, and there is a big cost to discarding that information.

However, the problems described here and in earlier chapters provide more than ample reason to stop holding teachers accountable for test scores in the ways in which we have. In later chapters I'll suggest alternatives.

10

WILL THE COMMON CORE FIX THIS?

In a word, no.

For a number of years, K–12 education has been roiled by the advent of the Common Core State Standards. The Common Core had its origin in a 2009 meeting of governors and state education chiefs from forty-eight states, the District of Columbia, and two territories. Their goal was to develop "a set of clear college- and career-ready standards for kindergarten through 12th grade in English language arts/literacy and mathematics . . . which are designed to ensure that students graduating from high school are prepared to take credit bearing introductory courses in two- or four-year college programs or enter the workforce."[1] Despite the intent to create standards that would be common across states, the Common Core was begun at the initiative of states, and their adoption by states remains voluntary, at least in principle.

However, the Obama administration did a great deal to foster the development of Common Core and to pressure states to sign on, and this pressure generated serious political blowback. Through its Race to the Top (RTT) initiative, the administration committed $350 million to the development of Common Core tests, providing much of the funding for the two interstate consortia that have been working on these assessments: the Smarter Balanced Assessment Consortium (SBAC) and the Partnership for Assessment of Readiness for College and Careers (PARCC). Perhaps more important, the administration used its RTT funding to pressure states to adopt the standards. The RTT offered states the prospect of large competitive grants at a time when state budgets were in dire straits because of the severe recession that began in 2008. The grant application required states to adopt challenging standards, and many state departments of education read this as meaning the Common Core.

The federal role in fostering adoption of the Common Core generated a conservative backlash. Education is traditionally under the purview of the states, and many conservatives bridled at the pressure from the federal Department of Education to adopt shared standards. Some states that had been on board initially later dropped them for this reason. Governor Mike Pence of Indiana led the way, signing legislation that ended Indiana's acceptance of the Common Core. Other nationally prominent Republican figures, such as Governor Nikki Haley of South Carolina, announced that they would fight the new standards.[2] Opposition to the Common Core became a plank in the 2016 Republican platform: "We likewise repeat our longstanding opposition to the imposition of national standards and assessments, encourage the parents and educators who are implementing alternatives to Common Core, and congratulate the states which have successfully repealed it."[3] The Trump administration has declared its opposition to the Common Core standards and has promised to repeal them, although it's not clear that it can. States will make the decision, and ESSA expressly prohibits any "officer or employee of the Federal Government" from taking "any action against a State that exercises its rights" to retain or drop the Common Core standards.[4]

Despite this political opposition, backing for the Common Core remains substantial and widespread. Statements of support have been offered by many diverse organizations in education, including the two main teachers' unions (the American Federation of Teachers and the National Education Association), the National Association of State Boards of Education, the College Board, ACT, the Council for Exceptional Children, and the National Parent Teachers Association.[5]

How the Common Core will fare over the long term remains unclear, but as I am writing, forty-two states and the District of Columbia continue to work on implementing the Common Core despite the controversy it has sparked. The two consortia established to develop new shared Common Core tests have fared far less well. In 2010 thirty-two states participated in SBAC and twenty-six in PARCC. (States could participate with both consortia.) By 2015 SBAC had shrunk to sixteen states and PARCC to only six. This doesn't mean that many states decided not to test the Common Core. States that retained the Common Core but dropped out of the consortia, such as New York and Kentucky, hired testing companies to develop their own state-specific tests aligned with the Common Core.

○ ○ ○

The controversy about the Common Core, however, is not just about the federal role in education, and leaving that issue aside, the arguments don't follow clear political lines. The substantive arguments pro and con are too numerous to delineate fully here, but I will note a few. One of the supporters' main arguments has been that earlier standards were fragmented and were neither appropriately focused nor sufficiently rigorous to prepare students for the modern workplace or further education. Supporters laud what they see as more rigor, including an emphasis on higher-order skills, such as problem solving, critical thinking, and communication. In the case of mathematics, supporters have been enthusiastic about the Common Core's emphasis on students' understanding and a greater focus on coherence in the curriculum.

The reasons for opposition have been diverse. The elementary-grades English language arts standards have been widely criticized as age-inappropriate and for placing too great an emphasis on nonfiction. The math standards have been criticized, ironically, both for insufficiently preparing students for college and for an excessive focus on formal mathematics. The new tests linked to the Common Core have been a substantial trigger for opposition. While supporters see better tests, opponents see tests that are too time-consuming and too difficult. Some opponents say the Common Core and the associated tests will widen the gaps between advantaged and disadvantaged students.

Diane Ravitch, who in recent years has become one of the nation's most prominent critics of test-based accountability, has also been a vociferous opponent of the Common Core. One of her criticisms is unusual and bears highlighting: she argues that the Common Core has been imposed on teachers and students without any evidence of the effects this will have. She wrote:

> The Common Core standards have been adopted in 46 states and the District of Columbia without any field test. They are being imposed on the children of this nation despite the fact that no one has any idea how they will affect students, teachers, or schools. We are a nation of guinea pigs, almost all trying an unknown new program at the same time.
>
> Maybe the standards will be great. Maybe they will be a disaster. Maybe they will improve achievement. Maybe they will widen the achievement gaps between haves and have-nots. Maybe they will cause the children who now struggle to give up altogether. Would the Federal Drug Administration approve the use of a drug with no trials, no concern for possible harm or unintended consequences?[6]

My only quarrel with Ravitch is that she is casting this problem far too narrowly. It's not just the Common Core that has been dropped into schools wholesale before we gathered any evidence about impact; this has been true of almost the entire edifice of test-based reform, time and time again. I'll argue later that putting a stop to this disdain for evidence—this arrogant assumption that we know so much that we don't have to bother evaluating our ideas before imposing them on teachers and students—is one of the most important changes we have to make.

The arguments for and against the Common Core are very important, and I don't want to belittle them in any way. They deserve a thorough airing. Just not here. For present purposes, most of them, excepting Ravitch's argument, are a distraction. The question posed by the preceding chapters is narrower: to what extent—if at all—will the adoption of the Common Core, with or without a consortium assessment, address the problems I have described?

Unfortunately, the short answer is that both the Common Core and the development of new tests linked to them are largely irrelevant to those problems. In this respect they are the same old wine in new bottles, repeating the mistakes that contributed to the failures of test-based reforms. This needn't have been the case. The development of new assessments—particularly computer-administered tests, which both consortia have designed—offers a chance to chip away at the problems by making bad test prep more difficult, although better tests in and of themselves won't be nearly sufficient to solve the problems you've seen. However, as of now, the consortia haven't confronted the problem of Campbell's Law. PARCC has published nothing about inflation. SBAC's Race to the Top application, which is 168 pages long, mentions score inflation once—in an appendix table, where an initial step for 2010–12 includes this question: "Were plausible unintended consequences such as score inflation or impact on student achievement in non-tested content areas... considered?" But the application does not explain anything that was done either to avoid or to evaluate potential inflation, and the consortium has not explicitly addressed in in later publications.

That's not to disparage the consortia's efforts to improve tests. Both have put a great deal of work into efforts to develop tests that are in various ways better than those that were in use before. Not all of these have panned out, in my opinion, but some have. Still, these improvements just don't address the problems of bad test prep and score inflation.

Predictability

As you have seen, Campbell's Law shows up almost everywhere people have looked. However, the opportunities to game the system differ from one context to another. The roots of Campbell's Law in health care are quite different from those in airline on-time statistics.

In educational testing there are two major opportunities to game the system, if you leave aside the many different ways one can simply cheat. The first is the approach used in the El Paso and Houston cases I summarized earlier: exclude potentially low-scoring kids from testing.

The second option is the one more commonly documented: taking advantage of the predictability of tests. Teachers can reallocate only if they know which content is likely to be emphasized on the next version of the test and which is likely to go largely or entirely untested. And coaching can work only if teachers know which details in the test are likely to show up again. You've seen numerous examples of this. If teachers know that the test will be multiple choice, they can waste instructional time teaching the strategies of process of elimination and plugging in possible answers. You've seen coaching strategies that work only because the new test is likely to use Pythagorean triples or present linear equations in the arbitrary form $y = mx + b$.

So how do we decrease bad test prep and score inflation? One response should be obvious: reduce the unnecessary predictability in the tests. For a number of reasons, there are limits to how far we can go in this direction. For example, if tests are too dissimilar from one year to the next, it becomes impossible to track trends over time. And one wouldn't want tests that randomly give more emphasis in some years to relatively unimportant content. However, a good bit of the predictability in tests is unnecessary. There is no good reason why linear equations should always appear as $y = mx + b$ and several reasons—not just the risk of inflation—that they shouldn't. Eliminating unnecessary predictability wouldn't entirely solve the problems I have laid out; it wouldn't eliminate bad test prep, score inflation, cheating, or the stress endured by teachers and students. However, it could chip away at the first two.

The consortia have not announced any intention of confronting this issue, even though computerized testing makes it easier to do so. In fact, they have followed approaches that could inadvertently worsen the problem. To explain requires a short dip into the esoterica of testing.

Both consortia use what are often called "task models" or "item templates" to generate items for parts of their assessments. That is, rather than writing new items from scratch each year, they create a template that specifies many aspects of the item that will remain constant over time. When a new item is needed, the item writers leave those attributes unchanged but alter one or more others. If a template is sufficiently tightly defined, a computer can generate new items without human intervention, which was one of the reasons they were first developed, some years before the Common Core was begun.

There are clear benefits to using task models, apart from making it easier to generate new items. The models help to make scores comparable in meaning from one year to the next, which is very helpful if you want to measure trends over time.

However, this approach holds an obvious risk: it makes the test more predictable, and that can bring opportunities for coaching and score inflation. That is, it can make items comparable not only in ways that you want but also in ways that you don't. To the best of my knowledge, this risk was first documented concretely more than a decade ago by researchers at the Educational Testing Service (ETS). ETS was one of the pioneers in the development of task models. These became increasingly important when ETS converted the Graduate Record Examination to a computer-based assessment, because this change required that ETS produce a larger number of items that were close substitutes for each other. Task models are a means of doing that.

The ETS researchers, however, were concerned that if people began to recognize the attributes of test items that were made similar by the task models, they could prepare by focusing on these rather than by learning the skills the items were supposed to measure. And this is precisely what they found. They administered to randomly selected groups of students both similar items and items designed to measure the same skills but dissimilar in appearance. Ideally, the appearance of the items wouldn't matter, but it did: students found the items that shared appearances with the first set easier. That suggests that students are learning to respond to the predictable but irrelevant characteristics of the items. The ETS authors warned: "It should be assumed that, if an item modeling approach is adopted, test preparation schools may soon alter their curricula to include instruction in item modeling. These schools could . . . teach item models."[7] In other words, they could coach, teaching students how to take advantage of the irrelevant features that are similar from item to item because of the task model. Just like Pythagorean triples.

This is not a reason to avoid using task models, but it makes it even more important to deal with the risk of unnecessary and harmful predictability. The consortia haven't yet said how—or even whether—they intend to address this.

On the positive side, there has been some discussion of these issues in individual states. For example, in designing its Common Core tests, New York State has been trying to reduce the unnecessary predictability of its tests, and the risk of inflation is one of its reasons for attempting this. However, this is the rare exception, not the rule, and the Common Core itself was not the motivation. It was just happenstance that the Common Core compelled New York to write new tests at a time when other factors had made the staff aware of the risks posed by predictability.

One Size Fits All

One reason for the failure of the reforms was the advocates' well-meaning but unrealistic one-size-fits-all approach. In setting arbitrary performance targets for students, they ignored the ubiquitous and unavoidable variation in student performance. In fixing performance targets for schools, they made the same error, ignoring differences in the circumstances facing teachers. Add sanctions to this, and the results were predictable: many of people who couldn't reach these targets by legitimate means resorted to illegitimate ones.

The jury is still out with respect to the impact of the Common Core on this problem. It may not have much of an effect at all, but if it does, it is more likely to worsen the problem than to lessen it.

The Common Core has just given the one-size-fits-all approach a more explicit and grandiose rhetorical wrapper. Go back to the original rationale: the new standards "are designed to ensure that students graduating from high school are *prepared to take credit bearing introductory courses in two- or four-year college programs or enter the workforce*" (emphasis added). It's hard to argue with this. It's a clear statement of one of the most important goals of education, although hardly the only one. But to meet this goal, the Common Core offers—with an exception I note below—*a single set of standards*. The standards are supposed to prepare students for just about anything other than being unemployed. There are no distinctions among the vast array of jobs that students might take. There is no distinction between students bound for college and those who aren't. As one advocate asserted some years ago when I raised this concern, "The Common Core has eliminated the distinction between college readiness and career readiness." Rhetorically, perhaps, but not in actuality. And the standards make no distinctions among the multitudes of occupations, which in some cases require dramatically different academic preparation. One size fits all.

The Common Core does make two concessions to the different paths students may follow. In high-school mathematics, the standards draw the traditional distinction between "additional mathematics that students should learn in order to take advanced courses such as calculus, advanced statistics, or discrete mathematics" and everything else,[8] and standards relevant to the advanced group are presented but flagged. The standards document for English language arts and literacy in history/social studies, science, and technical subjects acknowledges the difference between advanced students and others but doesn't include standards relevant to the advanced students. But with these two exceptions, the Common Core standards purport to be appropriate for everyone.

In one way the preparing-everyone-for-everything claim may not exacerbate the one-size-fits-all problem in elementary schools. When students are young, it *should* be unclear where they are headed in education and in life, and there are strong arguments against making assumptions about whether kids are headed to college or about the careers they will pursue. Preparing kids for whatever unknown paths may lie in front of them and keeping as many doors open as possible should be our goals.

The rhetoric becomes more problematic, however, when applied to testing in the elementary grades. Recall that the aim of the group initiating the Common Core was to create "college- and career-ready standards *for kindergarten through 12th grade*" (emphasis added). Some states have taken this rhetoric literally and claim that reaching the Proficient standard on their Common Core tests—even in the elementary grades—indicates whether a student is 'on track for college and careers.'[9] Even high-school and college-admissions tests predict performance in college only weakly, and it is simply an illusion to think that reaching a cut score on an elementary-grades test tells us much about whether a student will be prepared years later. This rhetoric may not matter, but it has the potential for making the one-standard-fits-everyone approach even more inappropriate for some students.

At the secondary level, the risks seem larger. In most schools, students follow a variety of different paths in selecting courses. This has posed a problem for test-based reform for decades. In the 1970s the reformers confronted this head on and designed their tests explicitly for lower-performing students. It was assumed by most people that these tests wouldn't be of much relevance to higher-performing students, and at the time that was widely considered to be fine. Starting in the 1980s, however, reformers decided that this wasn't acceptable, and they started the gradual process of implementing tests designed to hold schools accountable for the performance of all students. We've struggled with the consequences ever since. In most states, the solution was to use tests suitable for the large majority of students and simply not to worry if they were not all that appropriate for college-bound students—after all, college-admissions tests like the ACT and SAT can fill the gap for them—or for students at the bottom of the distribution.

The Common Core changes this in only one way: it offers a rhetorical justification for designing tests for the college bound and then using them for everyone else. A slow trend in this direction was apparent before the Common Core, as a handful of states and large districts (e.g., Chicago and the state of Kentucky) began requiring that all high-school graduates take a college-admissions test. There are praiseworthy motivations for this shift. One Kentucky legislator said to me, for example, "We have lots of kids in poor communities who never even thought about going to college. This will get them thinking about it, and it will show some of them that they have what it takes to succeed in college." The risk, however, is also clear: if the test contains material that teachers can't bring kids to master by legitimate means, some will turn to illegitimate ones.

Overreliance on Test Scores

The Common Core will do nothing to lessen the overreliance on test scores that has contributed so much to the failure of education reform.

Some states and districts have already begun taking steps to carve away at this problem—for example, by adding highly structured observations of teachers to their accountability systems. Moreover, the replacement of NCLB by ESSA gives states some leeway to modify their test-based accountability systems, and it mandates that states include at least one measure other than test scores, albeit without specifying what that other measure should be or how much it should count (other than mandating that it count less than scores).

Adoption of the Common Core, however, has nothing to do with these changes.

Excessive Pressure

So far, the Common Core has only worsened the excessive pressure to raise scores.

The Common Core does nothing to change the accountability system itself, of course. The NCLB rules stayed in place after states began adopting the Common Core, and whatever changes states may choose to make to their accountability systems in response to the increased flexibility offered by ESSA will not depend on the Common Core.

The Common Core standards have increased pressure in many places, however, because of the particular ways in which they have been tested. Here it is necessary to draw a distinction between the tests themselves and the performance standards—the cut scores—attached to them. One of the most common complaints about the Common Core is that some of the tests are too hard. However, if you read the press reports about this, you'll see that they focus on the percentages of students labeled as "proficient"—or conversely, failing—on the new tests. These cut scores, as you know, are arbitrary, and one could just as easily set performance standards on the new Common Core tests that are exactly as lenient or harsh as those that were layered onto the tests that preceded the Common Core. That is, you could set the new standards so that the same percentages of students reached them as in earlier cohorts. That would eliminate one of the ways in which the new tests are harder, and it would keep the failure rate the same, at least for the short term. However, as long as the arbitrary standards are harsher, they will exert more pressure.

The other aspect of difficulty is the actual content of the test. In some instances, the content of the Common Core tests is by design more advanced or in other ways more difficult. Regardless of where the cut scores are set, the more difficult content increases pressure on teachers because it is harder to teach. This may have good effects on teaching in some circumstances; after all, the tests are intended to prod teachers to teach more demanding material. The jury is out in this respect. But for my narrower question, the answer seems clear: the pressure teachers and principals feel to raise scores won't be lessened by the change to the Common Core.

A New Flavor of the Same Old Thing

The evolution of test-based reform has shown a dreary sameness for over thirty years, and the Common Core, unfortunately, fits the pattern to a T.

Each time the weaknesses of the reform have become apparent, the reformers have decided to try a new flavor of the same strategy, telling us in every instance that *this time* they have it right. The new variations usually involve new tests—performance assessments in one iteration, standards-based assessments in another, Common Core tests in yet another. The new approach often ratchets standards up further, either for low performers or for everyone. The reformers tinker with sanctions and rewards, usually increasing the pressure further but occasionally backing off a bit. Some iterations involve something unique, such as the recent absurdity of "evaluating" teachers with the scores of kids they don't even teach.

Yet underneath all of this ferment—some of which is in indeed important—the basic failed model of educational improvement has remained unchanged: set arbitrary performance targets on standardized tests; apply them uniformly, without regard to circumstances; and reward and punish. Whatever its other virtues and vices, the Common Core hasn't changed this. This approach hasn't worked before, and it won't work with the Common Core.

11

DID KIDS LEARN MORE?

What did we get in return for all of the stress, degraded instruction, bad test prep, score inflation, and outright fraud that test-based accountability has engendered? Did students actually learn more?

Yes and no. There are some bright spots, but the reforms didn't deliver the large gains in learning that would make us more competitive in international comparisons and a substantial reduction in the gap in achievement between advantaged and disadvantaged kids.

We know less about this most fundamental of questions than we should. While it's easy to find unequivocal pronouncements about the gains generated by the reforms—the newspapers are full of them once a year, and unfortunately some researchers have not been much more cautious—the honest answer is that it's very difficult to pin down with precision any effects the reforms had on actual student learning. One reason that we know less than we should—obvious, but often ignored—is that most of the abundant test score data available to us are too vulnerable to score inflation to be trusted.

There is a second reason for the dearth of information, the blame for which lies squarely on the shoulders of many of the reformers. Time after time they declared that they had figured out what would work, and they imposed it on students and teachers on a mass scale without taking time to evaluate their programs first. It's analogous to a drug company saying that they have figured out, based just on their own beliefs and logic, which drugs will be effective and safe, so they can skip the time-consuming and expensive burden of actually gathering some evidence before selling it to you. And it's not just that the reformers didn't take steps to evaluate their own programs. They also often implemented their programs in a way that made it harder for anyone else to evaluate them. We normally evaluate programs by comparing people who participate in them to similar people who don't, and that requires that we keep some people out of the program long enough to make this comparison. This is no different from evaluating drugs, which in most cases requires comparing outcomes for people with similar medical conditions who do and don't take them. But by and large, that didn't happen; the reforms were implemented quickly everywhere. Evaluators followed behind the elephant with a broom, searching for variations in how states and districts implemented the reforms to allow at least limited evaluations. Both the number and the quality of evaluations suffered as a result.

I won't repeat the mistake of pretending that we know more than we do. I'll limit myself to some broad conclusions that are warranted despite the incomplete data. That's enough to make it clear that the impact on students' learning has been far less than the reformers expected, and in my view, far less than would be required to justify the huge harms test-based accountability has caused.

Making Sense of the Evidence

I'll focus on achievement in reading and math. Although some states tested additional subjects, and NCLB and ESSA required testing in science in at least three grades starting in the 2007–8 school year, reading and math have been the primary focus of test-based reform since its inception, and most of the available evidence pertains to these two subjects.

To start, I need to distinguish between two questions. The easier question is what happened to student learning during the time of test-based accountability. The far more difficult question is *why* any such changes happened, and specifically whether they can be attributed to test-based accountability.

To answer the first question—whether the problems that motivated the reforms have been reduced substantially—we can look at trends in performance on tests that are not vulnerable to inflation because teachers aren't pressured to raise scores on them: primarily NAEP, but also the US samples of the major international assessments, TIMSS and PISA. (In some other countries the international tests may be more susceptible to inflation—in particular PISA, which is the focus of a great deal of attention in the media and among politicians in some countries.) It would be tempting to use these trend data to try to answer the second question as well—how much impact the reforms have had—and many people do, but they simply aren't up to the task. The reason is straightforward: simple trends on these tests reflect *everything* that can affect scores, not just the reforms. For example, there have been demographic changes in the school-age population, including increases in the proportion of students who are of Asian background and of Hispanic background. On average, these two groups score higher and lower, respectively, than non-Hispanic white students. Over the period of time I'll discuss here, the impact of these changes has been modest and doesn't affect any of my basic conclusions, but it has been sufficient that one can't simply take the numbers shown in trend data at face value. Similarly, trends reflect all other changes in educational practice that affect learning. This shortcoming isn't limited to testing; it's a common problem when we are trying to explain changes that occur over a substantial time. For example, adults lose muscle mass over the long term as they age. To find out whether an exercise and diet regimen helps to combat this, you wouldn't look only to see whether the people trying it gained muscle mass; it would be a sign of success if they just lost muscle mass more slowly than adults not following the regimen.

The question we most need to ask is therefore more subtle and much more difficult to answer: are scores going up *more than they would be in the absence of the reforms*? Or, for that matter, are they going down less rapidly than they would be? One can sometimes extract hints about this from trend data. In particular, it's helpful to look for the timing of any bend in the trend, such as a point when scores that are already increasing start improving more—or less—rapidly. For example, did scores start improving more rapidly in the years after the implementation of NCLB, when accountability became more uniform and pressure was ratcheted up in many states? However, to answer the causal question unequivocally, we need formal evaluation studies.

High-quality evaluations of the test-based reforms aren't common, once one removes the many that aren't useful because they tried to answer the question using scores on the high-stakes tests themselves. Moreover, the findings of some of the more trustworthy studies are inconsistent. This isn't surprising, given that the researchers had to work around the obstacles the reformers, perhaps inadvertently, had put in their path. Moreover, even perfect evaluations would show varying results because the implementation of the reforms varied considerably from place to place—for example, in the harshness of the performance standards states imposed. Some general patterns emerge nonetheless, and I'll focus on them.

Did Learning Improve?

Let's start with a simpler question: how much did learning in reading and math improve in recent years, for whatever reason?

Reading. In the case of reading, the answer is simple: trend data show that students' learning hasn't improved much, despite decades of unrelenting pressure to raise test scores in reading.

I've plotted trends on NAEP in figure 11.1, but interpreting this figure and those that follow requires a brief dive into technical matters. I say that figure 11.1 shows only small improvements, but how do I know how big the changes really are? The way I've drawn them makes them look small—the vertical scale leaves lots of empty space above the trends—but that is entirely arbitrary, and I did that only to make it easier to compare figure 11.1 with the much more positive news in the math trends that I'll show below. To know how big these changes are, one needs to understand the scale I've used. Test scores are reported on any number of different scales, and one extra point may be a big deal on one but a trivially small difference on another. For example, scores on the SAT math test run from 200 to 800; those on the competing ACT math test range from

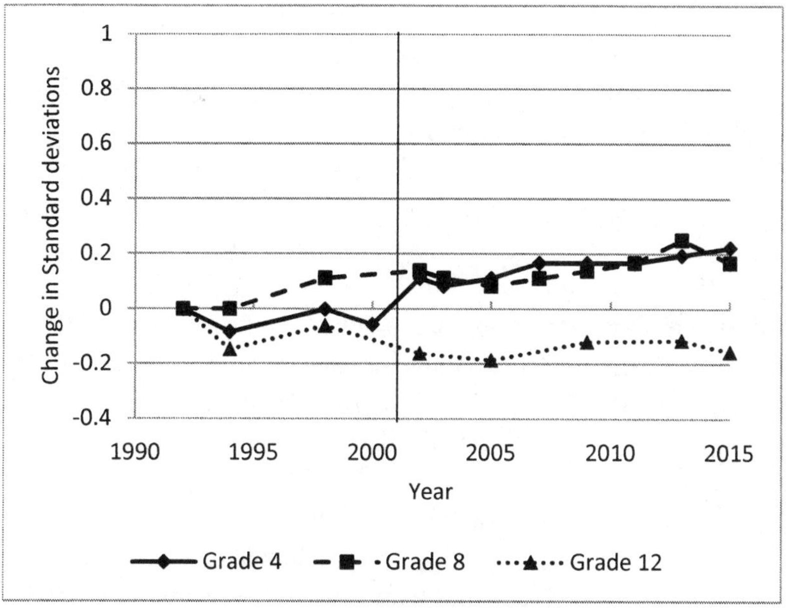

Figure 11.1. Trends in average NAEP reading scores, in standard deviations (SDs). Vertical line marks the first year of implementation of NCLB.

1 to 36. For our purposes, this poses two problems. First, one can't compare scores that are on different scales. Second, most people can't interpret the size of any given difference in scale scores. Is an increase of 5 points on the ACT math test large or small? Five points may sound small, but it actually isn't—on that particular scale. In contrast, the smallest difference even reported on the SAT scale is 10 points.

To get around these problems, I will put everything I describe onto a single scale that I used a few times earlier, called standard deviations. Specifically, I will set an average score to zero, and then all other values will be expressed in terms of differences from that average in standard deviation units.

This scale is unfortunately unfamiliar to most people, but it is the most often used in the social sciences, and for my purposes here, it has three very important advantages that offset its unfamiliarity. First, as you saw in earlier chapters, it allows us to compare across tests, regardless of the scale on which they are usually reported. If an admissions officer wants to compare a student's scores on the

ACT and SAT, one solution is to express both in standard deviation units. Second, with some complications, standard deviations can be translated into percentiles, as I did in earlier chapters. It doesn't matter what the test is; students with standard deviation scores of 0 and 1 are always at the fiftieth and eighty-fourth percentiles. Third, because the standard deviation scale is so widely used, it provides many useful standards of comparison. For example, while the black-white gap in math scores varies a good bit from test to test, it is often in the range of 0.8 to 1.0 standard deviation. It's 0.8 standard deviation on the fourth-grade NAEP test. Similarly, the gap between the United States and the highest-scoring East Asian countries in mathematics in TIMSS is typically close to 1 standard deviation. Since we are looking at reading trends, I'll use NAEP to give a more specific illustration of how we can use this scale. In the most recent NAEP fourth-grade reading assessment, the mean difference between black and white students was 26 points on the scale used to report NAEP results. The standard deviation of white students was 33 points. A student with the average score of black students would therefore be roughly 0.8 standard deviations below the average on the white distribution of scores, which means that this student would be at roughly the sixteenth percentile among white students.

With this background, let's look more closely at figure 11.1. The graph shows the change from the first year of data, so the value for that year is set at zero: no change. You can see that small improvements in reading in grades four and eight are matched by a comparable decline in grade twelve: the grade 12 line starts at zero—no change—in 1992 and drops, slowly and erratically, to –0.2 standard deviations by 2015. Grade 12 is the most important; what we care about most is the skills with which students leave school and enter either the workforce or postsecondary education. Nonetheless, it's important to note that the average scores in grades 4 and 8 increased by about the same amount as the twelfth-grade score dropped.

Because I've used standard deviations, I can easily translate these numbers into percentiles. In 2015, the average twelfth-grader would have outscored about 42 percent of students at the beginning of the trend, twenty-three years earlier. The average students in grades four and eight in 2015 scored better than about 58 percent of students 23 years earlier. Although I have to repeat my warning that trend data don't provide definitive answers to our second question—the actual impact of reforms—it may be a hint that these changes, both positive and negative, happened before the enactment of NCLB, which is also marked in figure 11.1.

Demographic changes in the student population did have some influence on these trends, but they don't account for the lack of progress in twelfth-grade reading. Over the twenty-three-year period, NAEP shows gains for only the smallest of the four main racial/ethnic groups: Asian/Pacific Islanders. The average scores of non-Hispanic whites and Hispanics were essentially unchanged (they actually declined trivially, but not by enough to be statistically trustworthy), while the average scores of black students dropped by 7 points—roughly 0.2 standard deviation.

Math. The trend data are much more positive in math than in reading, but the story is more complicated.

The best news is a rapid and very large increase in the average score of fourth-graders on the NAEP (the solid line at the top of figure 11.2). Between 1990, when the math framework for the current NAEP was introduced, and 2007, the average score increased by almost 0.8 standard deviation—in other words, by an amount roughly similar to the mean difference between whites and blacks or between the United States and countries like Korea on the TIMSS assessment. By any reasonable standard, this is a truly large improvement. If you exclude tests suffering from score inflation, this is one of the fastest rates of change in scores—either up or down—that we have seen in a large-scale assessment in the United States over more than half a century, and it was maintained for an exceptionally long period.

However, while the news is indeed good, it isn't as positive as it first seems. There are two big flies in the ointment.

The first big reason not to celebrate too much is that what we most care about is the skills students have when they leave school,

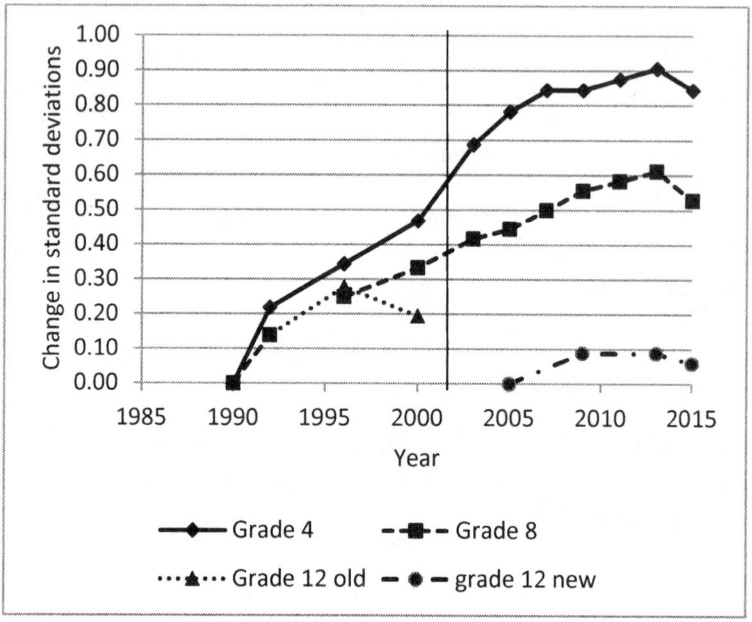

Figure 11.2. Trends in average NAEP mathematics scores, in standard deviations. Vertical line marks the first year of implementation of NCLB.

and it has been clear for a long time that the impressive math gains of fourth-graders don't persist: they wither as students progress through school. This is apparent from figure 11.2, which has the trends lines for the eighth and twelfth grades as well. You can see that the improvement in eighth grade, while still impressive, is only about two-thirds as large as those in the fourth grade. The real kicker, however, is the average scores of high-school seniors. This part of the figure has an additional wrinkle: the framework for the test was changed in 2005, so one can't compare the scores from that year and later to those from 2000 and earlier. Rather, one has to look at the two time periods separately. That shows a small improvement between 1990 and 1995 but essentially no improvement for the past decade.

The severity of this fade-out becomes even more apparent if you consider how students in the same cohorts perform in different grades. Leaving aside students who repeat a grade, the cohorts that showed no meaningful improvement in the twelfth grade between 2005 and 2015 are the same students who produced particularly large gains when they were in the fourth grade eight years earlier, contributing fully half of the total increase in scores. You can see this more clearly in figure 11.3, where I show the gain in scores those cohorts of students achieved over ten years in each of the three grades. Whatever happened to these kids when they were young didn't stick.

The second caution is not well known: the few other sources of uncorrupted test-score data show still sizable but much smaller gains in fourth-grade math than does the main NAEP upon which people usually rely. As good a test as it is, the main NAEP is just a sample, so we should look to see how well the NAEP trends are echoed in other data, just as we look for poll results to be mirrored in the findings of other polls. This is particularly important when we find a pattern that is unusual in terms of past experience, like the gains in NAEP fourth-grade math scores.

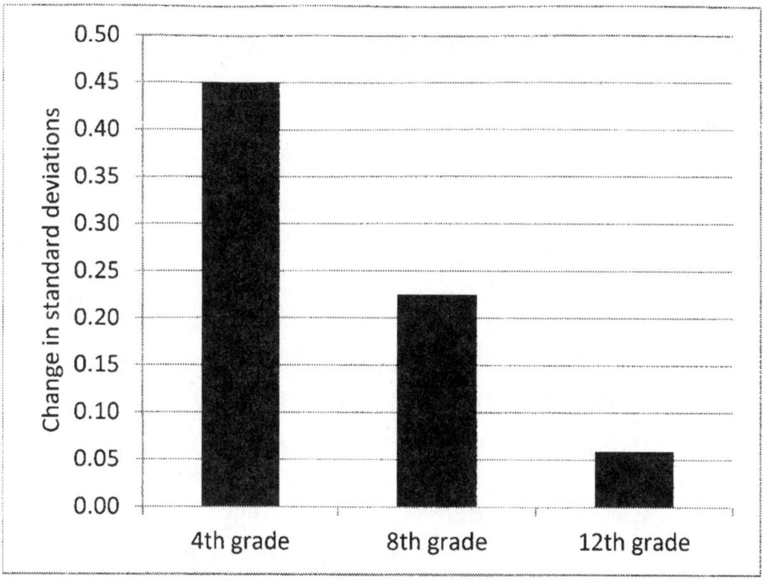

Figure 11.3. Ten-year gains in mathematics, by grade, for students in twelfth grade between 2005 and 2015.

While most available data are suspect because of score inflation, we have two comparisons that aren't: a second NAEP test and the US sample in TIMSS. Both show gains that are substantial but much smaller than those on the main NAEP.

The second NAEP test, called the Long-Term Trend Assessment (LTT), was started three decades ago, and it can be linked to even older data. In 1986 the average reading scores of nine- and seventeen-year olds (NAEP was then administered by age, not grade) dropped dramatically, by a seemingly implausible amount. The main NAEP is updated from time to time, and after the fact, experts agreed that much of this apparent decline in performance wasn't real; it was an artifact of changes made to the assessment.[1] In response, the Education Department has since administered the LTT, which doesn't change: the content, sampling, and administration are kept the same from year to year. (The one exception was in 2004, when a new version of the LTT was introduced.) The LTT is intended to provide a check on additional anomalous changes in performance on the main NAEP. It also provides data on longer-term trends; while the current version of the main NAEP shows trends from 1990 on, the LTT extends back to 1978. The drawback, however, is that the LTT is increasingly out of date in terms of content and format.

In fourth-grade math, the LTT shows improvement since 1990 almost exactly half as large as is shown by the main NAEP. I've shown this in figure 11.4, to which I will return in a moment for another reason. Particularly striking is the difference during the 1990s, when the main NAEP showed very rapid gains but the LTT showed almost no improvement at all. It's not uncommon for different tests to show different trends because they sample differently from the domain, but disparities this large are unusual in the absence of changes in the tested population, score inflation, or cheating. This discrepancy hasn't been examined in detail.

TIMSS was first conducted only in 1995, but between then and 2015 it has shown an improvement in fourth-grade math a bit more than half the size of the increase on the main NAEP. The design of TIMSS is different from that of NAEP—it's designed to

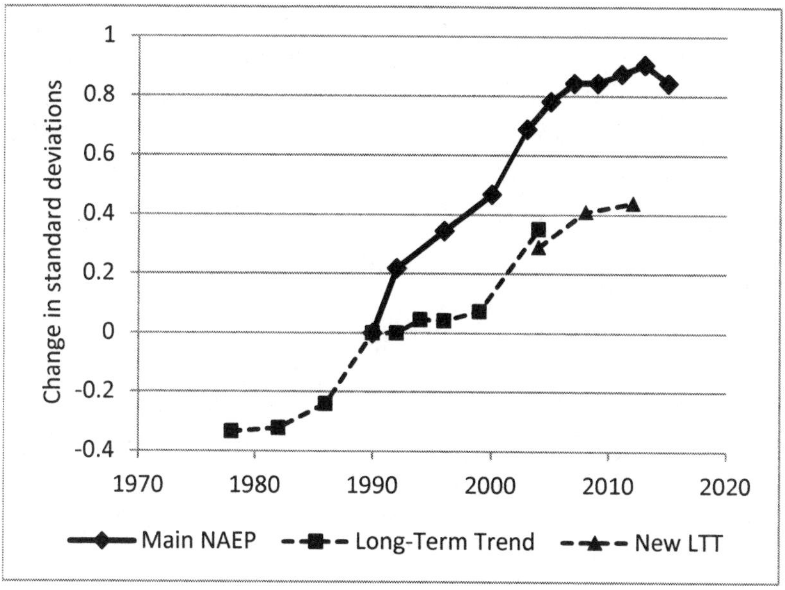

Figure 11.4. Fourth-grade math trends on the main NAEP, the original Long-Term Trend NAEP, and the new Long-Term Trend NAEP.

provide international comparisons—but the two tests are quite similar in some respects, and the NAEP and TIMSS estimates for gains in grade 8 are quite similar. I have not found anyone who can explain this large discrepancy.*

While very large NAEP gains in grade 4 math aren't replicated in other data, the bad news NAEP gives us for high-school math is. The most relevant comparison is the US sample for the other large international assessment, PISA. Overall, NAEP resembles PISA much less than it resembles TIMSS, and this is by design: PISA is intended to answer somewhat different questions. PISA

* The largest difference between the two assessments in mathematics appears to be the emphasis given to content strands: both are constructed of the same five strands, but the two tests give substantially different weight to some of them. However, this doesn't account for the difference in trends. I recomputed NAEP trends after assigning the TIMSS weights to each content strand. This did not appreciably change the NAEP trends.

samples fifteen-year-olds still in school rather than high-school seniors, and it emphasizes application of skills rather than mastery of the curriculum. Despite these differences, it tells the same story as NAEP: since its first implementation in 2003, PISA has shown no consistent improvement in the performance of our students in math.

○ ○ ○

What is the takeaway from this array of somewhat inconsistent data?

The main story is clear: for whatever reasons, performance in elementary-school mathematics has improved substantially—the gains on all three tests are sizable—but we can't be certain by how much. While it is all too tempting to treat the main NAEP as the "gold standard" and accept the very large gains on that assessment at face value, the fact is that we don't know what has caused the large discrepancies among the three different tests, and absent that, we don't really know just how big the improvement has been. More important, we have no evidence that these gains have persisted to high-school graduation.

I want to stress again that trend data alone can't answer our second question—the impact of test-based accountability—but the fourth-grade trends are relevant to this for two reasons. The first is that as I noted, timing can provide a hint, and the timing of the gains in math doesn't line up with the reforms. Go back to figure 11.4. NAEP shows that the improvements were under way at least as early as the first half of the 1980s, when test-based accountability was both uncommon and, where it existed, mild by comparison with today's policies. And both NAEP assessments show that the gains largely petered out within a few years of the implementation of NCLB.

But the conflicting data about grade 4 math are relevant to evaluations of the reforms for another, more direct reason: the most important evaluations of the reforms used scores on the main NAEP to evaluate impact. It's quite possible that their conclusions, to which I will return below, would be less positive had they used another test.

Trends in Achievement Gaps

The reformers didn't want only to raise everyone's performance. They wanted in particular to lessen inequities in student achievement. They wanted to bring the bottom up. This is why NCLB and ESSA focused especially on historically low-scoring groups, such as racial and ethnic minorities, students with disabilities, and economically disadvantaged students.

Whatever the impact of test-based accountability, the trend data don't show consistent improvement in achievement gaps. However, the story is somewhat complicated.

The gap between whites and blacks is clearly narrowing. That has been documented in many studies using a wide variety of data. However, this progress started—and largely ended—before test-based accountability became widespread. It was apparent in a variety of test data, including NAEP and the SAT, as early as the 1970s.[2] NAEP data suggest that in elementary-school math, the black-white gap reached an approximate minimum in 1986 and has fluctuated since, and the gap hasn't been statistically significantly different from its current size since 1978. Moreover, in more recent years, the only apparently substantial improvement was a one-time blip between the long-term assessments in 1999 and 2004. One-time changes of this sort are always questionable.

While the gap between black and white has been shrinking erratically, the gap between rich and poor students (measured as the gap between students from families at the tenth and ninetieth percentiles in income) has been *widening* consistently. Sean Reardon at Stanford has shown that this is apparent across a wide range of tests, and it began with students who entered school at least as early as 1980. The exception to this pattern is found in measures of readiness of students entering kindergarten, two of which showed a decrease in the gap between rich and poor between 1998 and 2010.[3] However, the gap at entry into school entirely reflects experiences outside of regular schooling, so it doesn't help clarify the impact of test-based accountability.

We can also simply compare the trends shown by low- and high-scoring kids. The news on this front isn't very encouraging. Some

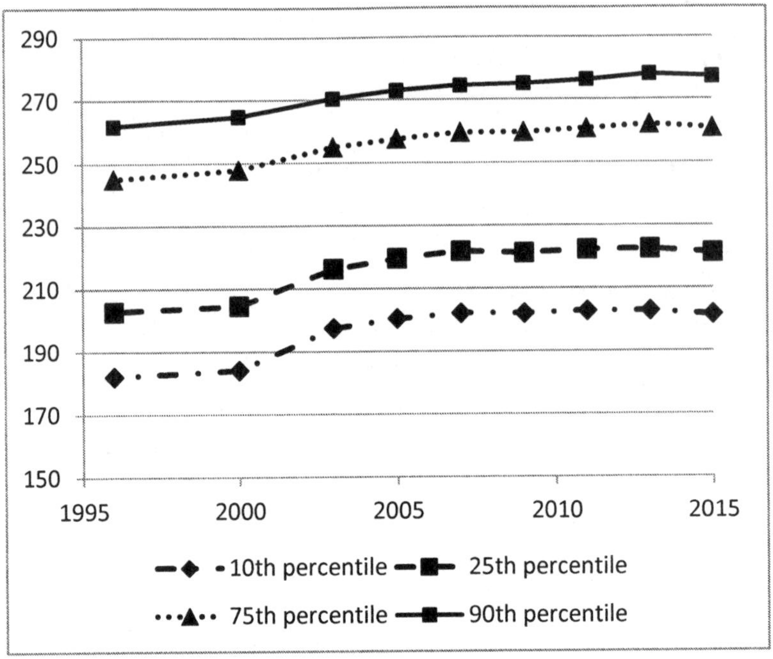

Figure 11.5. Trends in NAEP fourth-grade math scores, by percentile rank.

data do suggest a narrowing of the gap between low- and high-scoring students, but this improvement was small and erratic, and it doesn't appear at all in some of our trustworthy sources of test scores. I'll show this by comparing students at the ninetieth and seventy-fifth percentiles to those at the tenth and twenty-fifth percentiles, respectively.

I'll start with fourth-grade mathematics because it provides the best case for the reforms: by far the most positive trends overall, and—as slight as it is—some evidence of a narrowing achievement gap. On the main NAEP, the gap between the tenth and ninetieth percentiles shrank by 5 percent between 1996 and 2015, and the gap between the twenty-fifth and seventy-fifth percentiles shrank by 6 percent. TIMSS showed slightly more narrowing between 1995 and 2011. However, there is a warning sign: a closer look shows that the narrowing of the gap on NAEP occurred only during a single three-year period, between the 2000 and 2003 assessments. (There were no assessments in the intervening years.) I've plotted the data in figure 11.5, and it is immediately apparent that the trends for the four groups are essentially parallel other than during that three-year period.

And other data that warn us not to be too sanguine about this apparent improvement. The main NAEP shows no hint of this narrowing when these cohorts of students reached the twelfth grade. Once again, the improvement that appears the in the fourth-grade data doesn't persist as students move through school. Moreover, the NAEP Long-Term Trend assessment showed no narrowing of these gaps at all among students of any age since the mid-1980s.

While I should repeat my warning that trend data aren't sufficient to evaluate the reforms, the timing of this one-time narrowing between high- and low-achieving fourth-graders on the main NAEP isn't consistent with the reforms. The main change in these years was the enactment of NCLB, which wasn't signed into law until 2002 and therefore had very little time to affect schooling or performance by the time of the NAEP testing that began in January 2003.

How Much Did the Reforms Contribute to Trends in Achievement?

These data make it clear that we haven't ended up even close to where the reformers wanted us to be, but they don't answer the harder question: just how much did test-based accountability affect these trends?

The evidence is unfortunately weak. Many studies estimate the impact on scores on the tests used for accountability, but for reasons that should now be obvious, these can't be trusted. Studies that used other outcomes, often NAEP, dodged that bullet, but the rapid implementation of the reforms severely limited the design of these studies.

The best summary of the credible research is a book published by a study panel of the National Research Council (NRC), the research arm of the National Academies of Science. The NRC panel was intentionally designed to include both supporters and opponents of test-based accountability. (I was a member of the NRC study panel.)

The NRC panel concluded that test-based accountability systems had a modest positive impact on some aspects of student learning:

"School-level incentives like those of the No Child Left Behind Act produce some of the larger estimates of achievement effects [compared with other systems of test-based accountability], with effect sizes [across grades and subjects] around 0.08 standard deviations, but the measured effects to date tend to be concentrated in elementary grade mathematics."[4] This is consistent with the simple trend data, which showed sizable gains in fourth-grade mathematics, smaller gains in eighth-grade math, and no substantial improvements in twelfth-grade math or in reading in any grade.

But test-based accountability gets credit for only a modest portion of the improvements shown in math. The panel's positive conclusion about the effects of reform on elementary math scores relied heavily on a study by Tom Dee and Brian Jacob that estimated impact of strong schoolwide test-based accountability to be about 0.23 standard deviation.[5] Given that they relied on the main NAEP, which showed the largest overall gains in scores, this estimate corresponds to a bit over one fourth of the total gains shown by fourth-graders.

And while the Dee and Jacob study indicates that the reforms contributed to the gain in elementary-school mathematics, *we don't know how much of this reflects better teaching or an overall increase in students' learning*. We know that in response to test-based accountability, many teachers shifted a good bit of instructional time from untested subjects, including science, art, music, and physical education, into math and reading, in some cases nearly or even entirely eliminating instruction in those other subjects. This reallocation of instructional time reallocates student achievement, making students learn more math at the cost of learning less in subjects like science and social studies. It robs Peter to pay Paul, simply transferring students' learning from one subject to another. And the fact is that we simply don't know how much of the gain in math stems from better instruction and how much from reallocation.

Formal evaluations provide limited evidence about the effects of the reforms on achievement gaps, but there is some indication that the reforms may have contributed to a narrowing of some of the gaps in elementary-school mathematics. A number of the studies that have made this claim used scores on accountability tests as their outcome, which renders them useless for answering our question; they can't distinguish between greater real gains by low-scoring groups and more severe score inflation. However, a few avoided this failing. For example, the Dee and Jacob study that the NRC report emphasized, which used NAEP as an outcome, found greater effects on fourth-grade math scores for students eligible for free lunch (the usual proxy for poverty). They also found larger effects for black and Hispanic students in some cases, but this depended on the analytic method they used.[6] Whatever the impact of the reforms on the achievement gaps that concern us, the trend data show that it wasn't sufficient to bring about a substantial narrowing.

Putting the Pieces Together

The decisions we face would be simpler if the evidence were all on one side of the argument: big benefits of the reforms with minimal side effects, or major side effects with no benefit at all. As is often the case, this decision is not that simple.

But it's close.

It's no exaggeration to say that the costs of test-based accountability have been huge. Instruction has been corrupted on a broad scale. Large amounts of instructional time are now siphoned off into test-prep activities that at best waste time and at worst defraud students and their parents. Cheating has become widespread. The public has been deceived into thinking that achievement has dramatically improved and that achievement gaps have narrowed. Many students are subjected to severe stress, not only during testing but also for long periods leading up to it. Educators have been evaluated in misleading and in some cases utterly absurd ways. Careers have been disrupted and in some cases ended. Educators, including prominent administrators, have been indicted and even imprisoned.

The primary benefit we received in return for all of this was substantial gains in elementary-school math that don't persist until graduation. This is true despite the many variants of test-based accountability the reformers have tried, and there is nothing on the horizon now that suggests that the net effects will be better in the future.

12

NINE PRINCIPLES FOR DOING BETTER

I share the goals of many of the advocates of test-based accountability. They were convinced—by good, uncorrupted test-score data, such as NAEP and international assessments—that the performance of American students isn't as good as it should be and that we need to find ways to improve it. Some of them exaggerated the problem, but they were right in insisting that the American school system is not as strong as it could or should be. They were determined to address the glaring inequities in achievement affecting minority students, students with disabilities, students with limited proficiency in English, and students in poverty—problems also clearly shown by uncorrupted scores. This is a hugely important problem, and their efforts were long overdue. And they wanted schools to be evaluated on what they produce, which would have been an important step forward had they not carried it to such extremes and taken such a narrow view of what schools *should* produce.

You've seen that despite those good intentions, test-based accountability has failed. It was predestined to fail because it was based in good measure on a number of unrealistic assumptions. And it's not only hindsight that allows me to say this. Warning flags about some of these assumptions were hoisted decades ago.

In this chapter I'll lay out design principles for doing better; I'll turn to concrete suggestions for implementing these principles in the next chapter. To put these design principles into sharper relief,

I'll contrast a number of them to the assumptions that underlie test-based accountability. Advocates of test-based accountability may argue that I am oversimplifying their ideas. In some instances they would be right. One can find exceptions to what I describe, some of which are quite important, but those exceptions—and the details of the most sophisticated of the programs—shouldn't obscure the general thrust of the test-based accountability movement and the ways in which we need to change course.

Pay Attention to Other Important Stuff

The first principle should be obvious by now: pay attention to the other important stuff.

In some ways, the most fundamental assumption undergirding test-based accountability was that student performance as measured by standardized tests was sufficient to measure the quality of schools—or at least close enough to warrant subjecting schools to severe sanctions. To be precise, this is really three assumptions rolled into one: that student achievement in a modest number of subjects covers enough of what we want from schools, that standardized tests are sufficient to measure that portion, and that one can conclude that differences in measured achievement map neatly onto differences in school quality. All three of these assumptions are unwarranted.

This is one instance in which I am oversimplifying. Efforts to use other indicators, such as measures of school climate or opportunity to learn, are now widespread. However, these were not the core of the reforms. Many of these efforts are relatively recent, and while they have serious consequences for the evaluation of teachers in some systems, they typically carry far less weight than test scores in assigning sanctions and rewards to schools. The bottom line is that it is scores, more than anything else, that drive what happens in schools. And at least in terms of federal policy, this overreliance on student's test scores isn't likely to change greatly in the near term. ESSA's much-publicized retreat from a test-score-only approach requires only a single additional measure of school quality, doesn't mandate any particular one, and requires that it be given much less weight than test-based indicators (in high schools, in combination with graduation rates).

To give the reformers their due, their assumption that accountability could focus largely—or in many cases entirely—on measures of student performance was partly an overreaction to the also unreasonable view that was widely held beforehand: that schools and educators could be evaluated without any consideration at all of what students actually learned. Nonetheless, the reformers' assumption is simplistic, and it has done a good deal of damage.

I don't know whether many of the reformers explicitly discounted other important goals of education or other aspects of good education. Perhaps Arne Duncan's staffer, when he angrily demanded to know what I meant by "other important stuff," actually had some other important stuff in mind himself. He didn't say, and neither did anyone else in the room. Perhaps the problem was just a widespread myopia; perhaps so many people were saying test scores would do the trick that people were led not to think much about the other important stuff. Perhaps they believed that if scores improved, the rest of what is important would follow along. Or perhaps some actually did discount the importance of other goals. I suspect it was a mix of all of these, but we'll never know. For practical purposes, it doesn't matter. The other important things clearly *didn't* follow along. And even what scores purport to measure—certain aspects of learning in some domains—didn't really improve much either.

Even when the other important stuff—goals other than student learning in tested subjects—is left aside, overconfidence in standardized tests set the reformers up for failure. As you know, experts in measurement have been warning for well over half a century that standardized tests can only measure a portion of the domains they target, such as math. I noted earlier that there has been real progress in recent years in expanding the range of what can be assessed with standardized tests, but the envelope has been stretched much less than advocates would like, and we shouldn't let this progress distract us from the main issue: even the best tests still leave a great deal unmeasured. And there simply aren't good standardized tests for most teachers. That the reformers ignored long-standing warnings about the limitations of tests in subjects such as math—warnings, I remind you, not from the antitesting crowd but from people who earned their living selling tests—was bad enough. That they plowed ahead even when they had no appropriate tests whatever is truly hard to fathom. I was asked whether I would consider being an expert for the plaintiffs in the lawsuit contesting Florida's policy of evaluating teachers using the scores of other teachers' students. (I agreed but wasn't chosen.) I told one of the attorneys that it was hard to imagine being in the role of expert, which is to dispense arcane knowledge that others in the courtroom don't have, when any reasonably intelligent fourth-grader would recognize that Florida's policy is absurd.

And finally we have the big leap, inferring that variations in scores (or in value added, or some other measure based on scores) indicate differences in school quality. We have known for decades that much of the variability in student performance has nothing whatever to do with the quality of schools they attend. That's not to say that schools don't have a big impact on what students learn and therefore on test scores. Of course they do. But factors outside of school also have a very large effect. I used to joke that students in the schools my kids attended could be locked in the basement all day and would still do fine on tests. The schools were among the highest scoring in the state, and they served a neighborhood chock full of parents with advanced degrees—lawyers, doctors, biomedical scientists who worked down the road at the National Institutes of Health—who were determined to provide every advantage to their children. Quite apart from the home environment these parents provided, they worked hard to compensate for any weaknesses in school quality—for example, by hiring tutors or reteaching the material themselves. And as my son pointed out, what parents provided wasn't the whole story; peers were a big influence as well. Years later my son commented that he couldn't recall a single person who went to high school with him who didn't go on to a four-year college or university. Perhaps even more important, academic achievement conveyed status in his schools.

Here again, supporters of the reforms will say that I am overstating my case. Some states and districts have tried to account for a few student background characteristics in their accountability models. But these efforts are hardly universal, they are mostly quite limited, and they coexist with elements of the reforms that counter them—for example, NCLB's and ESSA's requirements that the same standards be used to evaluate all students other than those with severe cognitive disabilities. Some will also counter that value-added approaches strip out some of the effects of out-of-school factors, and indeed they do, but to a lesser degree than many believe.

To make schools better, we have to pay attention to the other important stuff. And not token attention. The important stuff, the things we most want to see in schools, needs to be front and center. An accountability system will work as intended only if we decide what we most want to see in schools and then design the system to encourage it. Or to be more precise, because all systems will encounter Campbell's Law to some degree: we need to focus on the other important stuff if we want the system to give us much of what we want with only modest undesirable side effects. When we can't figure out a way to encourage something important, we must at least not impose incentives that discourage it. Math log isn't going to happen in many classrooms if we give teachers strong incentives to allocate that time and effort to something else, as we have in recent years.

Specifying what we most value will be very tough work, and we will encounter frequent and sometimes vehement disagreements. However, we have to agree on more goals than we have in the past, some of which will be much more difficult to measure than students' learning. We can't make the mistake again of settling on just a few goals that are uncontroversial—who can argue with more learning in math and reading?—and pretending that the other important stuff will come along of its own accord. It won't. And we should be able to agree on much more. We know that there are important subjects that the tests used for accountability don't cover. We don't want our kids to loathe school or be turned off by learning;

after all, their well-being will depend on a huge amount of learning they will need to do after leaving school. We want them to be able to work collaboratively when jobs require it. We want them to be able to adapt their knowledge and skills to meet the changing demands that will confront them throughout their lives. And we can agree on more than this.

Monitor More than Student Achievement

The second principle, which is already widely acknowledged but not taken seriously enough in most quarters, is that monitoring schools effectively will require much more than measures of student achievement. By this I don't mean the approach in ESSA, which is to select one thing out of the array of available measures and add it to test scores. That's not enough to meet the first principle: measure what matters, and give these measures the importance they warrant. In particular, meeting this second principle will require evaluating teachers' practices as well as student performance. Unfortunately, this will sometimes be difficult, and how far we go in this direction will be limited by practical considerations, but we will have to go much farther than we have to date.

Set Reasonable Targets

The third principle, which sounds obvious at first blush but is inherently difficult and will prove controversial, is that once we have measures in place, we have to set reasonable targets.

The advocates of test-based accountability seemed to believe that once tests were in place, any old target for improvement was fine. I don't mean that policy makers were indifferent to the harshness or leniency of performance standards. Anything but. Sometimes they would argue for more demanding standards, hoping that this would give teachers stronger incentives to improve. In other instances they did precisely the reverse, keeping targets modest because they wanted to avoid what they considered to be intolerably high failure rates in the short term. But in virtually no cases I have encountered were performance targets set on the basis of what teachers in various settings could realistically be expected to accomplish. Once policy makers had set performance standards, they just assumed that teachers would find a way to reach them, regardless of how high the targets were or how quickly teachers had to reach them.

Instead, we need to set *targets that the majority of educators can reach by legitimate means*. If there is any single lesson to be taken from the dismal accounting in the previous chapters, it is that if you put enough pressure on people to meet goals that they can't reach by doing what you want, they will do what you don't want rather than fail. Some years ago I was on a panel that met with some congressional staffers to discuss one of the early efforts to reauthorize NCLB. One of the staffers had been an inner-city teacher before coming to work on the Hill. When the discussion turned to NCLB's incentives to engage in bad test prep, she interjected, in a truly plaintive tone, "What were we to do? I understood that what I was doing [bad test prep] wasn't what I should do. But how else could I achieve the score gains that were demanded of me?"

It may not be apparent why this seemingly obvious principle might be controversial. There are two reasons. Some will resist it because setting reasonable targets—avoiding the pretense that we can improve schools faster than we actually can—may be less useful politically than promising huge improvement. This is not the objection that should concern us.

A second objection should concern us a great deal and will prove difficult to address: the principle of reasonable targets will be seen as competing with the goal of greater equity. One reason policy makers set unrealistic uniform targets was their laudable goal of reducing inequities in education, such as the average gaps between rich and poor. There were two reasons their approach to this problem was naive. First, some of the causes of these gaps lie outside the control of educators. Second, most of the variation among students lies *within* groups, not between them. Even if we found good enough methods for addressing inequities in the education offered to disadvantaged students and mustered the political will to implement them, students would still vary greatly—even though that variation would no longer be associated with ethnicity, disability, and so on. We've seen some of the consequences of ignoring these facts: more reliance on bad test prep and more score inflation in disadvantaged schools, and an illusion of improved equity when there was in reality little or even no progress.

Thus the third principle is actually more complicated: we have to set reasonable targets *while still exerting pressure to lessen inequities in education*. In my opinion, addressing this tension will be one of the most difficult challenges in designing a sensible replacement for our current system. Dealing with it adequately will require both knowledge about individual schools and human judgment. We have no reasonable alternative but to confront this challenge directly, however, as we have already seen the damage done by failing to do so.

Stop Just Kicking the Dog Harder

Years ago, early in the era of test-based accountability, Linda Darling Hammond aptly referred to it as the "kick the dog harder model of education reform." The reformers' implicit assumption seemed to be that many teachers knew how to teach more effectively but were being withholding, and therefore confronting them with sanctions and rewards would be enough to get them to deliver. They downplayed the fact that some teachers simply don't have what they need to produce considerably higher achievement—whether it be the skills, good curriculum materials, an orderly and well-managed school environment, or other supports. Here again many supporters will cry foul, and they will have a point; I'm oversimplifying. If you look across the many test-based reform efforts, you will find quite a variety of efforts to provide teachers or students with some support to help them reach the targets. For example, some states and districts put in place remedial instruction outside of regular school hours. Some also provided teachers with instructional support. A good recent example is the "engageNY" website created by the New York State Education Department to help teachers learn to adapt to the Common Core Standards; the site contains curriculum materials that are widely accessed by teachers from around the nation. I don't mean to disparage these efforts in any way, but despite them, Darling-Hammond's characterization was spot on. The exceptions are scattered and limited efforts, not core, shared parts of the reforms, and a great many teachers have been left in the lurch, hunting for something they could do to meet their targets.

The fourth principle is then simple: stop just kicking the dog harder. Accountability for performance, by itself, won't succeed in many schools. If we are going to make real headway, we are going to have to confront the simple fact that many teachers will need substantial supports if they are going to markedly improve the performance of their students. The need for support is increasingly widely recognized, and there have been diverse efforts to provide it. However, the needed supports are likely to be both more varied and more expensive than we have so far acknowledged.

Don't Expect Schools to Do It All

The fifth principle is closely related to the fourth: don't expect schools to do it all. Even if we provide needed supports, pushing teachers to work harder or more effectively during regular instructional time won't suffice to make the improvements we want—in particular, sizable improvements in equity. This may be one of the instances in which the reformers are owed the most credit; the need for interventions outside of regular schooling, such as quality preschools, is increasingly widely recognized. However, there is a long path from recognizing the need for additional programs to implementing them adequately. And the range of services needed is broad. One can't expect students' performance in school to be unaffected by inadequate nutrition, insufficient health care, home environments that have prepared them poorly for school, or violence on the way to school. This also takes us back to the problem of setting realistic targets. How much and how quickly one can reasonably expect performance in school to improve—and therefore, how demanding one can make targets for teachers without pushing them to do what we don't want them to do—will depend in part on what is being done outside of schools.

Pay Attention to Context

Many of the reformers who pushed test-based accountability believed that schools can be evaluated without anyone ever actually looking at them. For the most part, the reforms have been built with indicators that the reformers assumed—erroneously—can be interpreted accurately by someone sitting at a desk somewhere else, often hundreds of miles away. And they assumed that these indicators can be interpreted correctly with meager or even no consideration of the context in which they are produced.

The sixth principle for doing better is therefore to pay attention to context. To intervene effectively, we need to know more than how the students in a school perform; we need to know something about *why*. This is true of both schools that do poorly and those that do well. Some schools perform poorly because of staff who are so weak that they should be replaced. Others perform poorly because their teachers need additional training. Some have teachers who need incentives to aim higher—who do need us to kick the dog harder. Yet others perform poorly for reasons unrelated to the quality of teaching—perhaps a high rate of student transience, a high rate of absenteeism, students with unstable or otherwise problematic home situations, and so on. These all call for different interventions. Years ago I was on a committee that the commissioner of education in New York at the time, Rick Mills, created to advise him on how to deal with alternative high schools that were requesting a waiver from state testing requirements. One of the high schools served a large number of students who had immigrated to the United States as adolescents. These students had not yet had much time to learn English, and adolescents tend to learn a new language more slowly than younger students do. These students simply didn't have the mastery of English needed to do well on the state's end-of-course high-stakes tests. It would make no sense to respond to low scores in that school in the same way one would respond to a school in which teachers are using weak curricula or ineffective teaching methods.

And this is no less true of high-performing schools. It's just as risky to assume that schools with high-scoring students deserve all the credit for their student performance as to give schools with low-scoring students all the blame. Context—in this case, all of the other advantages that students in many high-scoring schools have—can hide all manner of problems in instruction. In the middle school my kids attended, which I have mentioned was one of the highest-performing in the state, one of the English teachers routinely—and I really do mean routinely—introduced grammatical errors into her students' writing when she "corrected" it. Parents actually noticed her errors and commented on them on back-to-school day. The kids performed fine anyway. (My wife took on that reteaching assignment; each time, she explained the errors and appropriate alternatives.)

Accept the Need for Human Judgment

An additional assumption that underlies test-based accountability is that one can evaluate schools adequately without human (and in particular, professional) judgment. This is more than a doubtful assumption; it is something of a motivating principle of test-based accountability. Many of the reformers simply don't trust educators to evaluate schools, and they designed their reforms to run, not walk, in the other direction. Their distrust isn't baseless by any means. The reformers were confronting a system in which almost all teachers, regardless of their competence or behavior, were rated as acceptable year after year. In many systems it has been extraordinarily difficult to remove an ineffective teacher, and the personal costs to an administrator who tries can be huge. Annual ratings are just the tip of the iceberg; many administrators are reluctant even to intervene to address concrete and known problems. (When I explained problems in my kids' classrooms to administrators, the response I received most often—so often that I began to wonder whether administrators in that district were trained to give it—was "I'm sure that what you saw wasn't typical." I was told this once after observing the exact same problem in all six math lessons I had observed.) And as I noted earlier, some economists have noted that subjective evaluations are particularly problematic in a civil service system, such as public schools—although I should add that I never heard any policy makers voice this last concern.

So it's not entirely surprising that many of the reformers were reluctant to rely on professional judgment, and I share many of their concerns about it, but they haven't found an adequate substitute.

Their abhorrence of professional judgment has led some reformers to opt for standardized measures of all manner of things, even when there is good reason not to. For example, "grit"—essentially perseverance, although some insist there is a difference—has become a buzzword in education, and perhaps it should be: many children do need help learning to persevere in the face of difficulty, failure, or boredom, and school can help teach them this. The response adopted by many schools, including several districts in California, has been to administer standardized measures of attributes such as self-control and conscientiousness to elementary-school students. Once again, policy makers are using student performance as a proxy measure for school quality, and once again, they are relying on a standardized measure rather than judgment. The problem: the measures are no good for this purpose. Angela Duckworth, the psychologist most responsible for putting the notion of grit up in lights—and whose work on grit and self-control won her a MacArthur "genius" award—was quoted in the New York Times as saying, "It is a bad idea, . . . All measures [of these attributes] suck, and they all suck in their own way."[1] One of the many ways they are inadequate is that they can be faked. Marty West, a colleague of mine at Harvard, had this to say in the same article: "You think test scores are easy to game? They're relatively hard to game when you compare them to a self-report survey." And even if students don't deliberately fake their answers to make their schools look good, Duckworth pointed out that using the measures for accountability creates an incentive for "superficial parroting" of the socially desirable answers.

However well motivated this avoidance of human (or at least adult) judgment may be, it won't work. And as I will explain in the next chapter, our avoidance of professional judgment stands in stark contrast to the approaches taken in some high-achieving countries, such as Singapore and the Netherlands.

The seventh and perhaps most controversial of the principles, then, is that we need to accept the need for human judgment in evaluating schools. This is in some ways unfortunate, given the difficult problems inherent in relying on judgment, but there really is no practical alternative. We will need to find better ways to use judgment, not avoid it.

Create Counterbalancing Incentives

Suppose one decides to pay workers who replace car windshields on a piecework basis. There are good reasons to do this; it gives the workers an incentive not to slack off, and it may attract harder-working applicants. The drawback, however, is obvious: it also gives the workers an incentive to do sloppy work, if doing so speeds them up. That was of course one of the main flaws of the Soviet economic model. One way to deal with this perverse incentive is also obvious: have someone else inspect the installations for quality. This works, of course, only if the inspector has an incentive to fail poorly done installations, even if it reduces the shop's output. The inspector's incentives have to offset the perverse effects of the installers.' If the inspector's pay, like the workers', is based on the number of installations, you might as well skip the inspection stage and save the money.

One of the reasons that test-based accountability has failed so badly is that the advocates who designed it seemed not to perceive the need for any serious counterbalancing incentives. On the contrary, the system gave everyone in the system the exact same incentives: to raise scores and not to worry about how. It has been in no one's self-interest to avoid bad test prep, and it is no accident that in many instances, districts and states have actually provided teachers with materials to facilitate bad test prep. And it is similarly no accident that some of the big cheating scandals haven't started at the initiative of a few unscrupulous teachers (although that has happened as well); they have been instances of systemic corruption in which superintendents have pushed principals to cheat, and principals have done the same to their teachers.

Despite the pressures they face, a great many of educators have resisted the temptation to behave badly in response to the incentives they have been given, but the experience of recent years shows that it is foolish to count on this. To minimize Campbell's Law and maximize real improvements in schooling, we need to create countervailing incentives. If teachers have an incentive to cut corners by using bad test prep, someone else in the system should have an incentive to curtail it. If principals have an incentive to eliminate recess to squeeze out a little more time for test prep, someone should have an incentive to put a stop to this.

This is one more way—setting reasonable targets is another—we have to design the system to anticipate Campbell's Law.

Monitor, Evaluate, and Revise

A final assumption of the advocates of test-based accountability was that their reforms wouldn't be subject to Campbell's Law and that we could dispense with evaluating them carefully before imposing them on millions of students and teachers. Many of the reformers would bridle at this and reply that of course they evaluated their programs. They might argue that evaluation was the core of their reforms; they focused on test scores, which made their reforms self-evaluating: scores would do double duty, serving both as an incentive to teachers and as an indicator of improvement. But scores didn't provide an honest evaluation of the programs, of course, because of score inflation.

Why didn't the reformers recognize the failure of scores to provide trustworthy information about their programs? We can't entirely know, but from my experience, I believe it was mix of several things. Some people simply didn't know about Campbell's Law, either in general or in the specific forms it takes with testing. Many clung to the fallacious assumption that if tests are designed to include only good stuff, inflation won't be a problem. This is nonsense, but it has proven to be a very hard misconception to dislodge, and many people still believe it. And some—I've experienced this firsthand many times—willfully ignored evidence of Campbell's Law even when confronted with it. Perhaps a decade ago, I was asked to participate in a meeting hosted by the *Boston Globe* to offer advice about how its journalists and editors might present test scores in their articles. During the discussion, someone else raised the problem of score inflation and pointed out that it has major implications for their reporting. I responded by noting briefly a few of the key findings of research. A very prominent education reformer—I'll leave him unnamed—gave me what I took to be a condescending look and replied, "That's just a matter of opinion."

But the failure to evaluate the reforms also reflects a peculiar arrogance, a notion that reformers are smart enough to design their programs without major flaws—despite the fact that each iteration is based on a recognition of the shortcomings of the previous one they designed. One anecdote sums this up well. Years ago I attended a meeting at which a group was hashing out the early forms of the "college and career readiness" notion of school reform that has since morphed into the Common Core. With three exceptions—another researcher, a tech entrepreneur, and me—everyone in the meeting was from the world of education policy and reform. At one point one of the reformers stood next to a whiteboard and sketched out an elaborate system of pathways, sanctions, and the like. After he had gone on for quite some time, the entrepreneur interrupted him and asked, "Do you have some basis for all of that, or are you just making it up?" The room was quiet for a moment, and then the policy maker conceded that he was making it up. The conversation then resumed as if the interruption hadn't happened.

There is nothing wrong with making it up, of course. Good ideas have to start somewhere. What was wrong is that no one recognized the corollary: if he was making it up, he didn't know how well or poorly it would work. That leaves us with the obligation—particularly given that kids are affected, an ethical obligation—to test those ideas before imposing them wholesale on teachers and students.

This brings me to the final principle: because Campbell's Law always shows itself—and because we will always be designing interventions with less hard information than we ideally would have—we need to be on the lookout for problems. We need to evaluate what we do, and we need to do it on a far greater scale than we have to date. This will be costly both politically and financially, but we simply have to do it, for both ethical and practical reasons. A number of times I have referred to an evaluation of the innovative Kentucky accountability system that was put into place in the 1990s. Here I would like to give credit to the person who was in many ways most responsible, because his actions serve as a model for what we need to do in the future. At the time, the deputy commissioner in Kentucky, Ed Reidy, was my primary contact in the Kentucky Department of Education for the evaluation I was running, which was only one of many that the department allowed. I had a frank conversation with Ed about the risks my study and others posed for the department's policies. His response was simple: his job was to serve students, and he had an ethical obligation to learn whether the department's policies were helping students and to change course if big problems became apparent. I can point to a number of other policy makers who have taken similarly principled stands, but unfortunately this hasn't been our typical way of proceeding. It needs to be.

13

DOING BETTER

When I have attended meetings at which policy makers were designing test-based accountability systems for schools and teachers, most participants quickly got down into the weeds and fretted about details. How many items should be on part A of the math test? If we are going to use a proficiency index that awards each school some number of points for each student, how many points should a school get for students at each one of our performance standards? When we implement our arbitrarily chosen standard-setting method, how should we structure the proceedings?

The big questions occasionally came up, but they rarely became the center of discussion. The assumptions I laid out in the previous chapter may deserve some of the blame. But to be fair, the participants in these meetings didn't have a lot of wiggle room. For example, NCLB didn't ask states to debate whether it made sense to hold almost all students to the same performance standard; it mandated that they do so. So in these meetings people spent time worrying about the smaller things over which they *were* allowed control.

This won't do. I'm not saying that the details about which people have worried are not important. They often are. For example, as you have seen, decisions about how to set standards can have a tremendous impact. And even technical decisions that might seem too arcane to matter can have a practical impact. They warrant careful attention, but they pale in comparison to the fundamental issues, and it doesn't make sense to focus on details before we answer the big questions: how we might put into practice the principles I sketched in the previous chapter.

○ ○ ○

Early in my career, I was an analyst in one of the policy-analysis units of the Congressional Budget Office, an organization that prides itself on even-handed and thorough analysis. The T-shirts for our softball team showed two fists, one with the thumb pointing up and the other with the thumb pointing down. Around it was our motto: "CBO: on the one hand, on the other." It was an ironic reference to a comment by Ed Muskie, then a senator from Maine, who once complained that he was so tired of hearing "on the other hand" that he wanted to find one-armed social scientists to testify at hearings. This frustration was nothing new; a story has it that decades earlier, President Truman was so frustrated by the evenhandedness of Edwin Nourse, the first chair of the Council of Economic Advisors, that he said he wanted to find a one-handed economist.[1] The message of our T-shirt was this: we know it's annoying to hear the caveats, but they are a necessary part of the package, an essential component of the honest answers that are our stock in trade.

I've several times excoriated some of the reformers for assuming that whatever they dreamed up would work well, without turning to actual evidence. I won't repeat that blunder, and unfortunately, avoiding it requires that I use both arms to write this chapter. One reason is that there are big gaps in what we know, but there is another reason as well: tradeoffs. Many of the decisions we face will entail substantial, sometimes truly painful, tradeoffs. To do better in meeting one important goal will often entail giving up something significant with respect to another. Sometimes we can find ways to lessen these tradeoffs, but they can't be eliminated. Even if we come to agreement on a general approach, we may disagree on specifics because we assign different priorities to the many goals of education reform. Even if we had perfect knowledge about how the system would work, there would be no single optimal solution.

This leaves ample room for debate about how to move forward, but it doesn't justify standing pat and continuing with what we have been doing. The failures of recent policies have been too severe. However, these uncertainties make it all the more important that we carefully monitor the effects of whatever we do and be prepared to admit the need for midcourse corrections.

How Is It Done Elsewhere? Systems Very Unlike Ours

It's with some apprehension that I will very briefly sketch how monitoring and accountability are carried out in a few other countries. The reason I am hesitant is that international comparisons of this sort are routinely misunderstood and misrepresented, and I don't want to lure you into making that mistake. Often a commentator will pick a country that does well on an international test, usually PISA or TIMSS, then choose some aspect of that country's education system that appeals to that particular observer, and pronounce it to be one of the causes. In fact, they are just speculating. That's not to say that they are wrong; they may not be. But they rarely have enough evidence to back up their claims. The major international comparative assessments, such as PISA and TIMSS, are designed to provide descriptions of performance and of educational systems. They aren't designed to provide solid evidence about causes of differences among countries, and for the most part they don't. And it is almost certainly the case that things not measured in these studies—including factors completely unrelated to education policy, such as the esteem societies confer on teaching—contribute substantially to performance differences among countries.

Nonetheless, these international comparisons can be helpful in two ways. First, they open our eyes to the wide variety of options for running school systems. The countries I will describe—Finland, the Netherlands, and Singapore—all produce levels of student learning that by some measures exceed ours by quite a margin, but none of the three has an educational accountability system remotely like ours. That should help put to rest the common assertion that we need to continue with what we have been doing because our schools aren't producing enough student learning. Second, these comparisons are an excellent source of ideas and hypotheses. Can we say with any certainty how much the Dutch system of school inspections has contributed to the strong average achievement of Dutch students? Unfortunately, no. Can we say that the Dutch inspectorate, if transplanted to the United States, would have the same impact in Chicago that it has in Amsterdam? Again, no. However, it does provide a model well worth trying—and evaluating carefully—in the American context.

Let's start with Finland, which in recent years has been a darling of the education policy community in the United States. Finland is an appealing example for many because it scores near the top in the PISA international comparisons of math but has a system that looks nothing like the high-pressure systems of many of the East Asian countries that dominate these comparisons. To start, Finland has no high-stakes testing at all other than matriculation exams at the end of high school. Evaluation of education is largely left to the professional judgment of local educators. Equality of educational opportunity is a primary goal, and there are virtually no private schools. Teaching is a highly regarded and well-paid occupation, and teacher training institutes turn away a substantial share of their applicants. At one time or another, observers have pointed to most of these as putative causes of the strong performance of Finnish students.[2]

Although Finland is the European country most discussed in the United States, the performance of Dutch students on the PISA assessment is quite similar. The Dutch system, however, is fundamentally different from the Finnish and gives us other options to consider.

The Dutch educational system is exceptionally decentralized, even more so than the US system. For a century the Dutch constitution has given any citizen the right to establish, design, and manage a school. The national government establishes both learning goals and mandatory procedures for evaluation, but schools are governed by boards that are independent of the national government and increasingly independent of local governments as well. Parents have free choice among schools. Public and private schools both receive public funding, which follows the student. To a substantial degree, schools are free to choose among methods—including tests—to monitor their students and their own performance.

The Dutch system uses a complex mix of centralized and decentralized approaches for monitoring both student achievement and the quality of schools. Moreover, laws passed over the past several years are instigating substantial changes to several aspects of the system. Simply to describe all of the elements of this system would require far more space than I have here. Instead I'll describe a few key elements.[3]

Unlike Finland, the Netherlands has a long-standing tradition of assessing student achievement with standardized tests. The Dutch system is segmented, with several different types of schools at every stage after primary, and end-of-sector tests contribute to the decision about where students should be placed in the next stage. However, teachers' judgments are considered along with performance on the tests in making these decisions. Tests are also—and increasingly—used both to monitor students' growth over time and to describe school performance. Schools have choice in selecting tests other than the high-school leaving exams, but for purposes of monitoring the learning of younger students, almost all chose an assessment system produced by Cito, a testing firm, which provides reports to parents several times a year. Scores are made available to the public along with a great deal of additional information, both in publicized data sources and in the reports of inspectors, to which I will return in a moment.

External monitoring by means of tests is complemented by locally determined monitoring and evaluation. Schools are required to establish their own goals and specify measures for monitoring their progress toward them. These goals typically include but go beyond scores on externally supplied tests. This local accountability is not token. The Dutch system has a tradition of bottom-up rather than top-down reform, and local accountability, including the local choice of measures, is consistent with this.

For my purposes—thinking about alternatives to our failed test-based accountability—a critical question about the Dutch system is how schools that operate in such a decentralized system and have so much freedom to set goals and monitor performance are held accountable. There are at least two powerful accountability levers embedded in the Dutch system: inspections and market pressure.

Inspections in the Netherlands are carried out by a national agency, the Inspectorate of Education. Inspectors consider test scores, but a great deal of their focus is on elements of practice and classroom climate. The inspectors have fifteen indicators for evaluating lessons they observe, including "teacher explains things clearly," "pupils are involved in education activities," "teacher gives pupils feedback on learning . . . ," and "teacher adapts instruction to differences in development between pupils."[4] In recent years the inspectorate has moved to target inspections particularly on schools that appear to be performing poorly.

The second source of accountability is the market pressure created by parental choice of schools. Parents have a wealth of information—not just scores but inspection reports and detailed descriptive information about schools—to help them make their decisions.

For present purposes, several attributes of the Dutch system stand out. To start, the system is based on the principle that bottom-up innovation is as at least as important as top-down reform. Students in the Netherlands are tested more than those in many countries, and test scores matter for monitoring both students and schools. However, in evaluating both students and schools, the Dutch follow E. F. Lindquist's advice: scores on externally designed standardized tests are never used alone. The Dutch also avoid using a fixed cut score on a single test to evaluate either students or schools.

The point at which tests are most important for students is at the end of secondary school, when the Dutch system, like the Finnish and many other European systems, requires high-school leaving exams. However, in each subject, the leaving exam includes school-based assessments as well as a centrally designed standardized test. The system does impose a single cut score to determine whether a student has earned a diploma, but this cut is applied to the *set* of exams, both school-based and centrally designed, so strong performance on one of the assessments can compensate for weaker performance on another.

In sum, scores on standardized tests enter into the evaluation of Dutch schools, but they play a much more modest and nuanced role in the Netherlands than in the United States. They are presented to the public with a great deal of other information, and they are used by the central authority—the inspectorate—only in conjunction with other measures of school quality. The system relies heavily on local evaluations of quality, not just centrally imposed standardized tests. The system focuses heavily on measures of practice, not just outcomes. And it relies very heavily on professional judgment—both that of school personnel and that of external inspectors. Finally, by imposing inspections, the Dutch system avoids one of the most central failures of our system: it imposes countervailing incentives. Inspectors have no incentive to give high marks to a school that produces high scores by engaging in bad practices.

Finally, let's look at Singapore. Developed East Asian countries largely dominate international comparisons in mathematics, and Singapore often ranks at or near the top. For example, in the 2012 PISA assessment Singapore was the highest-scoring country in mathematics, followed by Hong Kong, Taiwan, and Korea.[5] This high level of achievement is all the more noteworthy because at the time of independence in 1965, a substantial share of Singapore's population was illiterate.

Singapore's education system stands in marked contrast to that of the Netherlands: it is highly centralized, and the national Ministry of Education maintains control over many aspects of the system. The ministry's goals have shifted over time, initially focusing on the mass education needed for economic survival and then turning more toward educational attainment—how far students progress in school—and the higher skills needed for a knowledge-based economy.[6] Most recently, in 2011, the ministry began a shift toward a more student-centered, holistic, and flexible education, with a focus on "character and values" as well as academic achievement.[7]

The evolution of Singapore's education policy—and in particular, the adoption of student-centered, holistic education as a central goal a few years ago—is important for this discussion for two reasons. First, the view of the ministry—which I share—is that a shift to more holistic goals for education requires that the importance of tests be reduced. Second, this new goal is consistent with the rich, judgment-based evaluation of teachers conducted routinely by the ministry.

First, the tests. All students in Singapore are given standardized tests, but they encounter truly high-stakes tests far less often than American students, at only a few points in their careers: at the end of primary school and after four years of secondary school. Students attempting to enter tertiary education also must take a set of matriculation exams called the "A levels," modeled after the similarly named exams in the United Kingdom.

Despite the low frequency of high-stakes testing, performance on tests is extremely important to students, parents, and educators in Singapore because scores govern students' placements and progression through the educational system. As in some other East Asian countries, many students in Singapore devote considerable time to study in private test preparation schools, known in Singapore as "tuition." In the eyes of many educators, parents, and other observers, the pressure to score well on tests and the resulting cramming have gotten out of control. For example, under the headline "Tuition Has Become an Educational Arms Race," a 2016 article in the *Singapore Times* reported that seven of every ten parents of children *from preschool* though secondary school send their children to private cramming schools; it concluded, "Parents know it doesn't improve their children's grades but they send them for tuition anyway because other children have it."[8] (I felt much the same when my kids were at the age at which most students from upper-middle-class families spend time and money on test prep for college-admissions tests.)

While both Singapore's system and ours are highly test driven, they are test driven in very different ways. To oversimplify only a bit, in the US system—if you leave aside college-admissions testing—the pressure to score well is top down: federal and state policy makers impose pressure on educators to raise scores. Although some high-stakes tests—in particular high-school exit tests—have direct consequences for students, most don't, and educators are left to find ways to pressure students to do well on them. Parents are largely bypassed in this system, and while many worry about the scores their children receive, they aren't for the most part the source of the pressure felt by educators. In fact, in recent years, parents in some locations have fought to reduce the pressures created by testing. The most striking example is what is now called the "opt-out" movement: the growing number of parents who simply refuse to let their children take their school's high-stakes tests. In contrast, in Singapore, as in some other Asian countries, testing is high stakes because of the importance of scores for selecting students for later schooling, and parents, wanting to keep doors open for their children, end up being a primary source of the pressure felt by both educators and their children.

Policy makers in Singapore are working to lessen the importance of testing, but it remains to be seen how successful they will be. For example, under a new policy, performance on each of the Primary School Learning Examination (PSLE) subject-area tests will be reported only in terms of eight broad bands that include anywhere from five to ten scale scores.[9] This will force more consideration of other factors by those selecting students for secondary schools, because many applicants will be tied in terms of their scores on the PSLE. This approach shares some of the disadvantages of our reporting in terms of performance standards, and some Singaporean parents are already expressing concerns about it, but it nonetheless shows the seriousness of the ministry's efforts to reduce overreliance on scores.[10] This push to reduce the emphasis on test scores is a major part of the recent focus on holistic education. This was made explicit in a 2016 speech by Ng Chee Meng, the acting minister of education (schools), who argued that the nation needs "a paradigm shift away from an over-emphasis on academics to better prepare our children and our people for the future." He noted that they need to learn "broader competencies to navigate the demands of life and work" and that "the education that we gift our children should be holistic. Every child should be provided with opportunities to discover and develop his or her strengths and interests, in multiple domains."[11]

This doesn't sound much like making kids memorize that on a particular test the symbol *b* is usually (and arbitrarily) used to represent the intercept, or like depriving them of other subjects to maximize the time available to cram for math and reading tests.

The contrast between Singapore and the United States comes into even clearer focus when one compares approaches to evaluating teaching. Singapore has an elaborate, labor-intensive program for evaluating and improving teaching called the Enhanced Performance Management System (EPMS). Despite the importance of testing in Singapore, the EPMS makes no explicit use of test scores, although Singaporean educators have told me that within some schools, administrators do use them anyway in evaluating teachers. The EPMS embodies three of the principles I enumerated in the previous chapter: evaluating a wide range of outcomes, relying on professional judgment, and providing high levels of support. The evaluation is remarkably broad and includes many aspects of learning, many facets of teaching practice ("nurturing the whole child," "cultivating knowledge," "teaching creatively," and more), as well as working well with both peers and parents.

It's telling that although EPMS ratings matter—teachers repeatedly rated as ineffective leave the profession—the EPMS is seen first and foremost as a system for facilitating the development of better teachers, and the ministry does not use the word *evaluation* or *accountability* in describing it. The EPMS evaluations are coupled with intensive support; for example, new teachers are given a reduced teaching load to allow them to observe more experienced peers and are assigned a senior mentor. Teachers are observed by their supervisors at least twice a year, sometimes more often, and the observations are followed with a discussion of both strengths and areas for improvement. In addition, school leaders observe teachers other than those whom they directly supervise.

The teaching profession in Singapore is also highly selective. Only very strong students are allowed to train for it.

○ ○ ○

What are we to make of this? Again I want to stress that we can't be certain what impact each of the elements of the Finnish, Dutch, and Singaporean systems has on the performance of their students, and without trying them here, we can't know how well they would transfer to the very different context in some US schools.

To be concrete, let's turn back to Finland. Until the advent of test-based accountability, most systems in the United States shared two of the characteristics of the Finnish system: a lack of high-stakes testing and reliance on local professional judgment. The reformers who brought us test-based reform argued that this system failed in the United States, and to some extent they were right: it's clear that in many schools, particularly many of those serving disadvantaged students, the system didn't work well. Clearly, just returning to those policies in and of itself won't get us where we want to go. Nonetheless, Finland is a very clear reminder that a system that relies on professional judgment rather than high-stakes testing *can* work well. We ought to be hunting in the Finnish example for the other factors that might have (I stress, *might* have) contributed in some measure to the greater success of this approach in the Finnish context. The selectivity, high pay, respect, and professional responsibility of the teaching profession are plausible candidates.

Despite these uncertainties, the systems in Finland, the Netherlands, and Singapore provide a rich array of alternatives to the failed American policies of recent years, and together they suggest approaches worth trying.

Options for Doing Better

In making specific suggestions below, I will frequently refer to "accountability." I don't mean by this a system—like our current one—in which each school and often each teacher has one or more numerical targets and reaps punishments or rewards on that basis. Rather, I am using the term in the more general sense of monitoring how well teachers and schools perform and using a variety of methods to induce—and enable—poor performers to do better. As a look at other education systems makes clear, that pressure can take many different forms, including feedback from superiors or other evaluators.

A few themes underlie many of the specifics I will propose. The first is *breadth*. One of the clearest messages from the research on Campbell's Law is that seriously incomplete measures generate severe distortions. Education is far too complex to permit a truly exhaustive system of measurement, but we need to make the system far broader than it has been in recent years. The second is *tradeoffs*. There is no panacea, and there are no options open to us that are free of substantial drawbacks. We need to confront these tradeoffs frankly. Our goal should be a system that—taken as a whole—has far smaller drawbacks than the failed system students and teachers have endured for years. The third theme is *balance*. Our current system is tremendously out of balance; the drive to raise scores outweighs everything else, in most places hugely. Even more important than the imbalance in what we measure is the imbalance in incentives. As I explained earlier, we have imposed on education a system that is devoid of counterbalancing incentives. In the Soviet Union this produced shoes no one wanted to buy; in the United States it produced the Atlanta cheating scandal. We need a system that has more balance in both what we measure and the incentives we create. This will necessarily be much broader than our current system, but it will also entail some truly difficult tradeoffs, and it will require venturing into partly uncharted waters.

1. We must measure what matters. The starting point has to be deciding what matters most. There is room to argue about this, and the list could become quite long, but I'll start with what I'll call the Big Three: student achievement, educators' practices, and classroom climate.

There isn't much controversy these days about the Big Three. Even within the constraints of test-based accountability, many states and districts are trying out ways of measuring both practice and classroom climate. There is, however, argument about how to measure the Big Three and about how much weight each should be given. In most districts, test scores still swamp everything else. Indeed, ESSA *requires* that test scores swamp everything else.

Let's start with student achievement. Perhaps surprisingly, I'll begin by saying that standardized tests should be a part of any system of monitoring and accountability. Many critics of our current system blame standardized tests, but for all the damage that test-based accountability has caused, the problem has not been testing itself but rather the rampant misuses of testing.

Why use standardized tests when we have so many other ways of measuring student achievement? The strongest argument for using tests in a system of monitoring is precisely the fact that they are standardized: ideally, students everywhere confront the same tasks, administered and scored the same way. This stands in stark contrast, for example, to high school grades, which vary in rigor from one school to another and even from one classroom to another. Standardized test scores mean—or ideally they *can* mean—the same thing regardless of where students attend school, and that in turn allows us to answer critically important questions, such as whether the achievement gaps between minority and nonminority students have really narrowed in recent years.

The rub, of course, is the caveat "ideally they can." You've seen that the pressure of accountability has undercut precisely this advantage of standardized tests. Even leaving aside cheating, some schools engage in far more bad test prep than others, often causing comparisons based on scores to be completely misleading. For example, as you have seen, in some places standardized tests have created an illusion that the achievement gap between disadvantaged and advantaged students has narrowed far more than it actually did. That's because of high stakes, not flaws in the tests.

So I should be more precise: we ought to start with standardized tests *if and only if we take steps to dramatically reduce bad test prep and inflated scores*. I'll come back to several steps we need to take in order to accomplish this. I am writing this with some trepidation, not because of concerns about tests but because I worry that policy makers won't resist the temptation to misuse them yet again or that they will fail to do enough to curtail fraudulent gains.

There is one additional caveat that you should anticipate by now: standardized tests won't suffice, even in the subjects for which they are well suited.

Some years ago I participated in a panel on testing hosted by a consortium of school districts in the Boston area. A high-school senior posed the most important question of the day. He attended Brookline High School, one of the region's high-performing (and advantaged) high schools, and he was clearly a very strong student; he was at the time trying to choose among three Ivy League universities that had accepted him. He said that one of the most valuable experiences he had in high school was a series of real experiments in science. Most "experiments" in science classes aren't actually experiments at all; they are just preplanned activities designed to demonstrate some fact or principle that the teacher and often the students know in advance. His experiments were the real deal: they entailed designing experiments, generating data, and analyzing them to investigate questions to which he didn't know the answer. This was truly excellent instruction in science of a sort that I, and I suspect most people in the room, believed ought to be made available to all students. His question for us was how the state test should be modified to capture that sort of learning.

My answer was that he was looking at the wrong tool. Yes, we can capture bits and pieces of that experience with standardized tests. For example, we can use them to evaluate whether he knows basic principles of scientific inquiry. However, that would not be enough to capture the quality of his work or what he learned from it. Moreover, adding a question or two on the principles of scientific inquiry to the state test wouldn't provide an incentive for his teachers to devote the time and energy to mentoring him as he did his experiments. It would be a lot easier and much faster for them to devote just a class or two to teaching the principles. That would leave more time for prepping students for the rest of the test. And by the same token, it wouldn't have given the student an incentive to devote the time and work to what he found to be his most valuable educational experience.

What's the solution? Precisely what the designers of standardized tests have been telling us to do for more than half a century, and what the Finnish, Dutch, and Singaporean systems do routinely: use local measures of student achievement—that is, measures not imposed from afar. These local measures include both the quality of students' work and their performance on tests designed by educators in their schools, both of which go into the grades that teachers assign. In addition to providing a far more complete view of students' learning, using these local measures—along with standardized tests when we have good ones—would give teachers more of an incentive to focus on the quality of assignments and schoolwork rather than just preparing students for a single end-of-year test.

Advocates of test-based reform might object that teachers still do use these local measures under the current regime. Of course they do. But these measures don't count. Good science experiments aren't what produces rewards or protection from the sanctions imposed under test-based accountability. The system treats them like math log—as something that won't be recognized or credited, regardless of whether it is good instruction.

But how can we trust that educators will demand enough of their students and apply sufficiently rigorous standards in evaluating their work? And how can we compare these local measures from one school to another? These are much more substantial objections. The unspoken premise of test-based reform is that we can't trust educators to impose appropriate and consistent standards. And in fact we can't simply send the Brookline student's grade of A on a science experiment to the state department of education, trusting that it means something similar to an A on a science assignment from one of the 237 other school districts in Massachusetts.

This is the first and one of the most difficult tradeoffs we face: to measure learning well and to give teachers better incentives, we will have to use measures that have other serious drawbacks—in particular, potential inconsistency from classroom to classroom and school to school.

There are ways to lessen this problem, but they are burdensome and not entirely satisfactory. One approach is to rely on professional judgment—that is, to have both assignments and grading standards a part of what observers evaluate. A second, common in some British Commonwealth countries, goes by the term *moderation* but might better be called *benchmarking*. In one form of benchmarking, teachers evaluate a sample of assignments and grades assigned in other schools to evaluate how comparable the assignments are and how consistent the grading is from teacher to teacher. When good standardized tests are available and are not corrupted by accountability pressure, scores can be used in benchmarking: if a teacher's or a school's grades are consistently higher than test scores suggest, that is reason to examine the work students are assigned and the standards used in grading it. These approaches can lessen inconsistencies in grading, but they won't eliminate them entirely.

But even using a broad and more burdensome set of measures of student learning doesn't get us where we need to go. I'll illustrate one reason by describing another math class session, this from the highest-track seventh-grade math class in one of the highest-achieving middle schools in Maryland, in the same district in which Norka Padilla taught. I'll do the teacher the favor of leaving her anonymous. Let's call her Ms. X.

On the day in question, the lesson was about arithmetic operations with mixed-sign numbers—for example, dividing a positive number by a negative one. This is not easy material to teach; it can be difficult to help students develop the intuition needed to understand why the procedures work. The class was structured around homework problems Ms. X had given the class the day before. She would call on a student and ask for the answer to a problem. If the student gave a wrong answer, she would call on the student directly behind the first. If that student also got it wrong, she would ask the class, "What is the rule?" Often hesitantly, someone would take a shot at it, often starting with something like "You take the number with the smaller absolute value..."

I was dismayed. I had been performing those arithmetic operations without any difficulty since I was in junior high school, perhaps even earlier, but I found myself hard pressed to state a rule for some of them. Memorizing the rules would not help students understand what they were doing.

That night, I asked my son, who was in the class, whether Ms. X had ever given them any concrete representations of any of these operations. My son asked what I meant, so I gave him several examples: moving both ways on a number line, credits and debits to a bank account, and so on. He said no, she just gave them rules to memorize. I learned over time that this was typical of the class.

The question you need to ask yourself is whether you would call this a good class if the students obtained high test scores at the end of the year. My answer is an emphatic no. It was a lousy class, and I would have pulled my son out in a heartbeat without even asking about test scores if I had been given the option. I doubt that what is called a *summative* test—an end-of-year test designed to measure the full year of learning—would have captured even how well the students learned to perform those arithmetic operations. After all, these students were in the highest-achieving track in the highest-performing middle school in one of the highest-performing districts in the state. They would do just fine on the test. All of the other factors that contributed to the students' strong performance would have masked the low quality of instruction.

But that's only one reason to look beyond test scores. A second is that the class was terribly dull, elicited little real thought and discussion from the students, and no doubt contributed to the all-too-common feeling that math is something aversive—best avoided when possible. That's why I would have pulled my son out, had I been given the opportunity. I would be hard pressed to find a clearer counterpoint to the excitement, intellectual engagement, and positive affect I had seen in Norka Padilla's class three years earlier.

So to evaluate the quality of Ms. X's class, you would have to go beyond measures of student learning and look at the other two of the Big Three: practice and climate. In this case the two were intertwined: Ms. X's practices were pedagogically weak, and they contributed to an aversive, boring atmosphere in the class. And measuring the quality of practice directly—rather than trying to infer it indirectly from test scores—has yet another benefit: it can help to tamp down inappropriate test preparation and score inflation. I'll come back to this.

I'll add one more to the Big Three: what are often now called "soft" or "noncognitive" skills—attributes such as persistence, the ability to work well in groups, and so on. E. F. Lindquist, the same pioneer of achievement testing who warned that tests must be used in conjunction with local measures of learning, also cautioned—more than half a century ago—that skills of this sort that can't be captured by standardized tests are a critically important goal of education.

This may strike some hard-headed advocates of accountability as "soft," but recent research has begun to confirm the wisdom of Lindquist's advice: soft skills affect how well students do long term, even after they leave school. And research suggest that teachers' influence on these soft skills is distinct from their impact on students' scores. For example, a 2016 study by Kirabo Jackson, an economist at Northwestern University, showed that teachers vary in their impact on absences, suspensions, high-school completion, and later college enrollment, separately from their influence on test scores.[12] While it is not at all clear yet how measures of these dispositions can be incorporated into an accountability system, it is certain that we want to encourage teachers to help students develop them, and holding teachers accountable for scores won't accomplish this. To make this concrete, think again about math log. One of the many reasons I was impressed by math log is that it seemed to foster both cognitive skills, reasoning about mathematics and explaining that reasoning, and softer skills: enthusiasm for mathematics and working well in small groups.

2. We need to measure the Big Three well. Let's assume we have agreement that we need to measure the Big Three. Disagreements will arise in deciding *how* to measure them.

One of the main motivations for placing so much emphasis on standardized test scores was the notion that educators can't be trusted to evaluate schooling or other educators. This same view seems to dominate recent efforts to measure practice and climate. In both cases, policy makers and researchers have turned to *standardized* measures—that is, methods that minimize the role of judgment by posing predetermined questions and providing uniform ways to score the answers. Practice is often measured with standardized observational systems such as the widely used CLASS (Classroom Assessment Scoring System) developed at the University of Virginia. As the university's website explains, "The CLASS™ tool includes four cycles of 15-minute observations of teachers and students by a certified CLASS™ observer. Those observations are then rated using a manual of behaviors and responses. . . . Research conducted in over 3,000 classrooms concludes that from Pre-K programs into the third grade, children in classrooms with higher CLASS™ ratings realize greater gains in achievement and social skill development."[13] CLASS is a measure that is applicable to any class, while other popular measures, such as the MQI (Mathematical Quality of Instruction) system developed by Heather Hill and colleagues at Harvard and the University of Michigan, focus on subject-specific instructional practices. For my purposes, what is most important about these measures is that they attempt to standardize the evaluation of practice, minimizing the role of judgment.

Increasingly districts are also turning to another type of standardized measure of practice and climate: surveys of students. As of 2015, thirty-three states either required or permitted including student surveys in teacher evaluations.[14] For example, the Tripod student survey, which was used in the Gates Foundation's influential Measuring Effective Teaching study and is administered in many districts, measures student perceptions of both their teachers' pedagogy and classroom climate. Students as young as third grade are given a variety of statements and asked to specify how true each one is. These examples give an idea of the range:

- My teacher gives us time to explain our ideas.
- Students behave so badly in this class that it slows down our learning.
- School work is interesting.

There are strong arguments in favor of relying on standardized measures of practice and climate. Standardization has the same advantages in these domains as it does in assessing student learning. If standardization works, a given score on a test or an observational measure of practice will have much the same meaning regardless of which school the student attends or which rater grades the work. Student surveys might seem more questionable—should one place more faith in evaluations by nine-year-olds than in those by trained professional inspectors?—but they have their advantages as well. Students can respond to the entirety of their experience in the class, while standardized observations and inspections are limited to a small sample of class time, which may happen to be atypical in some instances.

It has been well established that standardized measures can capture some of what is important in classrooms. Nonetheless, there are reasons not to put all of our eggs in that basket. To start, we don't yet know enough about how well the currently popular measures will work as part of a system in which they are a focus of serious accountability pressure—in particular, how severe both the distortions of practice and the corruption of the measures themselves will be. A given measure may work very well *under ideal circumstances* and nonetheless perform poorly under the pressure of accountability. After all, achievement tests work well in the absence of accountability pressure, but as you have seen, they often function terribly when the pressure to raise scores is strong.

Yet another reason not to trust that standardized measures will get us where we need to go is that they are almost certainly insufficient. A new study illustrates this concretely. In the 1990s, as part of TIMSS, researchers videotaped mathematics lessons in seven countries, including Japan. Because Japan is always one of the highest-scoring countries, the videos of Japanese lessons have been widely used as examples of effective mathematics instruction and are frequently contrasted with the practices recorded in American classrooms. I'm not a specialist in math education, but I too find a good deal to admire in the Japanese lessons. A doctoral student at Harvard, Katie Lynch, evaluated how these Japanese lessons rate on commonly used standardized measures of instructional practice. She had trained raters score the TIMSS videos using both CLASS and the MQI. Her findings were startling: the standardized measures showed the American lessons to be *superior* to the Japanese ones on many dimensions. For example, while the Japanese lessons scored highest on one CLASS dimension, analysis and problem solving, they scored lower than the US lessons in content understanding, quality of feedback, and instructional dialogue. On the MQI, the US lessons scored far higher than the Japanese lessons on the dimension of whole-lesson mathematical quality of instruction.[15] I doubt anyone who studies instruction will greet these findings by deciding that math instruction in the United

States is better than that in Japan after all. Nor is this an indication that the CLASS and MQI fail to measure important aspects of instruction. We have ample evidence that they do. A more reasonable explanation—although I am speculating—is that the standardized instruments were simply not sufficient to capture some of what is important.

None of this is an argument against using standardized measures of practice and classroom climate. Rather, I'm warning that we shouldn't assume that they will suffice and that we can't again make the mistake of ignoring Campbell's Law when using them.

The alternative to relying—or relying solely—on standardized measures is to do what the Dutch and Singaporean systems do: give a substantial role to the judgment of professionals. I doubt we will ever have an adequate system for holding educators accountable if we don't take this step. Education is simply too complicated to reduce it to a limited, predictable set of measures.

But which professionals? In the ideal world, much of this role could be given to school principals, but there are a number of reasons to be skeptical that this would be enough. The first I mentioned in an earlier chapter, and it applies to most public education systems: subjective evaluation of personnel is particularly risky in the public sector because the evaluators don't have money on the table and can more easily be tempted to base their evaluation on personal preferences rather than relevant performance. In addition, if the point of monitoring is to evaluate schools as well as individual teachers, principals will have an incentive to rate their staffs well. Two other reasons are specific to our system. First, a great many American principals haven't been trained to take on this responsibility. Second, years of test-based accountability have created perverse incentives for principals. They have been pressed to worry about how quickly scores increase but not to worry about how that is accomplished. Moreover, unrelenting pressure to raise scores has begun to corrupt the very notion of good teaching, and there is no reason to assume that principals—many of whom are promoted directly from the ranks of teachers—have been immune to this rot. Undoing this damage is likely to be both time consuming and difficult.

To make evaluations based on professional judgment meaningful and productive will therefore require three big steps: changing the incentives facing principals, retraining many of them, and relying in part on evaluations by professionals from outside the school. The last is precisely the approach followed in the Netherlands: evaluations of schools are conducted separately by both school personnel and the inspectorate.

I won't downplay how difficult it will be to do this well or how serious the risks are. Any system that relies on subjective judgment is open to both inconsistency and bias. Evaluations of this sort are costly and time intensive, and this increases the risk that observations will be too limited and may capture atypical lessons.

And inspections and observations too can be gamed. Some years ago I gave the opening talk at a meeting on educational accountability in the Netherlands. I noted how severe Campbell's Law has been in American test-based accountability, and I speculated that inspections might be a way to lessen this problem. After lunch, an official of the Dutch inspectorate who had missed my talk gave a presentation in which his first slide was a picture of a can of Campbell's soup. The theme of his talk: how teachers game inspections.

In addition, while imposing some oversight by outsiders may be necessary, it won't suffice if the incentives are designed incorrectly. Some years ago a colleague of mine was given permission to shadow "quality reviewers," outside observers—much like inspectors—sent by the New York City Department of Education to observe schools. I asked her to let me know if she saw them trying to counter bad test prep. She found the reverse: some of the reviewers *distributed* bad test prep materials. They saw their role as helping teachers raise scores—the primary measure of quality in the district—not making sure that they raised scores by means of better teaching.

So here again we face truly painful tradeoffs. Expanding what we measure and relying on professional judgment are necessary both to obtain a better view of the quality of schooling and to help balance incentives. Yet doing so will impose sizable burdens, including substantial financial costs and a large commitment of time to train and retrain the people doing the evaluation. And it will entail substantial risks—in particular, the risk of inconsistent and even biased subjective judgments. Minimizing these downsides will require careful design, ongoing monitoring of the system, and, undoubtedly, midcourse corrections. These costs, however, have to be compared with the damage created by our current system.

3. We must build a sensible accountability system. Measuring a broad range of important things is an essential first step, but it's not in itself enough to create reasonable incentives. I'll suggest four additional steps.

The first may seem self-evident, but it is routinely ignored regardless: *the system has to emphasize what's important.* The weight we give to various measures should, as much as possible, reflect their actual importance. It simply won't suffice to tell districts that they need to throw in one or more measures in addition to test scores. Unless the others are made to matter, test scores will still trump all the others. If the quality of instruction and classroom climate are truly important—and you can tell from the examples I have given that I believe they are—educators need to know that they really count.

The second step is to *create the counterbalancing incentives* that were largely lacking in the Soviet system and in our test-based accountability systems. Think of a hose that has a weak spot and starts bulging, threatening to burst, when the water is turned on. The sensible thing to do is to take some step to prevent the hose from bursting, such as wrapping the weak spot in duct tape. That bulge is analogous to the undesirable side effects that Campbell's Law tells us to expect. Applying pressure to control the bulges is analogous to imposing counterbalancing incentives.

The most obvious and biggest of the bulges, given the way we have been running schools, is inappropriate test prep. The first application of duct tape is making certain that whoever monitors a classroom—whether with some standardized instrument or by using judgment—is charged with evaluating aspects of good instruction, not just activities that will raise scores. However, given how badly corrupted instruction has become, I doubt that would be enough. The second application of tape would be charging the observers to check directly for inappropriate test prep.

Of course, teachers can easily game observations if they knew when the observations they will happen. One of my students, a former teacher, recently told me an anecdote about this. She taught in a school in which test prep dominated "instruction" day after day. One day, when an important outsider was scheduled to visit, the vice principal went to the teachers and told them to put aside test prep for the day and teach instead. (The point of the student's anecdote was something even worse: the corruption of the idea of teaching I described in an earlier chapter. One of her colleagues appeared puzzled because she believed that test prep *was* teaching.)

How can we reduce this gaming? Unscheduled observations would help, but they won't be enough, particularly to the extent that observers use known, standardized instruments. Teachers can prepare lessons that will score well and have them ready for unscheduled visits. Still, unexpected observations are an essential step. And as I mentioned, for all the questions raised by using surveys of students, they may help address this particular problem.

A third response to gaming observations requires *looking well beyond what happens on any single day in the classroom.* Bill Schmidt at Michigan State, who has devoted much of his career to international comparisons of both student achievement and curricula, argues that in many countries, evaluations of schooling include monitoring how well educators are teaching the intended curriculum—that is, the curriculum that is supposed to be taught. As you have seen, one of the most common inappropriate responses to test-based accountability has been to stop teaching the entire intended curriculum, cutting back on or entirely dropping whatever happens not to be on the test. The test essentially *replaces* the intended curriculum. To tamp this down, one has to compare what is called the "implemented curriculum"—that is, the content that is actually taught in a school—to the intended. Checking this would require that from time to time someone would have to examine teachers' syllabi, and often some of their lesson plans.

Monitoring how well the curriculum is taught is essential for a second, perhaps even more important reason: it is one way to combat the impoverishment of instruction in untested subjects that test-based accountability has caused. Recall that a common response by educators to testing in a limited number of subjects has been to take time away from other subjects, sometimes virtually or entirely eliminating them from instruction. No one in the current system has any incentive to tell teachers that a week of social studies isn't enough or that art class shouldn't be used to drill kids with math test prep materials.

A corollary is that *we need measures that are not too closely aligned with each other*—that is, that are not too similar. For those of you who are familiar with the last few decades of reform, this may seem to be a peculiar suggestion, as the education policy world spent a decade or more asserting in nearly perfect unison that the key to successful education was having everything—standards, curricula, instruction, and tests—closely aligned with each other. The ideal was that each of these should predict the next as well as possible, with no surprises. For example, some years ago I was in a position to suggest to a state education department items that they might use in their tests. One of the state's math standards explained a skill that students should have and happened to illustrate it with an example with two equations. I proposed an item that clearly focused on the skill but included a single equation. The staff of that state education department rejected the item, saying that the example that accompanied the standard showed two equations, not one. The real world, however, was never all that closely aligned with any of the standards or the test. After leaving school—and indeed, even while in school, if they move across state lines—students encounter the need to show knowledge and skills in forms that don't match the particulars of the state where they first went to school. If the students in this particular state later encountered a need for that particular mathematical skill, she couldn't count on confronting it only in situations involving exactly two equations. More generally, students haven't really mastered something unless they can demonstrate that mastery when faced with unfamiliar details. An excessive focus on alignment was just a recipe for Campbell's Law—specifically, for reallocation, coaching, and score inflation.[16]

What would it mean in practice to have measures that are not too tightly aligned? Two things. First, each measure in the system should be designed to capture important things that others miss. We don't need observations to tell us whether Norka Padilla and Ms. X successfully taught computational skills. Tests can do that. We need observations or other measures to capture the things that tests don't measure well, which in this case are the things that made their two classrooms so dramatically different in quality. We can use a test to find out whether the teacher of the Brookline student taught him the established scientific findings, the meanings of scientific terms, and some basic principles of scientific inquiry, but we need to see his work to judge how well he had learned to conduct experiments. The second and less obvious implication is that when different measures assess similar things, they should usually do it differently. For example, if we want students to be able to deal with simple linear equations, we shouldn't always confront them with equations in the form $y = mx + b$, and if we are concerned about students' ability to write, we need to give them tasks that aren't too similar to the tasks and scoring rules used in the end-of-year test.

Finally, *targets have to be reasonable*: the goals facing educators have to be ones that they can reach by legitimate means. This requires practical targets for both the amount of improvement and the time allowed to accomplish it. The time span must take into account the year-to-year fluctuations in scores that arise from both differences among cohorts of students and the often unavoidable trial-and-error in improving instruction, because ignoring these makes annual targets a recipe for failure. There is room to argue about how best to determine what is reasonable, but the principle is inescapable. If we demand more than educators can deliver by teaching better, they will have to choose between failing and cutting corners—or worse, simply cheating. This may sound obvious as a general principle, but in practice, it will be both controversial and difficult to implement. To begin, demanding big and rapid gains makes for good press and often good politics, so persuading policy makers to be realistic won't always be easy.

I noted in the last chapter the more difficult challenge: setting reasonable targets means setting *varied* targets. Reducing inequities in education has to remain one of our primary goals, but simply wishing away performance differences among schools and among kids within schools was more than unrealistic; it was destructive. It created enormous pressure to cut corners and to cheat, and it undoubtedly is one of the principal reasons we have seen fraudulent reductions in the gap between advantaged and disadvantaged students.

Here I really need my second arm: no one can yet say with any assurance how best to set realistic, varied targets while still creating the needed pressure to improve the schools serving kids who now do poorly. It's not that we lack ideas, and I will give a few suggestions in a moment. The problem is that we don't yet have good evidence about what will work best, in part because the law has largely forbidden states and districts to try and evaluate ways of doing this.

My first suggestion for how to address this dilemma works only for the subjects for which we have good tests: *set goals based on students' growth, not the level of their performance.* If the goal is to reduce inequity—and if one is satisfied with the progress of higher-scoring students—the targets for growth can be made more stringent for low-achieving students, *as long as they remain practical and needed supports are provided.* Turning back to my own time teaching remedial reading poorly: it would have been entirely reasonable to have pushed me to increase modestly the rate at which my dyslexic kids improved from one grade to the next, provided that I was helped to learn better pedagogical methods. This approach has numerous drawbacks: for example, annual growth estimates are very unreliable, and different ways of measuring growth often give different answers. Still, it is more reasonable than the current approach; it would have accomplished nothing productive at all to tell me that my students had to be "proficient" within a few years. They weren't going to be, unless I cheated.

But what about the great majority of teachers for whom there are no good tests that allow monitoring growth? This is another instance in which I believe we will need to rely to some extent on human judgment. How much improvement one can realistically expect depends a great deal on the context. To pick just one example, schools with high rates of student turnover will usually find it harder to make improvements than those serving more stable communities. Similarly, weak teaching contributes more to poor student performance in some schools than in others. I don't see how we can set reasonable targets—and how we can put the needed pressure on schools doing an inadequate job of serving low-scoring students—if we don't bother trying to sort this out.

4. Use tests sensibly. Time after time, as bad news about test-based accountability began to accumulate, its advocates have insisted that if we just substituted better tests—what they considered "better" varied from one instance to another—the system would right itself. They maintained that the negative effects on instruction and score inflation would be brought under control and that we would finally get the promised improvements in learning. This didn't happen, as you have seen. While I don't want to disparage efforts to improve tests, these arguments have missed the main story. The chief problem was never the tests themselves. It was the misuse of tests, which was often worsened by successive reforms.

I've already noted a number of steps toward a more sensible use of tests. We shouldn't rely on tests when we don't have appropriate and sufficiently high-quality tests to use. As much as is practical, we need to avoid relying on arbitrary performance standards, and we need to set realistic goals for improvement. We need to use test scores in conjunction with a wide variety of other measures, and we need to balance the incentives to raise scores. We need to take steps to reduce inappropriate test prep. Here I'll note a few more.

While improving the tests themselves won't solve the problems of test-based accountability, we do need to make one change in the design of assessments: we need to *make them less predictable* in order to whittle away at inappropriate test prep. In the distant, low-stakes past, predictability in a test wasn't as big a deal because teachers didn't have much of an incentive to teach to the tested sample rather than the entire domain. In fact, schools would routinely use the exact same test booklets for years, and test vendors released new editions only at intervals of six or seven years. Because of accountability pressures, predictability now matters a great deal, and even though states now use new test forms every year, the new ones often look a great deal like the old, right down to using b for the slope in $y = mx + b$. You've seen how educators and test prep firms have responded. To lessen this problem, we have to make tests less predictable. Here again, I need my second arm. There are technical constraints that limit how much we can vary the content of tests. Moreover, because no one worried about predictability until very recently—and most people in the field still don't, even though the reasons to worry are painfully obvious—we have only begun to work out the practical details, and it is not yet clear just how big a dent in Campbell's Law this can make.

My other recommendations are all matters of test use, not design.

We need to *stop pretending that one test can do everything*. It's now common to claim that a test designed and used for accountability can also provide honest monitoring of progress and good diagnostic information for teachers. This is hardly surprising; accountability testing has already swallowed a great deal of school time, and with our current incentives, few people want a second measure that might distract from the all-important goal of ratcheting up scores on the accountability test. However, it just isn't so, particularly given the pressures in our system to raise scores. As you have seen, Campbell's Law has made scores on accountability tests misleading—often dramatically misleading—indicators of progress. And using the high-stakes test to diagnose students' weaknesses strengthens the already intense incentives to focus instruction on details of that test, further worsening Campbell's Law.

A corollary is that we need to *curtail sharply the use of the "interim" or "benchmark" assessments* that are widely used to predict how students will score at the end of the year. Many of these tests are just facsimiles of parts of the end-of-year summative test, designed to mirror not only the content of the summative test but also how that content is presented. Currently students in many districts spend a huge amount of time over the course of the school year taking them. This is a waste of instructional time, and it is a recipe for score inflation. Obviously, tests used during the course of the year should reflect the same curriculum—the same domain—as the summative test, but they shouldn't be mirror images. They shouldn't be test prep.

Finally, a recommendation for a truly fundamental shift: we should consider turning the current approach on its head and *treating scores as the starting point rather than the end of evaluation.* I've stressed repeatedly that scores alone, whether high or low, aren't enough to tell us *why* students are performing as they do. Low scores, however, are an indication of likely problems. Rather than treating these low scores as sufficient to label a school a failure, we could use them to target other resources used for evaluation. The Dutch Inspectorate does precisely this: low-scoring schools are more often inspected.

5. Provide support to teachers. Teachers can't do it all—especially teachers in many low-performing schools. This fact is widely accepted in principle, but it is often ignored in practice. We will need to take this far more seriously than we have if we are to achieve the large gains in student learning, and in particular the big improvements in equity, that reformers have promised us for years.

The supports we should provide are of three types. The first is *better initial training*—called "preservice" training in the field—and retraining for teachers already in the workplace. Many teachers simply don't have the skills needed to produce the improvements we want, particularly for disadvantaged children. It's telling that despite the much greater selectivity of the teaching field in Singapore, the primary function of the country's labor-intensive EPMS system is the improvement of teachers' practices. There is nothing new about this recommendation. For decades, American experts in teacher training, such as Linda Darling-Hammond, have been pointing to the need for better training and internships.

The second category is *in-school supports*: supplementary classes, longer schooldays, smaller classes, and the like. The third is *out-of-school supports*. One that has received a great deal of attention in recent years is high-quality preschool, which can improve the long-term prospects of disadvantaged kids.

Why are recommendations for more support controversial? One reason is money. It is vastly cheaper to buy a test, set arbitrary targets, and pretend that the problem is solved. A second is timing. It takes time for these supports to work. Test scores can be improved very rapidly—even in the space of only two or three years—if one turns a blind eye to fraudulent gains.

There is one additional, less obvious reason why the importance of support might be controversial: its implications for setting targets. Just as the improvements we can reasonably expect depend on the circumstances confronting any given school, they depend on the amount of support we are willing to provide to the educators who work in it. For example, consider two hypothetical elementary schools that are located in very poor neighborhoods and that largely serve highly disadvantaged students. Assume that the teachers in the two schools are comparable in quality. Students in the first school have access to high-quality preschools, health screening, and a school breakfast program. The second school has none of these. It would be unrealistic to expect students in schools like the second to match the performance of kids in schools like the first, and expecting similar performance would necessarily cause you to conclude—falsely—that teaching in the second school is of lower quality. Once again, this points to the importance of knowing about the context in which a school operates and to the need for professional judgment.

6. Monitor and make midcourse corrections. I've repeatedly said that one of the most important reasons for the failure of test-based accountability was the reformers' unwillingness to evaluate their policies before imposing them wholesale on teachers, principals, and kids. We can't make that mistake again. We need to test out new approaches before we take them to scale. We need to monitor and evaluate these approaches—routinely—once they are put in place. And we need to make midcourse corrections when problems are uncovered, as certainly will happen.

What do we need to look for? I'll single out a few particularly important things.

To start, we need to monitor directly the effects of reform on teachers' practices and other aspects of schooling. We can't repeat the mistake of assuming that increases in test scores or other outcomes for which educators are held accountable signify improved practices. On the positive side, we need to evaluate the extent to which the changes we hope for are actually made. On the negative side, we need to look for the inevitable distortions of practice that Campbell's Law describes.

Then we need to be on the lookout for the second part of Campbell's Law: the corruption of the measures used for accountability. Just as test scores became inflated as a result of test-based accountability, other measures used in its replacement will inevitably be threatened to some degree. We need to monitor the extent of that corruption, and we need to identify the contexts in which it is particularly severe—just as we have learned that schools serving disadvantaged students suffer more severely from Campbell's Law under the pressures of test-based accountability.

And—here I need my second arm yet again—the uncertainties and tradeoffs entailed in my own recommendations point to things that we need to monitor. I'll note two that are particularly important. First, many of the supports I suggested are expensive and labor intensive, and this makes careful evaluation of their impact essential. Second, the tradeoffs and uncertainties that accompany the use of professional judgment are well known, and it won't be clear at the outset how well a new system will minimize the undesirable side effects.

Monitoring and evaluation, however, won't help unless we have a clear commitment to making changes as unwanted findings come to light. When Campbell's Law appears, we need to take steps to tamp it down. If we find that some forms of expensive or burdensome support don't have much payoff, we need to modify or abandon them. If evaluators are ineffective or abuse their power, we need to change the way we use professional judgment.

It may be politically difficult to make this commitment. A program is easier to sell if one doesn't admit doubts about it, and midcourse corrections can be both politically costly and disruptive. But it can be done. Earlier I noted that years ago Vermont embarked on a truly innovative program of using portfolio assessments in addition to standardized tests. When Rick Mills, the commissioner of the Vermont Department of Education, proposed the portfolio program, I told him that because he was breaking new ground, he shouldn't believe anyone who claimed to know with any certainty how well the program would work. His response was to explain this publicly and often and to commit his department to making changes as needed. And he stuck to it. He allowed my group at RAND to monitor the functioning of the program without any restrictions. When we encountered a serious problem—teachers' evaluations of the portfolios were so inconsistent that the scores couldn't be used for many of their intended purposes—he called a press conference in which he released our findings and then turned to changes that he would make in response. (He also put me on the spot: cameras rolling, he introduced me as head of the evaluation group and said, "Ask him whatever you would like.")

14

WRAPPING UP

Almost thirty years before I started writing this book, I predicted that test-based accountability—then in its early stages, and still far milder than the system burdening schools today—wouldn't succeed. I said that many educators would face only three options: cheat, find other ways to cut corners, or fail. As successive waves of "reform" ratcheted up the pressure to raise scores, the risks only became worse, and others and I repeated the warning.

Educators have done all three. I take no comfort in having been right.

○ ○ ○

But neither anyone else in the field nor I correctly predicted just how extreme the failures of test-based reform would be. I anticipated cheating, but not on the scale of the scandals that have begun to come to light. I expected that many teachers would resort to bad test prep, but I didn't anticipate that states and districts would openly peddle it to their teachers. I expected that test prep would displace some amount of instruction, but I didn't foresee just how much time testing and test prep would swallow or that filling students' time with interim tests and test prep would become the new normal. And I didn't foresee that test-based accountability would fundamentally corrupt the notion of good teaching, to the point where many people can't see the difference between test prep and good instruction. I predicted score inflation, but I found its magnitude in some settings jaw-dropping. It never occurred to me that teachers would be “evaluated” based on the scores achieved by other teachers’ students or that districts would have scramble to find any tests they could just so that they could claim to be evaluating teachers, even those teaching physical education or the arts, based on scores on standardized tests.

○ ○ ○

I’m far more interested in charting a better way forward than in pointing fingers, and as I have made clear, I have no interest in impugning the motives of the people responsible for the current system. On the contrary, many of them had the best of intentions. However, we need to look back at the causes of the failures in order to avoid repeating them in the future.

Looking back on the past three decades of test-based accountability, I have to qualify my early prediction that many teachers would fail. In an important sense educators *didn’t* fail. Teachers and principals didn’t manage to make the improvements in education that the policy makers claimed, but they did precisely what was demanded of them: they raised scores. Reformers may take umbrage and say that they certainly didn’t demand that teachers cheat. They didn’t, although in fact many policy makers actively encouraged bad test prep that produced fraudulent gains. What they did demand was unrelenting and often very large gains that many teachers couldn’t produce through better instruction, and they left them with inadequate supports as they struggled to meet these often unrealistic targets. They gave many educators the choice I wrote about thirty years ago—fail, cut corners, or cheat—and many chose not to fail.

○ ○ ○

This is not to say that educators are blameless, but if one wanted to ascribe blame, one would have to start far higher up the chain of command. The roots of the failures I’ve described go right to the top. Placing all the blame on educators would be more than mistaken; it would obscure much of what we need to do differently. We need changes in behavior—and incentives that will induce them—from top to bottom.

We should ask: why has this gone on so long? Apart from details, much of what I wrote in the first nine chapters of this book is old news. We have known for decades that teachers were being pushed into using bad test prep, that states and districts were complicit in this, that scores were often badly inflated, and even that score inflation was creating an illusion of narrowing achievement gaps. The first solid study documenting score inflation was presented twenty-five years before I started writing this book. The first study showing illusory improvement in achievement gaps—the largely bogus "Texas miracle"—was published only ten years after that.

In good measure, the failures of the current system have festered as long as they have because many of the advocates of test-based accountability simply didn't want to face the evidence. Certainly, some of those making decisions weren't aware of the evidence, and a few who were aware struggled within the constraints of current policy requirements to respond to it. However, many of the advocates were aware of the evidence but found ways to discount it—like the superintendent who said to me that he knew that there wasn't score inflation in his district because the gains were so large. Others persuaded themselves that however badly previous attempts at test-based accountability had worked, this time they had it right.

And I suspect many of them knew that test-based accountability isn't optimal but considered it good enough—and far less expensive and burdensome than better alternatives. That turned out to be a naive hope and a costly mistake.

○ ○ ○

Why now? Given how resilient test-based accountability has proved in the face of the bad news that has been accumulating for fully a quarter of a century, it's easy to be pessimistic that this ship can be turned around. Why push now for a change of course?

ESSA, the replacement for NCLB, doesn't represent anywhere nearly a big enough change of course. It maintains many of the core elements of the test-based reforms that preceded it, including NCLB. The specific changes included in ESSA—including the important ones, such as requiring states to use at least one indicator other than scores—are just very small steps, as a comparison with the recommendations in the previous two chapters makes clear. For example, ESSA only slightly broadens the focus from test scores, does nothing to confront Campbell's Law, doesn't allow for reasonable variations among students, doesn't take context into account, doesn't make use of professional judgment, and largely or entirely (depending on the choices states' departments of education make) continues to exclude the quality of educators' practice from the mandated accountability system.

Yet ESSA provides a reason to be guardedly optimistic: its enactment stemmed in some measure from a growing dissatisfaction with simple test-based accountability. NCLB was enacted with a remarkable degree of bipartisan support, but over time it lost most of its fans, and it's not an exaggeration to say that by the end it was detested by many people in the education world. Some of the criticism of NCLB in its latter days focused on the core failings of test-based accountability—in particular, the extent to which the pressure to raise scores had come to dominate schooling. It's remarkable that even Arne Duncan, who arguably did as much as any one person during the past decade to increase the pressure on educators to raise test scores, conceded that "testing issues today are sucking the oxygen out of the room in a lot of schools." Even though ESSA won't in itself do enough to reduce the distortions created by test-based accountability, this dissatisfaction with the past offers some hope that ESSA represents the beginning of a shift to a more sensible and productive approach.

And ESSA is not the only sign of growing dissatisfaction with test-based accountability and its effects. Many parents have become fed up with having their children in schools that are so dominated by testing. Perhaps the clearest sign is the "opt out" movement—parents who refuse to let their children take some standardized tests. This movement is still spotty. In many locations there is no real sign of it. However, in others it has profoundly disrupted high-stakes testing. In New York, for example, where the movement was the focus of a substantial media campaign, about one-fifth of the state's students didn't take the states tests in grades 3 through 8 in 2015 and 2016. While still limited in its reach, the opt-out movement is national in scope, and it has clearly touched a nerve. This may give more impetus to policy makers to consider alternatives to the current system.

○ ○ ○

Let's be optimistic and assume that ESSA and the opt-out movement are early signs of a growing dissatisfaction with test-based accountability and that we will finally have a chance to work on better alternatives. In the previous two chapters I've outlined both principles for doing better and a number of specific suggestions, but I'll end with a few themes that pervade both.

We need to approach the task of improving education with a great deal more humility than we have for the past three decades. Under the best of circumstances, education is an extraordinarily complicated system, and the scale and decentralization of the American system make it all the more so. There is a great deal we don't yet know about how this cumbersome and complex system will respond to new policy initiatives or new forms of practice. And like any other complex system, it will impose tradeoffs, often very painful ones. Some we can anticipate; others will surprise us. And there are many different ways to implement the suggestions I've made. Some will work better than others. None will work perfectly, and few if any will work as well as we would hope.

How can we best respond to these uncertainties? To start, we shouldn't—once again—overpromise. It's tempting and politically useful to claim that we have a new approach that will produce huge gains in performance, but doing so is both naive and destructive. We should set reasonable goals and try out a variety of specific approaches for meeting them, rather than pretending that we know in advance which will function best and how much improvement they will generate.

I do mean "try out," not "try." We're in the same position that Rick Mills was in when he introduced portfolio assessments in Vermont: to some extent we'll be plowing new ground, and we owe it to kids and their teachers to evaluate the specific options that states and districts design, discard the bad ones, and tinker with the better ones before implementing them wholesale.

And the need to monitor, reject, and revise won't end even then. One reason is that some of our plans, however well thought out, won't work. Campbell's Law is another reason: people will be inventive in finding the weaknesses in any system, and new bulges will keep appearing in the hose. And on the positive side, educators and others will continually generate ideas for doing better, and these new innovations will in turn need to be evaluated and revised. It's no accident that the governments of both the Netherlands and Singapore, which already had educational systems that produce very high achievement, have both made substantial changes to their management of schools in recent years.

Will it be difficult to implement these suggestions? Yes, very, and expensive as well. Is there room to argue about how best to put them into practice? A great deal, and we will undoubtedly make some mistakes regardless of wins those debates. And progress won't be fast; it will take quite some time simply to repair the damage that test-based accountability has produced, let alone to make the sizable improvements we want. But years of experience have shown that the alternative—dodging these difficulties and tinkering with what we have—is unacceptable.

NOTES

Notes to Chapter One

1 Los Angeles Times (2012). "On Politics in the Golden State," *Los Angeles Times*, June 18, 2012, http://latimesblogs.latimes.com/california-politics/2012/06/student-notebooks-standardized-testing.html.

2 For example, see Jessica Chasmer, "Common Core Testing Makes Children Vomit, Wet Their Pants: N.Y. Principals," *Washington Times*, November 25, 2014, http://www.washingtontimes.com/news/2013/nov/25/common-core-testing-makes-children-vomit/; Katrina vanden Heuvel (2013). "Stakes on Standardized tests Are Too High," *Washington Post*, April 30, 2013, https://www.washingtonpost.com/opinions/katrina-vanden-heuvel-stakes-on-standardized-testing-are-too-high/2013/04/29/16e9e9d8-b0d5–11e2-bbf2-a6f9e9d79e19_story.html.

3 Launa Hall, "This Ed-Reform Trends Is Supposed to Motivate Students. Instead, It Shames Them," *Washington Post*, May 19, 2016, https://www.washingtonpost.com/posteverything/wp/2016/05/19/data-walls/?utm_term=.86e09c9ec7c9.

4 Valerie Strauss, "Parent of Dying Boy Has to Prove Her Son Can't Take Standardized Tests," *Washington Post*, February 4, 2014, http://www.washingtonpost.com/blogs/answer-sheet/wp/2014/02/04/parent-of-dying-boy-has-to-prove-her-son-cant-take-standardized-test/.

5 Cook v. Stewart, No. 1:13-cv-72 (N.D. Fla. May 6, 2014).

6 US Department of Education, *U.S. States in a Global Context: Results from the 2011 NAEP-TIMSS Linking Study* (Washington, DC: US Department of Education, 2013), 1.

7 Wagner v. Haslam, 112 F. Supp. 3d 673 (M.D. Tenn. 2015).

Notes to Chapter Two

1 John Hassell, "Bush Hints at Compromise on Standardized-Test Plan," *Seattle Times*, March 15, 2001.

2 Everett F. Lindquist, "Preliminary Considerations in Objective Test Construction," in *Educational Measurement*, ed. E. F. Lindquist (Washington, DC: American Council on Education, 1951), 119–84.

3 H. D. Hoover et al., *Iowa Tests of Basic Skills Interpretive Guide for School Administrators, Levels 5-14* (Chicago: Riverside, 1994), 11.

4 Every Child Succeeds Act of 2015, Pub. L. No. 114–95, Title I, Part A, Sec. 1111(c)(4)(C)(ii)(II).

Notes to Chapter Three

1 http://www.kipp.org/our-approach/five-pillars.

2 Reeta Chakrabarti, "South Korea's Schools: Long Days, High Results," *BBC News*, December 2, 2003, http://www.bbc.com/news/education-25187993.

3 Sandra Davie, "Tuition Has Become an Educational Arms Race," *Straits Times*, July 9, 2015, http://www.straitstimes.com/opinion/tuition-has-become-an-educational-arms-race.

4 Chee Meng Ng, "MOE FY 2016 Committee of Supply Debate—Speech by Acting Minister for Education (Schools) Ng Chee Meng," Singapore Ministry of Education, April 8, 2016, https://www.moe.gov.sg/news/speeches/moe-fy-2016-committee-of-supply-debate—-speech-by-acting-minister-for-education-schools-ng-chee-meng, accessed June 20, 2016.

5 National Commission on Excellence in Education, *A Nation at Risk: The Imperative for Education Reform* (Washington, DC: NCEE, 1983).

6 Chris Pipho, "Tracking the Reforms, Part 5: Testing—Can It Measure the Success of the Reform Movement?" *Education Week* 4, no. 35 (198): 19.

7 Gordon Ambach, "Comments on 'Should Instruction Be Measurement-Driven?,'" paper presented at the annual meeting of the American Educational Research Association, New Orleans, April 1987.

8 Margaret E. Goertz, Mark C. Duffy, and Kerstin Carlson Le Floch, *Assessment and Accountability Systems in the 50 States: 1999–2000* (Philadelphia: Consortium for Policy Research in Education, University of Pennsylvania, 2001).

9 Ibid.

Notes to Chapter Four

1 Coral Davenport and Jack Ewing, "VW Is Said to Cheat on Diesel Emissions; U.S. Orders Big Recall," *New York Times*, September 19, 2015, http://www.nytimes.com/2015/09/19/business/volkswagen-is-ordered-to-recall-nearly-500000-vehicles-over-emissions-software.html?smid=nytcore-ipad-share&smprod=nytcore-ipad&_r=0.

2 "A Scandal in the Auto Industry: Dirty Secrets, *Economist*, September 26, 2015, http://www.economist.com/news/leaders/21666226-volkswagens-falsification-pollution-tests-opens-door-very-different-car.

3 Environmental Protection Agency, "DOJ, EPA Announce One Billion Dollar Settlement with Diesel Engine Industry for Clean Air Violations," October 22, 1998, http://yosemite.epa.gov/opa/admpress.nsf/b1ab9f485b098972852562e7004dc686/93e9e651adeed6b7852566a60069ad2e?OpenDocument.; Jack Ewing, Hiroko Tabuchi, and Ben Protess, "Volkswagen Said to be Close to Settling Justice Inquiry Into Emissions," *New York Times*, January 6, 2017, https://www.nytimes.com/2017/01/06/business/volkswagen-diesel-emissions-investigation-settlement.html.

4 Davenport and Ewing, "VW Is Said to Cheat."

5 Danny Hakim and Hiroko Tabuchi, "Volkswagen Test Rigging Follows a Long Auto Industry Pattern," *New York Times*, September 23, 2015, http://www.nytimes.com/2015/09/24/business/international/volkswagen-test-rigging-follows-a-long-auto-industry-pattern.html?_r=0.

6 Donald T. Campbell, "Assessing the Impact of Planned Social Change," in *Social Research and Public Policies: The Dartmouth/OECD Conference*, ed. G. M. Lyons (Hanover, NH: Dartmouth College, 1975).

7 Everett F. Lindquist, "Preliminary Considerations in Objective Test Construction," in *Educational Measurement*, ed. E. F. Lindquist (Washington, DC: American Council on Education, 1951), 152–53.

8 Sandeep Juahar, "Giving Doctors Grades," *New York Times*, July 22, 2015, http://www.nytimes.com/2015/07/22/opinion/giving-doctors-grades.html?smid=nytcore-ipad-share&smprod=nytcore-ipad.

9 David Dranove et al., "Is More Information Better? The Effects of 'Report Cards' on Health Care Providers," *Journal of Political Economy* 11, no. 3 (2003): 555–88.

10 All examples from the English National Health Service are taken from Gwyn Bevan and Christopher Hood, "What's Measured Is What Matters: Targets and Gaming in the English Public Health Care System," *Public Administration* 84, no. 3 (2006): 517–38.

11 Kathleen J. Mullen, Meredith B. Rosenthal, and Richard G. Frank, "Can You Get What You Pay For? Pay-For-Performance and the Quality of Health Care Providers," *RAND Journal of Economics* 41, no. 1 (2010): 64–91.

12 Cherly Jensen, "Risks Higher for Front-Seat Passengers in Some S.U.V. Crashes, Tests Show," *New York Times*, June 25, 2016, http://www.nytimes.com/2016/06/24/automobiles/risks-higher-for-front-seat-passengers-in-some-suv-crashes-tests-show.html?smprod=nytcore-ipad&smid=nytcore-ipad-share&_r=0, accessed June 25, 2016.

13 The examples here are taken from A. Nove, "The Problem of 'Succcess Indicators' in Soviet Industry," *Economica* 25, no. 97 (1958): 1–13; and Richard Rothstein, *Holding Accountability to Account: How Scholarship and Experience in Other Fields Inform Exploration of Performance Incentives in Education* (Nashville: National Center on Performance Incentives at Vanderbilt Peabody College, 2008), http://s4.epi.org/files/2014/holding-accountability-to-account.pdf.

Notes to Chapter Five

1 Jennifer Medina, "Reading and Math Scores Rise Sharply across N.Y.," *New York Times*, June 24, 2008, http://www.nytimes.com/2008/06/24/education/24scores.html?_r=0.

2 Jennifer Medina, "U.S. Math Tests Find Scant Gains across New York," *New York Times*, October 14, 2009, A1, http://www.nytimes.com/2009/10/15/education/15scores.html.

3 "Test Trouble," *New York Post*, October 17, 2009, http://nypost.com/2009/10/17/test-trouble/.

4 Medina, "U.S. Math Tests Find Scant Gains."

5 Ronald K. Hambleton et al., *Review of the Measurement Quality of the Kentucky Instructional Results Information System, 1991–1994* (Frankfort, KY: Office of Education Accountability, Kentucky General Assembly, 1995).

6 Daniel Koretz et al., "The Effects of High-Stakes Testing: Preliminary Evidence about Generalization across Tests," paper presented at the annual meeting of the American Educational Research Association, Chicago, April 1991, http://dash.harvard.edu/handle/1/10880553.

7 Daniel Koretz and Sheila I. Barron, *The Validity of Gains on the Kentucky Instructional Results Information System (KIRIS)* (Santa Monica, CA: RAND, 1998).

8 Stephen Klein et al., *What Do Test Scores in Texas Tell Us* (Santa Monica, CA: RAND, 2000).

9 Diana Jean Schemo, "Questions on Data Cloud Luster of Houston Schools," *New York Times*, July 11, 2003; Diana Jean Schemo and Ford Fessenden, "Gains in Houston Schools: How Real Are They?" *New York Times*, December 3, 2003.

10 Schemo, "Questions on Data"; Schemo and Fessenden, "Gains in Houston Schools."

11 Andrew Ho and Edward Haertel, *Metric-Free Measures of Test Score Trends and Gaps with Policy-Relevant Examples* (Los Angeles: National Center for the Study of Evaluation, University of California, Los Angeles, 2006).

12 For a qualitative study of teachers' focus on bubble students, see Jennifer Booher-Jennings, "Below the Bubble: Educational Triage and the Texas Accountability System," *American Educational Research Journal* 42, no. 2 (2005): 231–69. For a quantitative study of the effects on scores, see Derek Neal and Diane Schanzenbach, "Left Behind by Design: Proficiency Counts and Test-Based Accountability," *Review of Economics and Statistics* 92, no. 2 (2010): 263–83.

13 Julie Berry Cullen and Randall Reback, *Tinkering toward Accolades: School Gaming under a Performance Accountability System*, Working Paper 12286 (Cambridge, MA: National Bureau of Educational Research, 2002); David Figlio and Lawrence Getzler, *Accountability, Ability and Disability: Gaming the System?*, Working Paper 9307 (Cambridge, MA: National Bureau of Educational Research, 2002); Brian Jacob, "Accountability, Incentives and Behavior: Evidence from School Reform in Chicago," *Journal of Public Economics* 89, nos. 5–6 (2005): 761–69.

14 Manny Fernandez, "El Paso Schools Confront Scandal of Students Who 'Disappeared' at Test Time," *New York Times*, October 13, 2012, retrieved from http://www.nytimes.com/2012/10/14/education/el-paso-rattled-by-scandal-of-disappeared-students.html; Manny Fernandez, "Sentence Cut in Texas for School Official Jailed in Test Scandal," *New York Times*, December 12, 2013, retrieved from http://www.nytimes.com/2013/12/13/us/sentence-cut-in-texas-for-school-official-jailed-in-test-scandal.html?_r=0; Claudio Sanchez, "El Paso Schools Cheating Scandal: Who's Accountable?," National Public Radio, retrieved from http://www.npr.org/2013/04/10/176784631/el-paso-schools-cheating-scandal-probes-officials-accountability.

Notes to Chapter Six

1 Rachel Aviv, "Wrong Answer: In an Era of High-Stakes Testing, a Struggling School Made a Shocking Choice," *New Yorker*, June 21, 2014, http://www.newyorker.com/magazine/2014/07/21/wrong-answer, accessed June 24, 2016.

2 Kim Severson, "Systematic Cheating Is Found in Atlanta's School System," *New York Times*, July 5, 2011, http://www.nytimes.com/2011/07/06/education/06atlanta.html; Jennie Jarvie, "Judge in Atlanta School Cheating Scandal May Reconsider Tough Sentences," *Los Angeles Times*, April 20, 2015, http://www.latimes.com/nation/la-na-atlanta-cheating-resentence-20150420-story.html"; Sara Morrison, "Dozens of Atlanta Teachers Indicted in Cheating Scandal," *The Wire: News from the Atlantic*, March 29, 2013, http://www.thewire.com/national/2013/03/dozens-atlanta-teachers-indicted-cheating-scandal/63705/; Joy Remsovits, "Atlanta Cheating Scandal Unveiled by Reporters, *Huffington Post*, July 6, 2011, http://www.huffingtonpost.com/2011/07/06/atlanta-public-schools-cheating_n_891737.html.

3 John Perry and Heather Vogell, "Surge in CRCT Results Raises 'Big Red Flag,'" ajc.com (*Atlanta Constitution*), March 26, 2012, http://www.ajc.com/news/news/local/surge-in-crct-results-raises-big-red-flag-1/nQSXD/.

4 Erin Fuchs, "Here's How an Alleged Cheating Ring That Could Send Atlanta Teachers to Prison Was Uncovered," *Business Insider*, September 25, 2014, http://www.businessinsider.com/how-was-the-atlanta-cheating-scandal-was-uncovered-2014-9.

5 Joy Resmovits, "Atlanta Cheating Scandal."

6 Fuchs, "Here's How an Alleged Cheating Ring."

7 Resmovits, "Atlanta Cheating Scandal"; Kim Severson, "Systematic Cheating Is Found in Atlanta's School System," *New York Times*, July 5, 2011, http://www.nytimes.com/2011/07/06/education/06atlanta.html?_r=0.

8 Resmovits, "Atlanta Cheating Scandal"; Jarvie, "Judge in Atlanta"; Aviv, "Wrong Answer."

9 Alan Judd, "Beverley Hall Dies; Criminal Case—and Her Legacy—Unresolved," *Atlanta Constitution*, March 2, 2015, http://www.ajc.com/news/news/breaking-news/hall-dies-criminal-case-and-her-legacy-unresolved/nkMKf/; Aviv, "Wrong Answer."

10 Alan Blinder, "Atlanta Educators Convicted in School Cheating Scandal," *New York Times*, April 1, 2015, http://www.nytimes.com/2015/04/02/us/verdict-reached-in-atlanta-school-testing-trial.html.

11 Aviv, "Wrong Answer.

12 Ibid.

13 Ibid.

14 Ibid.

15 Ibid.

16 Ibid.

17 Blinder, "Atlanta Educators Convicted"; Jarvie, "Judge in Atlanta"; "Atlanta Cheating Scandal: Prison Time Cut by Half for Three Educators," NBC News, April 30, 2015, http://www.nbcnews.com/news/us-news/atlanta-cheating-scandal-three-former-educators-be-resentenced-n351251.

18 Benjamin Herold and Dale Mezzacappa, "2009 Report Identified Dozens of PA Schools for Possible Cheating," *Philadelphia Public School Notebook*, July 8, 2011, http://thenotebook.org/articles/2011/07/08/2009-report-identified-dozens-of-pa-schools-for-possible-cheating.

19 Craig McCoy and Kristen Graham, "Principal, 4 Teachers Charged in Cheating Scandal," *Philadelphia Inquirer*, May 9, 2014, http://articles.philly.com/2014-05-09/news/49720079_1_three-city-charter-schools-philadelphia-school-district-cheating-scandal.

20 Martha Woodall, "Two More Philadelphia School Officials Finished by Cheating Scandal," *Philadelphia Inquirer*, July 25, 2015, http://articles.philly.com/2015-07-25/news/64821714_1_berson-education-department-pssa.

21 Ibid.

22 Bill Turque, "Rhee Dismisses 241 D.C. Teachers; Union Vows to Contest Firings," *Washington Post*, July 24, 2010, http://www.washingtonpost.com/wp-dyn/content/article/2010/07/23/AR2010072303093.html.

23 Greg Toppo, "Memo Warns of Rampant Cheating in D.C. Public Schools," *USA Today*, April 11, 2013, http://www.usatoday.com/story/news/nation/2013/04/11/memo-washington-dc-schools-cheating/2074473/.

24 Chester E. Finn, "Three Cheers for Michelle Rhee," *National Review*, July 26, 2010, http://www.nationalreview.com/corner/233613/three-cheers-michelle-rhee-chester-e-finn-jr.

25 Jack Gillum and Marisol Bellow, "When Standardized Test Scores Soared in D.C., Were the Gains Real?" *USA Today*, March 30, 2011, http://usatoday30.usatoday.com/news/education/2011-03-28-1Aschooltesting28_CV_N.htm.

26 Ibid.

27 Ibid.

28 Bill Turque, "DCPS Leaves Consultant Caveon's Toolbox Shut in test Cheating Allegation Inquiry," *Washington Post*, May 23, 2011, https://www.washingtonpost.com/blogs/dc-schools-insider/post/dcps-leaves-consultant-caveons-toolbox-shut-in-test-cheating-allegation-inquiry/2011/05/21/AF889i9G_blog.html?tid=a_inl.

29 District of Columbia Office of the Inspector General, *Report of Investigation on the DC Comprehensive Assessment System Standardized Exams*

Administered by the District of Columbia Public Schools, OIG 2011-0318 (Washington, DC: Office of the Inspector General, August 8, 2012).

30 Jason Breslow, "Education Department Finds No Evidence of Widespread Cheating on D.C. Exams," *Frontline*, PBS, January 8, 2013, http://www.pbs.org/wgbh/frontline/article/education-department-finds-no-evidence-of-widespread-cheating-on-d-c-exams/.

31 The inspector general's reports are listed at http://www2.ed.gov/about/offices/list/oig/ireports.html.

32 John Merrow, "Michelle Rhee's Reign of Error," *Taking Note: Thoughts on Education from John Merrow*, April 11, 2013, http://takingnote.learningmatters.tv/?p=6232.

33 Sandy Sanford, *Project Brief Sheet for Erin: Erasure Study*, unpublished memorandum. This memo can be obtained from the *Washington Post* at https://www.washingtonpost.com/news/answer-sheet/wp/2013/04/13/yes-rhee-saw-the-test-cheating-memo/.

34 Merrow, "Michelle Rhee's Reign."

35 Valerie Strauss, "Why Not Subpoena Everyone in D.C. Cheating Scandal—Rhee Included?" Answer Sheet, *Washington Post*, April 12, 2013, https://www.washingtonpost.com/news/answer-sheet/wp/2013/04/12/why-not-subpoena-everyone-in-d-c-cheating-scandal-rhee-included/.

36 Emma Brown, "Teachers in 18 D.C. Classrooms Cheated on Tests Last Year, Probe Finds," *Washington Post*, April 12, 2013, https://www.washingtonpost.com/local/education/teachers-in-18-dc-classrooms-cheated-on-tests-last-year-probe-finds/2013/04/12/b1a57e7c-a3a3-11e2-82bc-511538ae90a4_story.html?tid=a_inl.

37 Eric Stirgus, "Cheating Shadow Also Lingers in Dougherty County, "*Atlanta Journal-Constitution*, April 1, 2015, http://www.ajc.com/news/news/cheating-shadow-also-lingers-in-dougherty-county/nkkJg/.

38 "Crescendo Schools' Charter Revoked after Cheating Scandal," *Huffington Post*, September 12, 2011, http://www.huffingtonpost.com/2011/07/13/crescendo-schools-charter_n_897481.html?ir=Education.

39 Alan Judd, "School Test Cheating Thrives While Investigations Languish," *Atlanta Constitution*, September 12, 2012, http://www.ajc.com/news/news/education/school-test-cheating-thrives-while-investigations-/nSHwF/; Alan Judd, John Perry, and Heather Vogell, "Cheating Our Children: Suspect Scores Put Award's Integrity in Question," *Atlanta Journal-Constitution*, April 28, 2012, http://www.myajc.com/news/news/local/cheating-our-children-suspect-scores-put-awards-in/nQTPY/.

40 Priya Mann, "Cheating Scandal Rocks Van Buren Public Schools District," *Click on Detroit*, January 26, 2016, http://www.clickondetroit.com/education/cheating-scandal-rocks-van-buren-public-schools-district.

41 Valerie Strauss, "And now a new standardized testing scandal," *Washington Post*, June 8, 2011, https://www.washingtonpost.com/blogs/answer-sheet/post/and-now-a-new-standardized-testing-scandal/2011/06/17/AGotFQaH_blog.html.

42 Michels, "Faking the Grade"; Claudio Sanchez, "El Paso Schools Cheating Scandal: Who's Accountable?," National Public Radio, retrieved from http://www.npr.org/2013/04/10/176784631/el-paso-schools-cheating-scandal-probes-officials-accountability.

43 "Lockland Schools Falsified Student Data, State Says," WLWT.com, July 25, 2012, http://www.wlwt.com/news/local-news/hamilton-county/Lockland-schools-falsified-student-data-state-says/15700928; "Ohio State Auditor Will Launch Investigation into School Cheating, Attendance Record Tampering," *Huffington Post*, July 27, 2012, http://www.huffingtonpost.com/2012/07/27/ohio-state-auditor-will-1_n_1711448.html.

44 Diana Jean Schemo, "As Testing Rises, 9th Grade Becomes Pivotal," *New York Times*, January 18, 2004, http://www.nytimes.com/2004/01/18/us/as-testing-rises-9th-grade-becomes-pivotal.html?pagewanted=2&src=pm&_r=1.

45 Paul Takahashi, "State Investigation Finds Cheating at Las Vegas Elementary School," *Las Vegas Sun*, April 16, 2014, http://lasvegassun.com/news/2014/apr/16/state-investigation-finds-cheating-las-vegas-eleme/.

46 Erica L. Green, "2011 School Test Scores Will Be Clean, Alonso Vows," *Baltimore Sun*, June 23, 2011, http://articles.baltimoresun.com/2011-06-23/news/bs-md-ci-school-cheating-announcement-20110623_1_abbottston-cheating-school-test-scores.

47 Judd, "Beverly Hall Dies."

48 Meghan Rolland, "Cheating on Oklahoma Exams Leads to Resignations, Retesting," NewsOK, January 11, 2012, http://newsok.com/cheating-on-oklahoma-exams-leads-to-resignations-retesting/article/3643775/?page=1; Linda Conner Lambeck, "Education Chief: Make Teachers Pay for Cheating," *CTPost*, August 3, 2011, http://www.ctpost.com/local/article/Education-chief-Make-teachers-pay-for-cheating-1718210.php.

49 Greg Toppo et al., "When Test Scores Seem Too Good to Believe," *USA Today*, March 17, 2011, http://usatoday30.usatoday.com/news/education/2011-03-06-school-testing_N.htm.

50 Elizabethe Holland, "District Finds Widespread Cheating at East St. Louis Elementary School," *St. Louis Post-Dispatch*, August 16, 2012, http://www.stltoday.com/news/local/education/district-finds-widespread-cheating-at-east-st-louis-elementary-school/article_bad6a78e-e7d1-11e1-aa08-001a4bcf6878.html.

51 Jodi Upton, Denise Amos and Anne Ryman, "For Teachers, Many Ways And Reasons To Cheat On Tests, *USA Today*, March 10, 2011, http://usatoday30.usatoday.com/news/education/2011-03-10-1Aschooltesting10_CV_N.htm.

52 "California Education Rankings: 23 Schools Stripped of API Ratings for Cheating," *Huffington Post*, October 29, 2012, http://www.huffingtonpost.com/2012/10/29/california-education-rank_n_2040412.html; Lisa Gartner, "Prince William Teachers Helped Students on Standardized Tests," *Washington Examiner*, June 14, 2016, http://www.washingtonexaminer.com/prince-william-teachers-helped-students-on-standardized-tests/article/2502933; Samreen Hooda, "New Jersey School Teachers and Principal Suspended for Helping Students Cheat," *Huffington Post*, August 30, 2012, http://www.huffingtonpost.com/2012/08/29/new-jersey-school-staff-s_n_1840582.html; Judd, "Beverley Hall Dies"; Emily Le Coz, "Clarksdale Teacher Charged In Cheating Investigation," *Clarion-Ledger*, April 23, 2015, http://www.clarionledger.com/story/news/2015/04/23/clarksdale-teacher-charged-cheating/26255241/; Upton, Amos, and Ryan, "For Teachers, Many Ways."

53 M. B. Pell, "More Cheating Scandals Inevitable, as States Can't Ensure Test Integrity," *Atlanta Journal-Constitution*, September 30, 2012, http://www.myajc.com/news/news/more-cheating-scandals-inevitable-as-states-cant-e/nSPqj/.

54 "California Education Rankings"; Jessica Williams, "State Documents Detail Standardized Test Cheating, Irregularities at New Orleans Schools, the Lens Reports," *Times-Picayune*, July 16, 2013, http://www.nola.com/education/index.ssf/2013/07/state_documents_detail_standar.html.

55 Government Accounting Office, *K-12 Education: States' Test Security Policies and Procedures Varied* (Washington, DC. GAO, 2013).

56 Brian A. Jacob and Steven D. Levitt, "Rotten Apples: An Investigation of the Prevalence and Predictors of Teacher Cheating," *Quarterly Journal of Economics*, 118, no. 3 (2003): 843, 846.

57 Daniel Koretz et al., *Perceived Effects of the Kentucky Instructional Results Information System (KIRIS)* (Santa Monica, CA: RAND, 1996).

58 Judd, "School Test Cheating Thrives While Investigations Languish."

59 Toppo et al., "When Test Scores Seem Too Good to Believe."

60 Judd, "School Test Cheating Thrives While Investigations Languish."

61 Richard Rothstein, "Taking the Fall in Atlanta," *Economic Policy Institute Working Economics Blog*, April 3, 2015, http://www.epi.org/blog/taking-the-fall-in-atlanta/.

62 A. Bidwell (2014). Duncan Relaxes Testing Push, But Teachers Want More. *U.S. News and World Report*, August 21, 2014, http://www.usnews.com/news/articles/2014/08/21/education-secretary-arne-duncan-loosens-reins-on-teacher-evaluations-testing, accessed May 22, 2015.

Notes to Chapter Seven

1 Walt Haney, "The Myth of the Texas Miracle in Education," *Education Policy Analysis Archives* 8, no. 41, doi:10.14507/epaa.v8n41.2000, accessed June 15, 2016; Linda McNeil and Angela Valenzuela, "The Harmful Impact of the TAAS System of Testing in Texas: Beneath the Accountability Rhetoric" (Austin: Department of Curriculum and Instruction and the Center for Mexican American Studies, University of Texas, 2000), http://eric.ed.gov/?id=ED443872, accessed June 15, 2016.

2 For a brief description of and citations to a number of these studies, see Brian M. Stecher, "Consequences of Large-Scale, High-Stakes Testing on School and Classroom Practice," in *Making Sense of Test-Based Accountability*, ed. Laura S. Hamilton, Brian M. Stecher, and Stephen P. Klein (Santa Monica, CA: RAND, 2002), 79–100. For more recent data, see Thomas S. Dee, Brian Jacob, and Nathaniel Schwartz, "The Effects of NCLB on School Resources and Practices," *Educational Evaluation and Policy Analysis* 35, no. 2 (2013): 252–79, and Richard J. Murnane and John P. Papay, "Teachers' Views on No Child Left Behind: Support for the Principles, Concerns about the Practices," *Journal of Economic Perspectives* 24, no. 3 (2010): 151–66.

3 For example, Murnane and Papay, "Teachers' Views," 159.

4 Jeff Rubinstein, *The Princeton Review: Cracking the MCAS Grade 10 Mathematics* (New York: Random House, 2002), 19.

5 Elaine Allensworth, Macarena Correa, and Steve Ponisciak, *From High School to the Future: ACT Preparation—Too Much, Too Lat*e (Chicago: Consortium on Chicago School Research, 2008).

6 Rubinstein, *Princeton Review*, 15.

7 Ibid., 56.

8 Steven Farr, *Teaching as Leadership* (San Francisco: Jossey-Bass, 2010), 45.

9 Paul Bambrick-Santoyo, *Leverage Leadership: A Practical Guide to Building Exceptional Schools* (San Francisco: Jossey-Bass, 2012); Doug Lemov, *Teach like a Champion 2.0* (San Francisco: Jossey-Bass, 2015).

10 Lemov, *Teach like a Champion*, 17.

11 The most recent of these studies is one of mine: Daniel Koretz et al., "Predicting Freshman Grade-Point Average from College-Admissions and State High-School Test Scores," *AERA Open*, September 2016, http://ero.sagepub.com/content/2/4/2332858416670601, doi:10.1177/2332858416670601, accessed December 5, 2016.

12 Lemov, *Teach like a Champion*, 123.

13 Bambrick-Santoyo, *Leverage Leadership*, 114; Paul Bambrick-Santoyo, *Driven by Data: A Practical Guide to Improve Instruction* (San Francisco: Jossey-Bass, 2010), 7.

14 Bambrick-Santoyo, *Driven by Data*, 8.

15 Farr, *Teaching as Leadership*, 21.

16 Ibid., 43.

17 Bambrick-Santoyo , *Driven by Data*, 16.

Notes to Chapter Eight

1 Nebraska Department of Education, "Nebraska State Accountability-Reading (NeSA-R) Performance Level Descriptors, Grade 6," https://www.education.ne.gov/Assessment/pdfs/NeSA_Math_Performance_Level_Descriptors.pdf.

2 Robert L. Linn, "Performance Standards: Utility for Different Uses of Assessments," *Education Policy Analysis Archives* 2, no. 31 (2003), http://epaa.asu.edu/ojs/article/view/259.

3 *Federal Register* 68, no. 54 (March 20, 2003): 13796–13801.

4 "The Honesty Gap," http://honestygap.org/, accessed May 24, 2016.

5 Robert L. Linn, "Assessments and Accountability," *Educational Researcher* 29, no. 2 (2000): 4-16.

6 Ibid., 11.

Notes to Chapter Nine

1 Michael Winerip, "Hard-Working Teachers, Sabotaged When Student Test Scores Slip," *New York Times*, March 4, 2012, http://www.nytimes.com/2012

/03/05/nyregion/in-brooklyn-hard-working-teachers-sabotaged-when -student-test-scores-slip.html?_r=0, accessed July 13, 2016.

2 "Tennessee Value-Added Assessment System," Tennessee Department of Education, http://tn.gov/education/topic/tvaas, accessed June 29, 2016.

3 Michael Winerip, "A Popular Principal, Wounded by Government's Good Intentions," *New York Times*, July 18, 2010, http://www.nytimes.com/2010 /07/19/education/19winerip.html?_r=0, accessed July 12, 2016.

4 Coleman James et al., *Equality of Educational Opportunity* (Washington, DC: US Department of Health, Education, and Welfare, Office of Education, 1966).

5 American Statistical Association, *ASA Statement on Using Value-Added Models for Educational Assessment*, April 8, 2014, 2, http://www.amstat .org/policy/pdfs/ASA_VAM_Statement.pdf, July 13, 2016.

6 Aaron Pallas, "Meet the 'Worst' 8th Grade Math Teacher in New York City," *Sociological Eye on Education* blog, Hechinger Institute on Education and the Media, May 15, 2012. Reprinted in the *Washington Post*, May 16, 2012, https://www.washingtonpost.com/blogs/answer-sheet/post/meet-the -worst-8th-grade-math-teacher-in-nyc/2012/05/15/gIQArmlbSU_blog .html, accessed July 14, 2016.

7 J. R. Lockwood et al., "The Sensitivity of Value-Added Teacher Effect Estimates to Different Mathematics Achievement Measures," *Journal of Educational Measurement* 44, no. 1 (2007): 47.

8 Daniel F. McCaffrey et al., "The Intertemporal Variability of Teacher Effect Estimates," *Education Finance and Policy* 4, no. 4 (2009): 572–606.

Notes to Chapter Ten

1 Common Core State Standards Initiative, "Frequently Asked Questions," http://www.corestandards.org/about-the-standards/frequently-asked -questions/, accessed July 13, 2016.

2 Motoko Rich, "Common Core School Standards Face a New Wave of Opposition," *New York Times*, May 29, 2014, http://www.nytimes.com/2014/05 /30/education/common-core-standards-face-a-new-wave-of-opposition .html?_r=0, accessed June 21, 2016.

3 Committee on Arrangements for the 2016 Republican National Convention, Republican Platform 2016, 33, https://www.gop.com/platform/, accessed July 19, 2016.

4 Advisor Asserts President Will Repeal Common Core," *Education Week*, February 14, 2017. http://www.edweek.org/ew/articles/2017/02/15/adviser

-asserts-president-will-repeal-common-core.html?qs=trump+common+core, accessed February 17, 2017. Every Student Succeeds Act, S.1177, 114th Cong., Section 8544 (2015).

5 Common Core State Standards Initiative, "Statements of Support," *New York Times*, http://www.nytimes.com/2014/05/30/education/common-core-standards-face-a-new-wave-of-opposition.html?_r=0, accessed July 21, 2016.

6 Diane Ravitch, "Why I Cannot Support the Common Core Standards," *Diane Ravitch's Blog*, February 26, 2013, https://dianeravitch.net/2013/02/26/why-i-cannot-support-the-common-core-standards/, accessed July 21, 2016.

7 Mary Morley, Brent Bridgeman, and René Lawless, *Transfer between Variance of Quantitative Items* (Princeton, NJ: Educational Testing Service, 2004).

8 Common Core State Standards Initiative, *Common Core State Standards for Mathematics*, 57, http://www.corestandards.org/wp-content/uploads/Math_Standards1.pdf, accessed July 25, 2016.

9 For example, see State University of New York, *New College Readiness Assessments for New York State*, August 2012, 1, http://system.suny.edu/media/suny/content-assets/documents/academic-affairs/assessment/Spring-2012-Update-on-College-Readiness-Assessents-in-New-York-State_FINAL.pdf, accessed August 4, 2016.

Notes to Chapter Eleven

1 Edward Haertel et al., *Report of the NAEP Technical Review Panel on the 1986 Reading Anomaly, the Accuracy of NAEP Trends, and Issues Raised by State-Level NAEP Comparisons* (Washington, DC: US Department of Education, Office of Educational Research and Improvement, 1989).

2 Daniel Koretz, *Trends in Educational Achievement* (Washington, D.C., Congressional Budget Office, 1986).

3 Sean F. Reardon, "The Widening of the Achievement Gap between the Rich and the Poor," in *Whither Opportunity*, ed. Greg J. Duncan and Richard. J. Murnane (New York: Russell Sage Foundation, 2011), 91–116; Sean F. Reardon and Ximena A. Portilla, *Recent Trends in Income, Racial, and Ethnic School Readiness Gaps at Kindergarten Entry*, Working Paper 15-02 (Stanford, CA: Center for Education Policy Analysis, Stanford University, June 2016).

4 National Research Council, Committee on Incentives and Test-Based Accountability in Education, *Incentives and Test-Based Accountability in Education* (Washington, DC: National Academies Press, 2011), 4.

5 Ibid., 60; Thomas S. Dee and Brian A. Jacob, "The Impact of No Child Left

Behind on Student Achievement," *Journal of Policy Analysis and Management* 30, no. 3 (2011): 418–46.

6 Dee and Jacob, "Impact of No Child Left Behind," table 6.

Notes to Chapter Twelve

1 Kate Zernicke, "Testing for Joy and Grit? Schools Nationwide Push to Measure Students' Emotional Skills," *New York Times*, February 29, 2016, http://www.nytimes.com/2016/03/01/us/testing-for-joy-and-grit-schools-nationwide-push-to-measure-students-emotional-skills.html?_r=0.

Notes to Chapter Thirteen

1 Justin Martin, *Greenspan: The Man Behind Money* (Cambridge, MA: Perseus, 2000), 88–89.

2 Anu Partanen, "What Americans Keep Ignoring about Finland's School Success," *Atlantic*, December 29, 2011, http://www.theatlantic.com/national/archive/2011/12/what-americans-keep-ignoring-about-finlands-school-success/250564/, accessed September 8, 2016.

3 For a more detailed explanation of the Dutch system, see the following source, from which I abstracted my discussion: Deborah Nusche et al., *OECD Reviews of Evaluation and Assessment in Education: Netherlands* (Paris: OECD Publishing, 2014), http://dx.doi.org/10.1787/9789264211940-en.

4 Ibid., 102.

5 OECD, *PISA 2012 Results: What Students Know and Can Do* (Paris: OECD Publishing, 2013), 1:19.

6 Char Boon Goh and S. Gopinathan, "Education in Singapore: Developments since 1965," in *An African Exploration of the East Asian Education*, ed. B. Fredriksen and J. P. Tan (Washington, DC: World Bank, 2008), 80–108, http://hdl.handle.net/10986/6424.

7 Singapore Ministry of Education, "Education System," https://www.moe.gov.sg/education/education-system, accessed September 12, 2016.

8 Sandra Davie, "Tuition Has Become an Educational Arms Race," *Singapore Times*, July 9, 2015, http://www.straitstimes.com/opinion/tuition-has-become-an-educational-arms-race, accessed September 13, 2016.

9 Singapore Ministry of Education, "Changes to PSLE Scoring and Secondary One Posting," https://www.moe.gov.sg/news/press-releases/changes-to-psle-scoring-and-secondary-one-posting, accessed September 30, 2016.

10 For a discussion of parental concerns, see Calvin Yang, "PSEL Changes: Parents Worry about Broad Bands for Scores," *Straits Times*, July 17, 2016, http://www.straitstimes.com/singapore/education/psle-changes-parents-worry-about-broad-bands-for-scores, accessed September 30, 2016.

11 Ng Chee Meng, "MOE FY 2016 Committee of Supply Debate—Speech by Acting Minister for Education (Schools) Ng Chee Meng,'" https://www.moe.gov.sg/news/speeches/moe-fy-2016-committee-of-supply-debate—-speech-by-acting-minister-for-education-schools-ng-chee-meng, accessed September 13, 2016.

12 Kirabo Jackson, *What Do Test Scores Miss? The Importance of Teacher Effects on Non-Test Score Outcomes*¸ NBER Working Paper 22226 (Cambridge, MA: National Bureau of Economic Research, 2016),

13 University of Virginia, Curry School of Education, *Classroom Assessment Scoring System*, http://curry.virginia.edu/research/centers/castl/class, accessed October 4, 2016.

14 National Council on Teacher Quality, *2015 State Teacher Policy Yearbook, National Summary* (Washington, DC: NCTQ, 2015), 79.

15 Katherine Lynch, *How Well Do High Performing TIMSS Countries Measure Up?*, Working Paper (Cambridge, MA: National Center for Teacher Effectiveness, Harvard University, 2016).

16 For more discussion of this, see Daniel Koretz, "Alignment, High Stakes, and the Inflation of Test Scores, in *Uses and Misuses of Data in Accountability Testing*, Yearbook of the National Society for the Study of Education (Malden, MA: Blackwell, 2005), col. 104, pt. 2, 99–118.

INDEX